IMAGES
of America

CHICAGO HEIGHTS REVISITED

IMAGES
of America

CHICAGO HEIGHTS REVISITED

Dominic Candeloro and Barbara Paul

ARCADIA
PUBLISHING

ISBN 978-0-7385-0129-1

Published by Arcadia Publishing
Charleston, South Carolina

Printed in the United States of America

For all general information contact Arcadia Publishing at:
Telephone 843-853-2070
Fax 843-853-0044
E-mail sales@arcadiapublishing.com
For customer service and orders:
Toll-Free 1-888-313-2665

Visit us on the Internet at www.arcadiapublishing.com

Cover: Sunday, May 23, 1937, was Legion Day in Chicago Heights. Drum and bugle corps from the surrounding area, the three Chicago Heights Legion posts, and the Veterans of Foreign War combined to create this spectacular event. This photo, taken from the second floor of Chicago Heights City Hall, shows spectators on the library steps, along the curbs, and seated in their automobiles, which were reverse-parked to offer a view of the parade passing through the "Heart of the City."

Contents

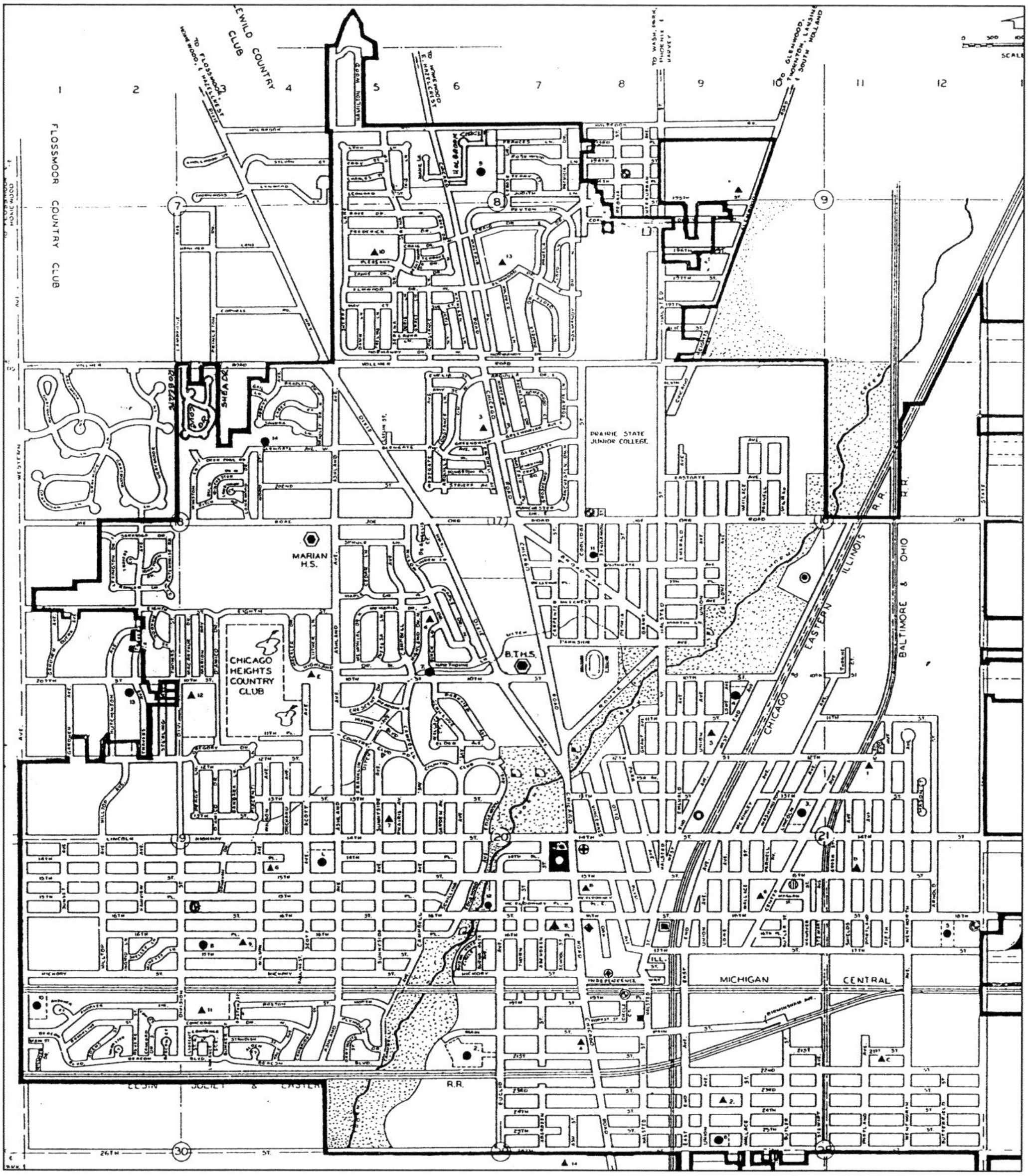

This modern-day map of Chicago Heights reveals the importance of railroads on the south and East Side. The prominence of Thorn Creek's parks and forest preserve running northwest through the center of the city and the contrast between the pre-World War II city's rigid grid with the post war (northern) curved street plan is marked. Note also, in the lower center, the intersection of the Lincoln and Dixie transcontinental highways making Chicago Heights the "Crossroads of the Nation."

Introduction

The first volume of *Images of America: Chicago Heights* was an enormous success. The acceptance and popularity of the book exceeded all our expectations. It is very gratifying for us to have so many people reading and talking about a past we love so much. The proceeds from the sale of the book helped the Historic Preservation Committee fund a survey of the Euclid Area, historic city tours for students, Porch Fest, and other projects.

This second volume expands on the original book. We take a look back to the early part of the century, then go into the period from 1930 to 1970 in some detail. Again we have focused our attention on the old downtown; for many of us, that configuration of shops, hotels, restaurants, and public buildings was the heart and soul of our city. For us older folks, the downtown *was* Chicago Heights. We have also tried to cover the neighborhoods and the social scene, to the extent that we had photos to illustrate those themes.

What emerges from this collection of images is a multi-varied portrait of a lively city striving as one to win World War II, even while supporting a large spectrum of differing religious, social, and ethnic institutions. The people of Chicago Heights have a strong attachment to their neighborhoods and their city. They are proud of their past and ready for their future, and we are privileged to be able to document their exciting story. We acknowledge the contributions again of the members of the Historic Preservation Committee: Elizabeth Booth, James and Colleen Calabrese, Barbara DeMith, Genevieve Ford, Joseph Hawkins, Earlene Levesque, Madeline Mancini, Ester Montalvo, Marie Patton, Barbara Paul, Dollie Pinnow, and Jeanne Rafaj. We thank the following who responded to our appeal for photos: Helen Albrecht, John Andrade, Gloria Barrett, Elizabeth Booth, Robert Borak, Ray Deabel, Nora Farabaugh, Carol Mancini Formentini, Theresa Giannetti, Kenneth Hall, Delphine Hannig, Joseph Hawkins, Clarence Helmrath, Maurine Hjemvick, Edward Hoertlein, Dorothy Komer, Andrew Kristina, Velia Leli, Scott Logan, Rita Lustig, William O. Maier , Harold Martin, K. Ethel Merker, Peter Mitkus, Charles Nardoni, Joe Pagoria, Gina Ristenpart, Sandy Robey, Gwen Techman, Clara Tiberi, Patricia Trainor, Genevieve Wlos, and Alic Wegley. Joe Pagoria, a retired *Star* photographer, contributed negatives of his photos of the Rau's Store and City Hall at Christmas, the 1940s photo of the Mound, St. Anne's Church, and Jenson Auto.

Special thanks to Geri Biamonte for her help in preparing the manuscript; to the staff of the mayor's office (Claudia Ruiz, Paulnita Rees, and Maria Zerante) and the library (Carolyn Wagner) for their aid to the authors; and to Steve Modzelewski and Carol Candeloro, who helped with proofreading. Thanks to Mayor Angelo "Sam" Ciambrone for having the vision to launch the Historic Preservation Committee and for his help in identifying many of the photos.

History is sometimes an elusive subject—an amalgam of our personal memories, our interests, and the documents and photos that survive. In this book we make no pretense of presenting the definitive story of our town. Other people in another time with access to different sources would (and will) come up with alternative views of our past. We encourage dialogue, and we challenge those with additional sources to join us in our quest to capture our local heritage.

Again, we encourage readers to explore in depth the holdings of the Chicago Heights Free Public Library including the files of the *Star*, an extensive obituary index, F.S. Beeson's *History of Chicago Heights 1833-1938* (which was done for the Federal Writers' Project), local citizenship documents from 1903 to the 1950s, an archive of over 1,000 photos, city directories, and other local history materials housed in the library's History Room. For further information, contact the Library staff at (708)754-0323 or fax your request to 754-0325. You may communicate with us on the World Wide Web at ChicagoHeights.net, www.SLS.Lib.IL.US/chs/, D-Candeloro@goust.edu, and www.ecnet.net/users/gcandel/hom.html. We also invite all our readers to become active participants in the Chicago Heights Historic Preservation Committee, which meets the second Tuesday of each month at the library.

Dominic Candeloro
Barbara Paul

February 2000

One

1900–1930

In the period 1900–1930, "progress" was the key word in Chicago Heights. From 1900 to 1910 the population increased 185 percent. Exciting things were happening in Chicago Heights. New and expanding factories like Inland Steel, Victor Chemical, American Stoveboard, and Midwest Forging attracted thousands of new residents. These were new immigrants excited about their new country, eager to work hard at their new jobs, and ready to re-establish their families in Chicago Heights. The city was led by businessmen with vision who dreamed of building up their new enterprises. Confidence, assurance, and civic pride ran high in Chicago Heights during that era. To the modern reader, it would have been a great time to be alive . . . except for the 1918 Flu epidemic, the high rate of infant mortality, and outdoor toilets.

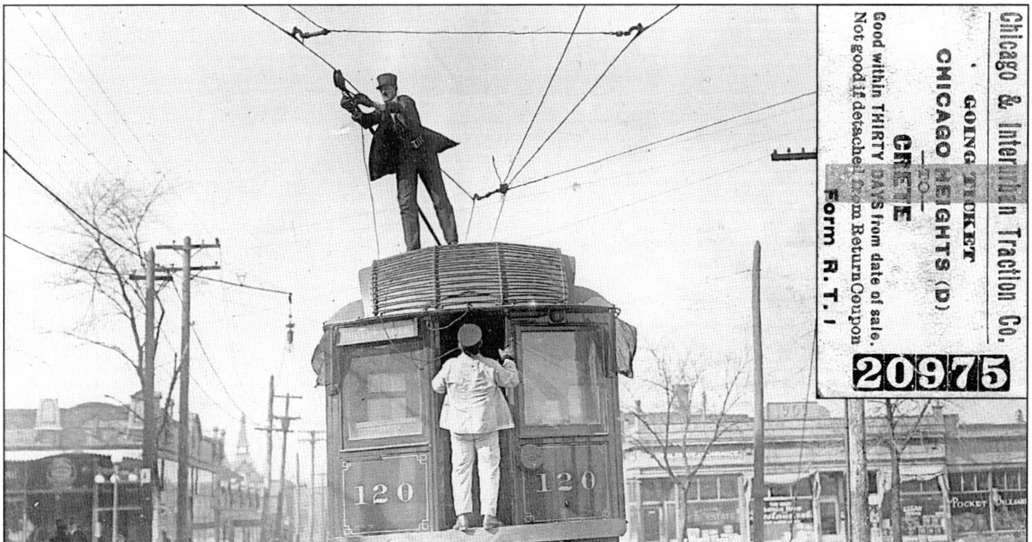

Above, a conductor adjusts the contacts for the Chicago and Interurban Transit car #120 on an impromptu stop along the Halsted Street route that led from Chicago to Chicago Heights and on south to Kankakee. The ticket stub is a souvenir from March 22, 1918.

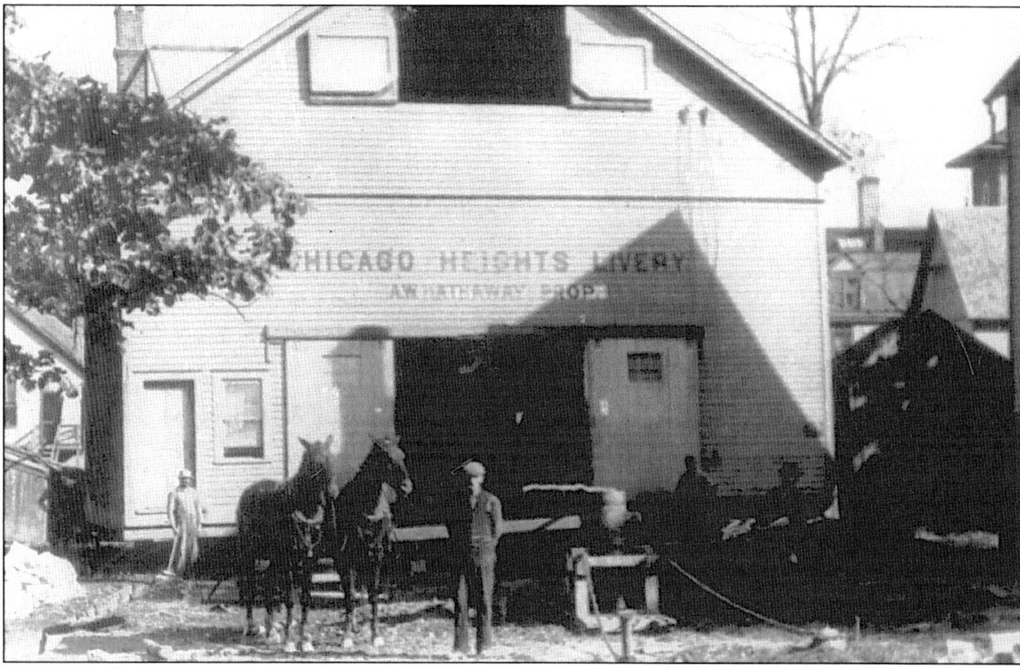

During the early development of the city, increased demand for residences and improved property often required the moving of buildings. Here, the Chicago Heights Livery Barn is being moved by E.E. Somes and his crew to 55 E. Hickory Street.

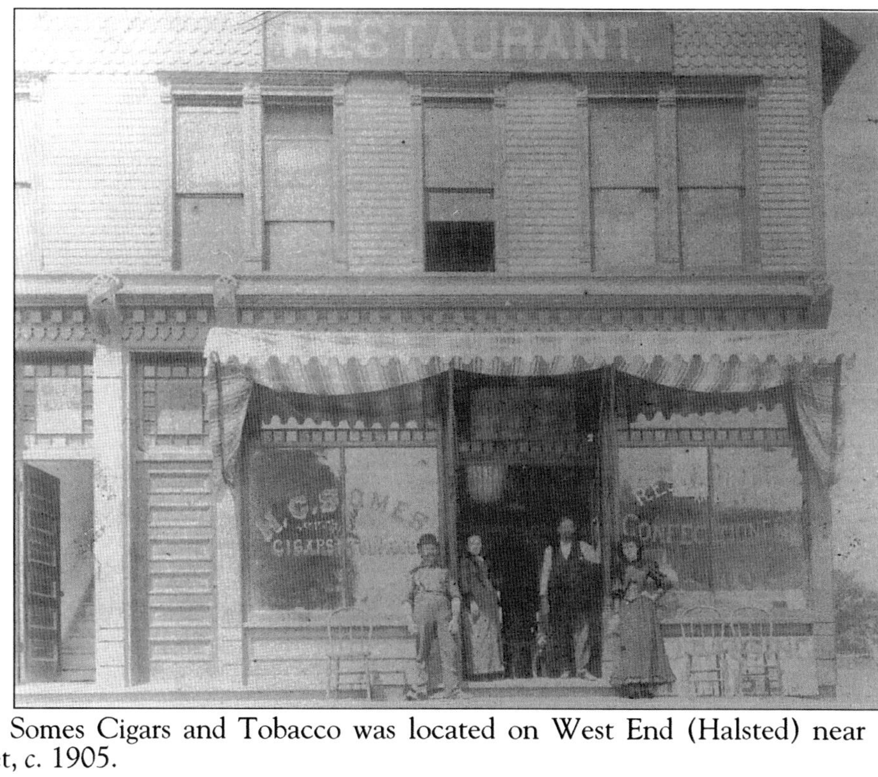

H.C. Somes Cigars and Tobacco was located on West End (Halsted) near Illinois Street, *c.* 1905.

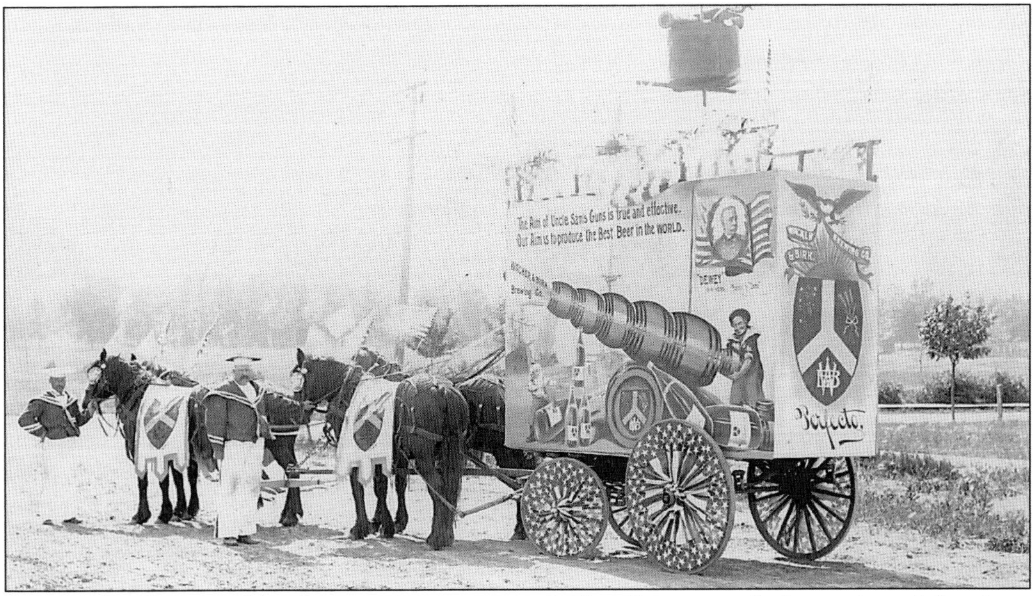

Emmet Koelling and his beer wagon were undoubtedly a crowd pleaser in celebrations around the turn of the century. "The Aim of Uncle Sam's Guns is True and Effective. Our Aim is To Produce the Best Beer in the World," and "Dewey—Our Hero" were the slogans of the Wacker and Birk Brewing Company.

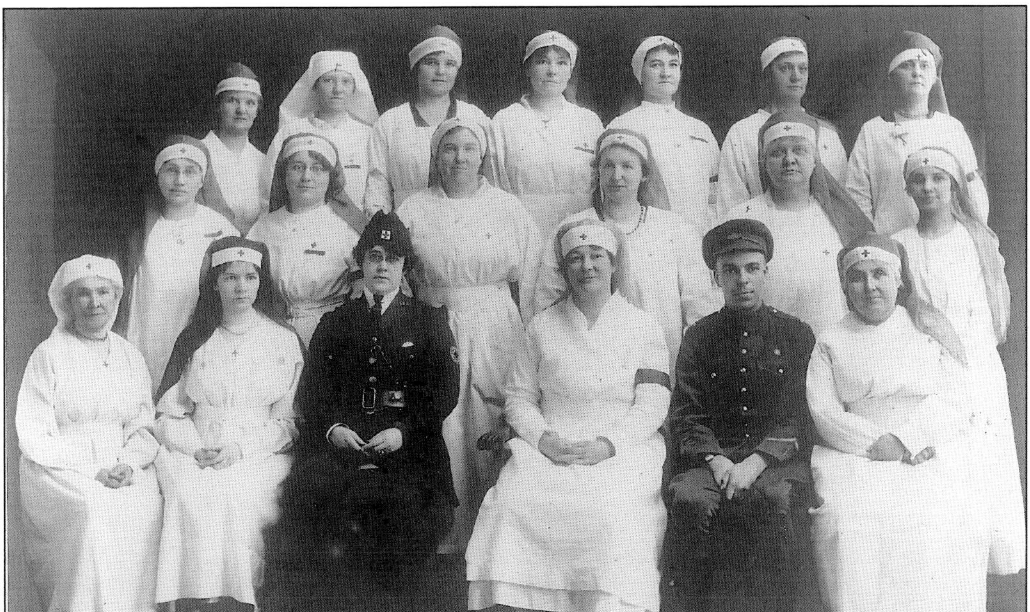

Among the Women's Red Cross Corps during World War I are as follows, from left to right: (front row) Mrs. Anna G. Clayton, Mrs. Mildred Smeck, Mrs. Edna Hawes, Mrs. Martin Strand, unidentified, and Mrs. Irving Kelley; (middle row) Mrs. John Gravelot, Mrs. Rufus Orr, Mrs. C.R. Sage, Mrs. W. O. Robbins, and Mrs. H. Donaldson; (back row) Mrs. W. H. Stolte and Mrs. Ellis Klinger. Note that many married women of that era were identified with "Mrs." and their husband's first name.

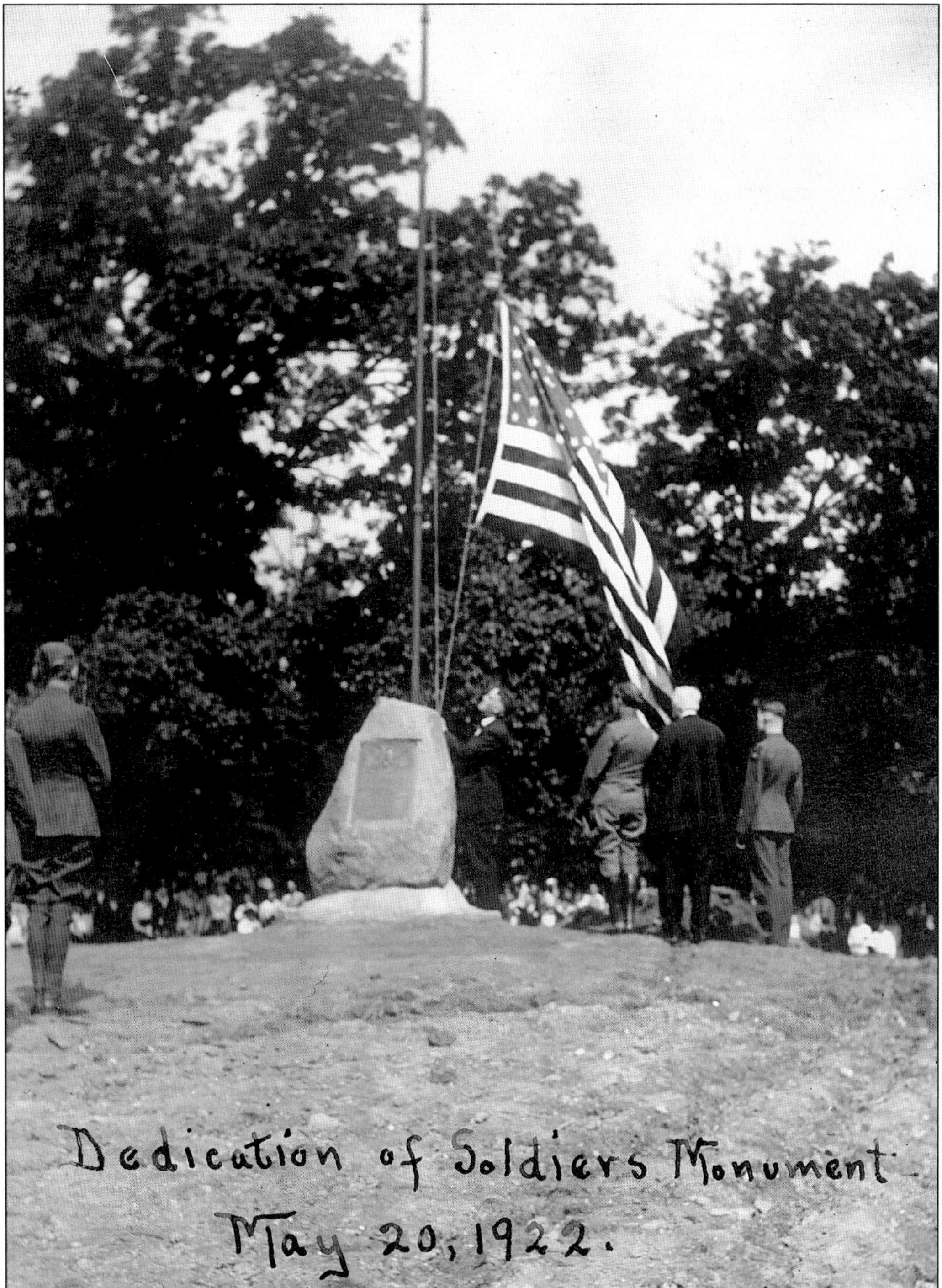

This photo was taken at the Saturday, May 20, 1922, dedication of the Soldiers Monument at the Crossroads in Chicago Heights. Since that time, this spot has become the traditional gathering place for Memorial Day, Veteran's Day, and Christmas tree lighting ceremonies.

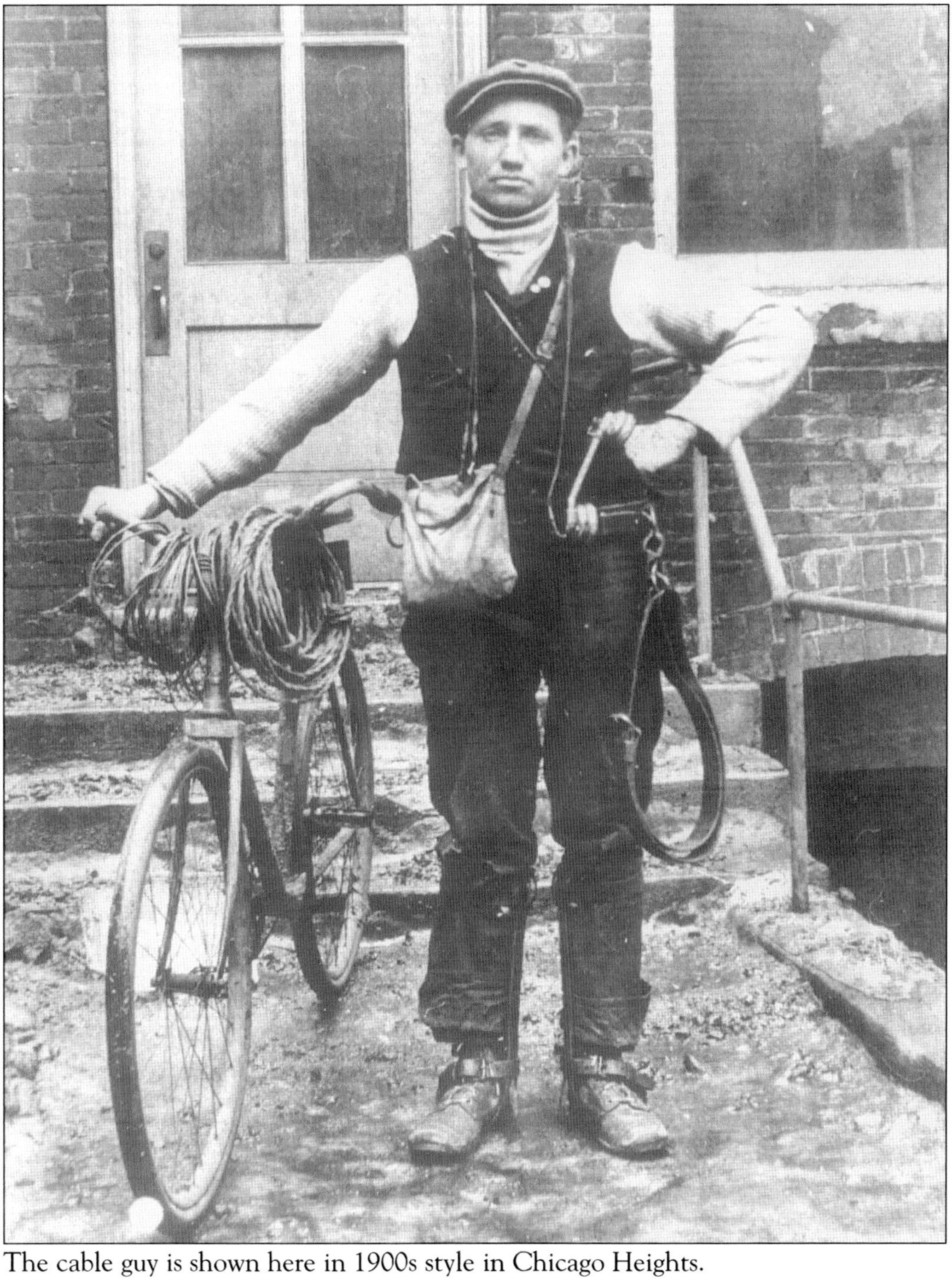

The cable guy is shown here in 1900s style in Chicago Heights.

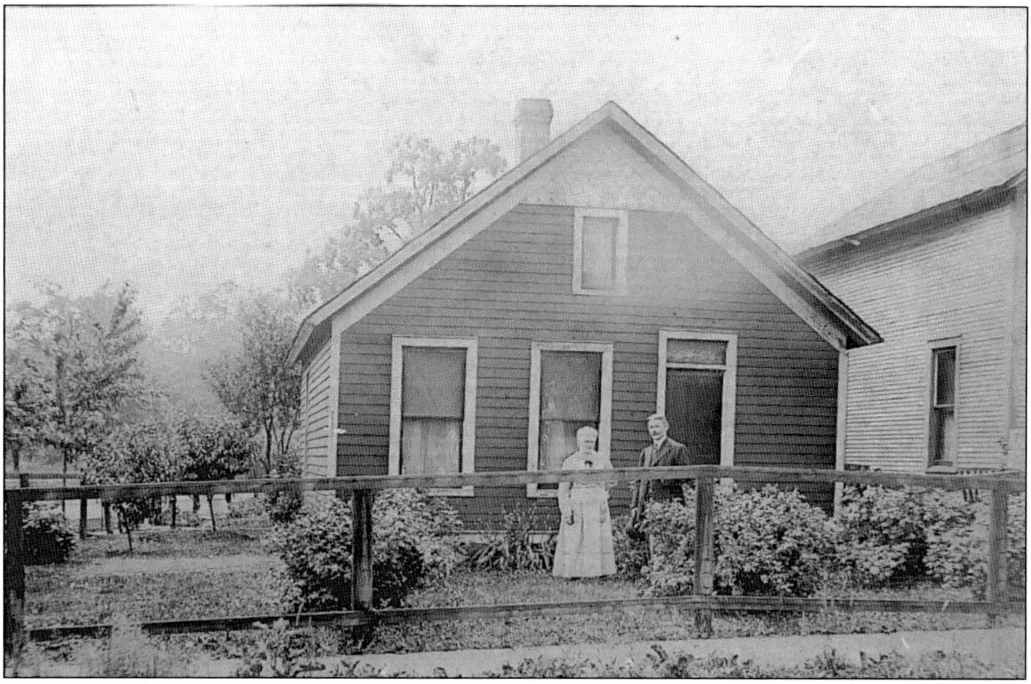

Richard and Alma Agrell are pictured in front of their home on Park Avenue.

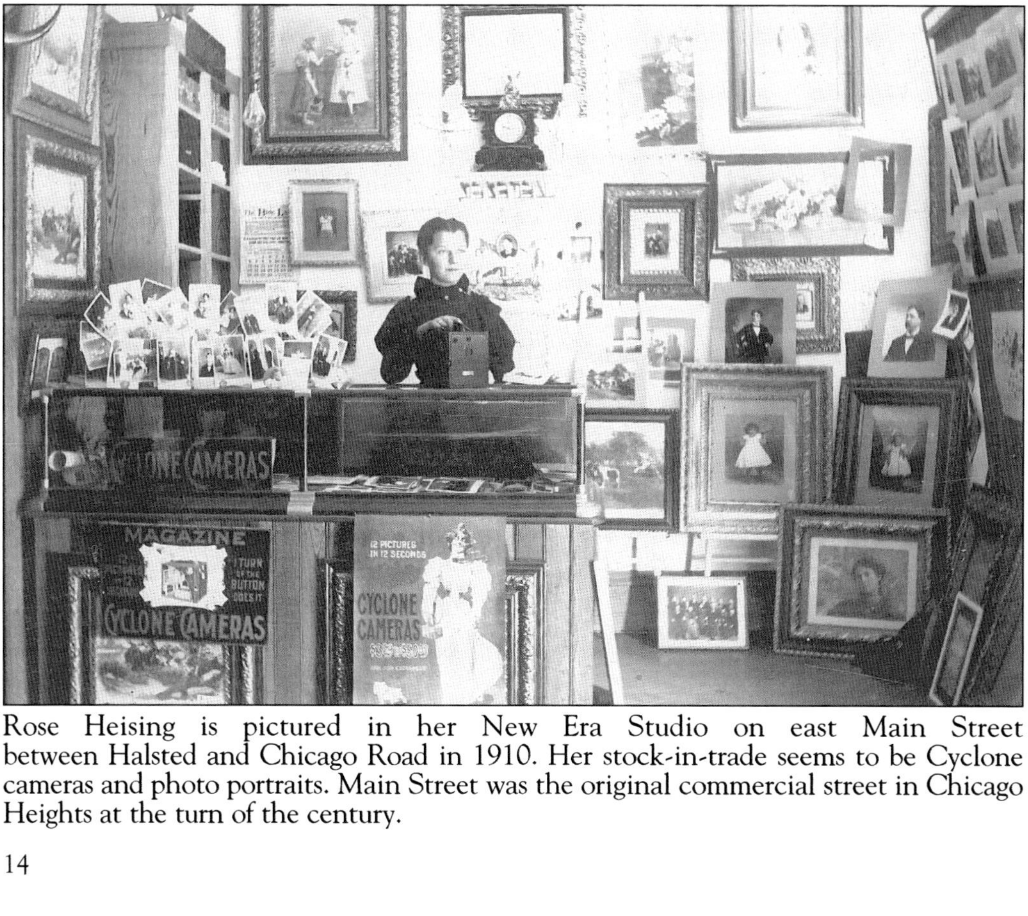

Rose Heising is pictured in her New Era Studio on east Main Street between Halsted and Chicago Road in 1910. Her stock-in-trade seems to be Cyclone cameras and photo portraits. Main Street was the original commercial street in Chicago Heights at the turn of the century.

Two

INDUSTRY

From 1890 to 1960, Chicago Heights was a blue-collar town. The list of Chicago Heights manufacturers and the number of workers they employed is quite impressive. Victor Chemical had 900, Flinkote 650, AMSCO 600, Calumet Steel 450, Inland Steel 375, and Hotpoint 325. The overwhelming majority of the jobs were accessible to anyone with a good work ethic, a strong back, and a good pair of hands. Workers who started work at a factory at age 18 often retired from that same factory 40 years later, and dissatisfied workers could easily find work in other factories if they chose.

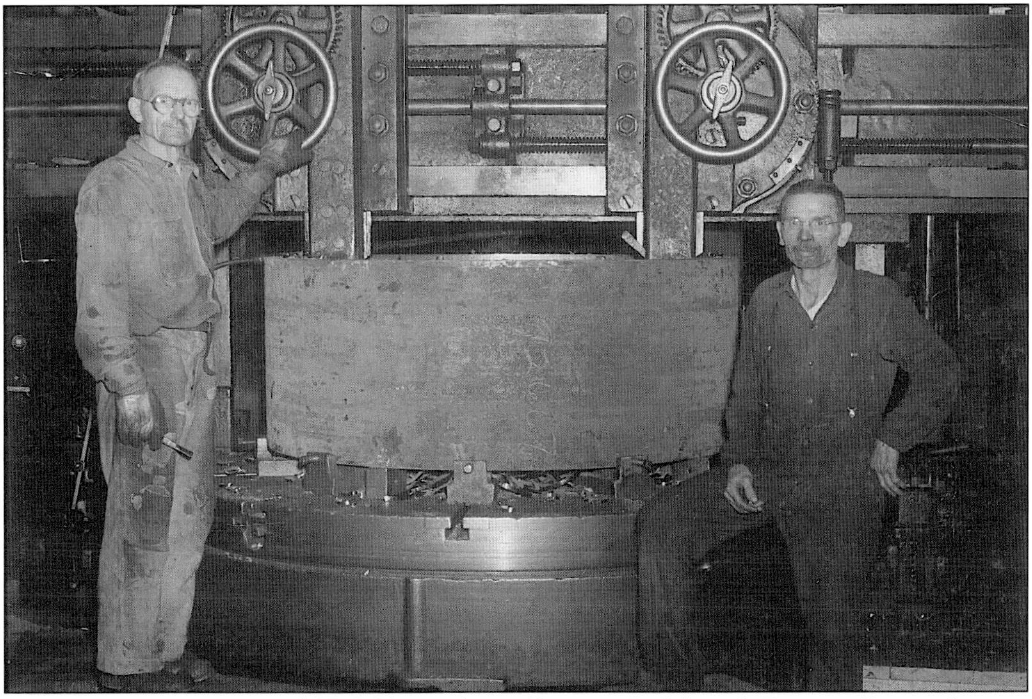

American Locomotive (ALCO) workers George Stahl and Barney Stuempl were recognized as long-time employees in a 1944 ALCO publication. They began working in the boring mill in 1910. ALCO was one of the many heavy industries in Chicago Heights that supported the war effort in the 1940s.

Chicago Heights Industries And Their Products

Industries in the Chicago eights area employ approxi- iately 7.835 people from the city nd outlying communities, ac- ording to figures released by . P. MacNicol, Secretary of the Ianufacturers' association of is city.

The cost of raw materials, with alue added through manufact- ring, estimated Mr. MacNicol, mounts to more than $50 mil- on with the annual payroll otaling close to $25 million.

Listed here are the industries ith their products and approxi- iate number employed:

American Locomotive company, 3rd street and Euclid avenue; ocomotive springs and tires—60.

American Manganese Steel di- ision, American Brake Shoe ompany, 389 East Fourteenth reet; manganese steel castings nd steel welding rods—600.

American Stoveboard company, ixteenth and State streets; stove- oards—25.

Armour Fertilizer Works, Tenth nd State streets, sulphuric acid nd fertilizer—150.

F. H. Ayer Manufacturing com- any, 2015 Halsted street; gen- ral machinists—35.

Bennett Industries, Inc., Peo- ne; steel storage tanks, drums, ructural steel—125.

Bisbee Linseed company, 2012 utler street; linseed oil, meal nd cake—50.

Calumet Steel division, Borg- Varner corporation, Eleventh treet and Wentworth avenue; teel bars, sections, tubing and ence posts—450.

Carb-Rite company, Nineteenth nd Halsted streets; carbon riquettes—10.

Cardox Corporation, Monee; ire extinguishers—100.

Chicago Heights Pattern and Iodel Works, 216 Morgan street; ood patterns—25.

Chicago Heights Trading com- any, 1632 Wentworth avenue; ructural and sheet steel—20.

Chicago Table company or merican Bed company, 1805 ast End avenue; furniture—50.

Columbia Tool Steel company, 92 East Fourteenth street; alloy nd carbon tool steels—250.

Concrete Joist and Products company, 535 East Sixteenth street; concrete joists and blocks —15.

Dowell, Inc., East End avenue and Sauk Trail; chemicals—15.

Edgewood Textile Mills, Inc., 7 East Nineteenth place; bed spreads and drapery material—10.

Flintkote company, Seventeenth street and Wentworth avenue; prepared roofing, asphalt shingles, siding and wallboard —650.

Forster Textile Mills, Inc., Seventeenth street and Union avenue; bed spreads and drapery material—100.

Funk Forging company, Seventeenth street and Fifth avenue; steel forgings and metal specialties—25.

General Transformer company, 18162 Harwood street, Homewood; radio and television transformers —300.

Gold Seal Asphalt Roofing company, Eleventh and State streets; prepared roofing, asphalt shingles and siding—200.

Gould-National Batteries, Inc., Twelfth street and McKinley avenue; storage batteries—225.

Benjamin Harris & company, Thirteenth and State streets; nonferrous metals, smelting and refining—165.

Highway Steel Products company, 1326 McKinley avenue; highway reinforcing steel, beverage venders, lawn rollers, etc. —85.

Hotpoint, Inc., Fourteenth and Arnold streets; commercial cooking equipment—325.

Illinois Shade Cloth corporation, Seventeenth street and Union avenue; window shades and shade cloth—125.

Inland Steel company, Main street and Birmingham avenue; steel bars, shapes, reinforcing bars and fence posts—375.

Industrial Oil and Varnish company, 70 East 23rd street; oil and varnish—5.

International Minerals and Chemical corporation, Sixteenth and State streets; plant food—35.

Jasica Wood Products company, 1116 Union avenue; wood products and specialities—5.

Keystone Asphalt Products company, East Sixteenth street; mastic board and asphaltic products—75.

Kimble Glass division, Owens-Illinois Glass company, Twelfth and Arnold streets; glass bottles and specialties—250.

Mohawk Tablet company, Seventeenth street and East End avenue; stationery—100.

Mid-West Forging and Manufacturing company, East Sixteenth street; metal sign stands and forgings—100.

Midwest Plastic Products company, 1801 Chicago road; plastic sheet stock and tubing—15.

Nagle Pumps, 1249 Center avenue; power pumps—20.

Nebraska Bridge Supply and Lumber company, East End avenue and Sauk Trail; show fencing—20.

Neil Box Company, Inc., Seventeenth street and Center avenue; boxes—10.

Ramapo Ajax division, American Brake Shoe company, Twelfth and Washington streets; railway track material—225.

Steger Furniture Manufacturing company, 3321 Chicago road, Steger; radio and television cabinets—400.

Steger Products Manufacturing corporation, 3317 Chicago road, Steger; wheel toys, radio and television cabinets—200.

Thrall Car Manufacturing company, 26th and Wallace streets; railway equipment—50.

Tile-Tex division, The Flintkote company, 1232 McKinley avenue; asphalt composition and plastic floor and wall tile—350.

Triem Steel and Processing, Inc., 26th and State streets; steel processing, pickling and oiling—25.

Victor Chemical Works, Eleventh and Arnold streets; chemicals —900.

Wardway Paint Works, Tenth and Washington streets; paints —100.

Weber Costello company, Twelfth street and McKinley avenue; school supplies and geographical globes—140.

Wesco Waterpaints, Inc., Matteson; cold water paints—60.

Western Metal Abrasives company, 101 East Main street; abrasives—25.

This 1950s clipping lists the major manufacturers in the city. Employment was even more impressive when business, commercial, and service occupations were included. The business district benefitted, since even those workers who lived outside of Chicago Heights generally shopped, banked, and sought entertainment in town.

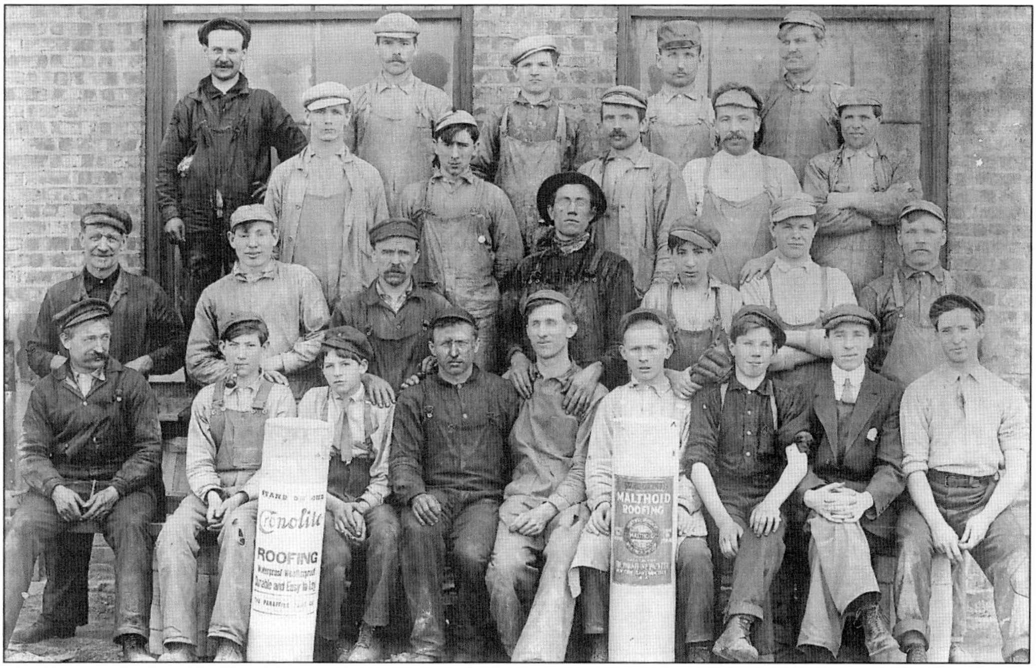

In the 1920s, Flinkote employees included men and boys of various ages. By 1927, it had purchased two roofing firms in Ohio and had announced plans to expand the Chicago Heights factory—making Flintkote the largest exclusive manufacturer of roofing materials in the world. By the 1950s the plant, located at 17th and Wentworth, employed 650 people.

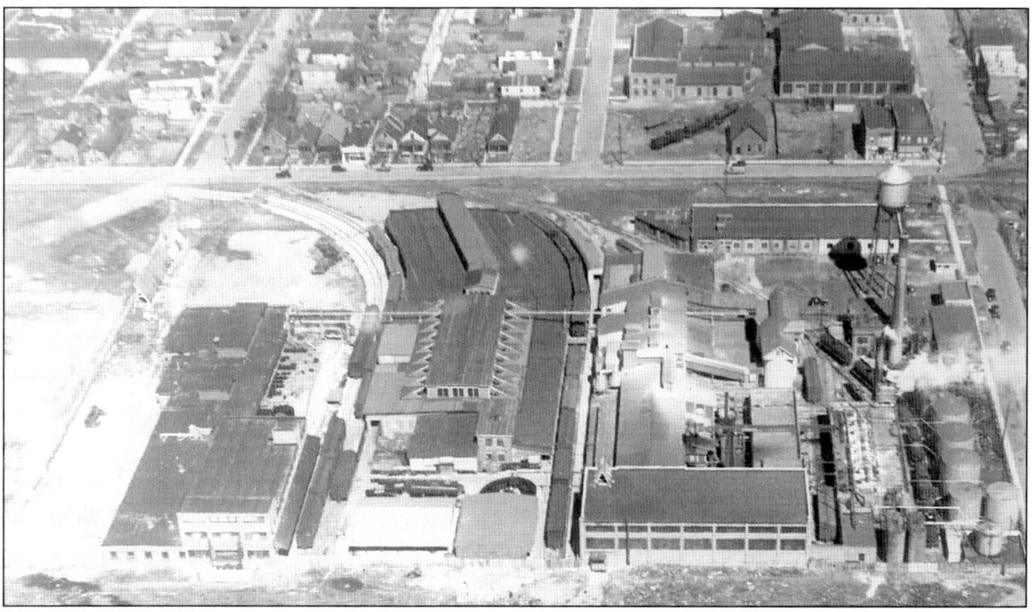

The Flintkote Company started operations in Chicago Heights in 1920. This 1939 photo shows the importance of rail spurs to Flintkote and to Funk Forging (upper right). Also pictured at the top—the 7th building from the right (on 17th Street)—is the birthplace of Mayor Angelo Ciambrone and, next to it, the old Savoia's Restaurant.

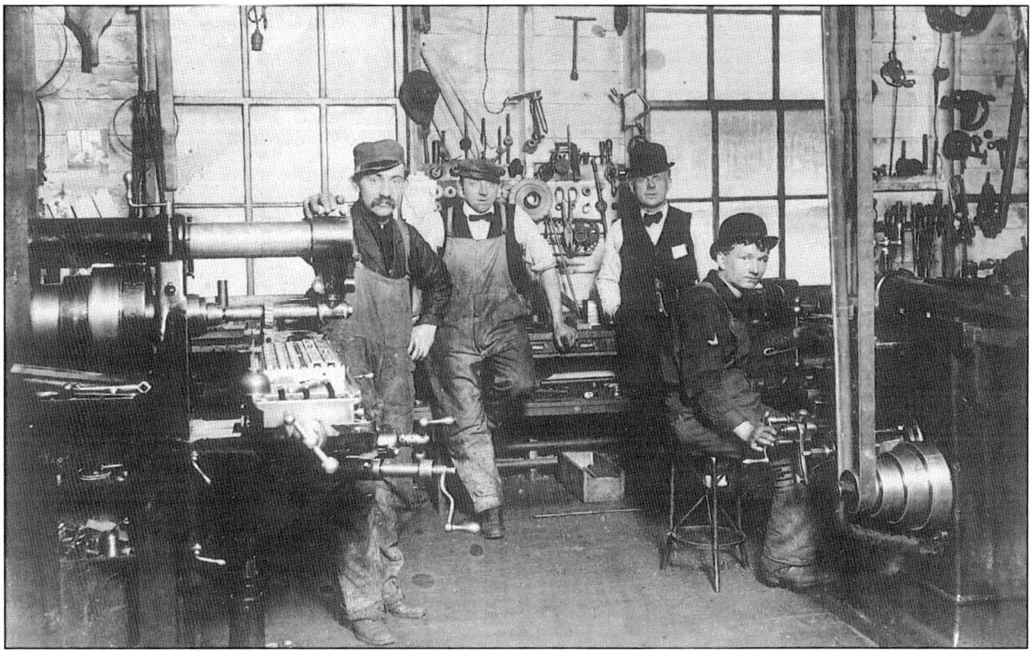

The F.H. Ayer Manufacturing Company was founded in 1898 by Fred H. Ayer and continues to operate today. Pictured are the following, from left to right: Frank W. DeBolt, Julius Mason, Fred Ayer, and Willie Corkhouse. Note the belt powered machinery.

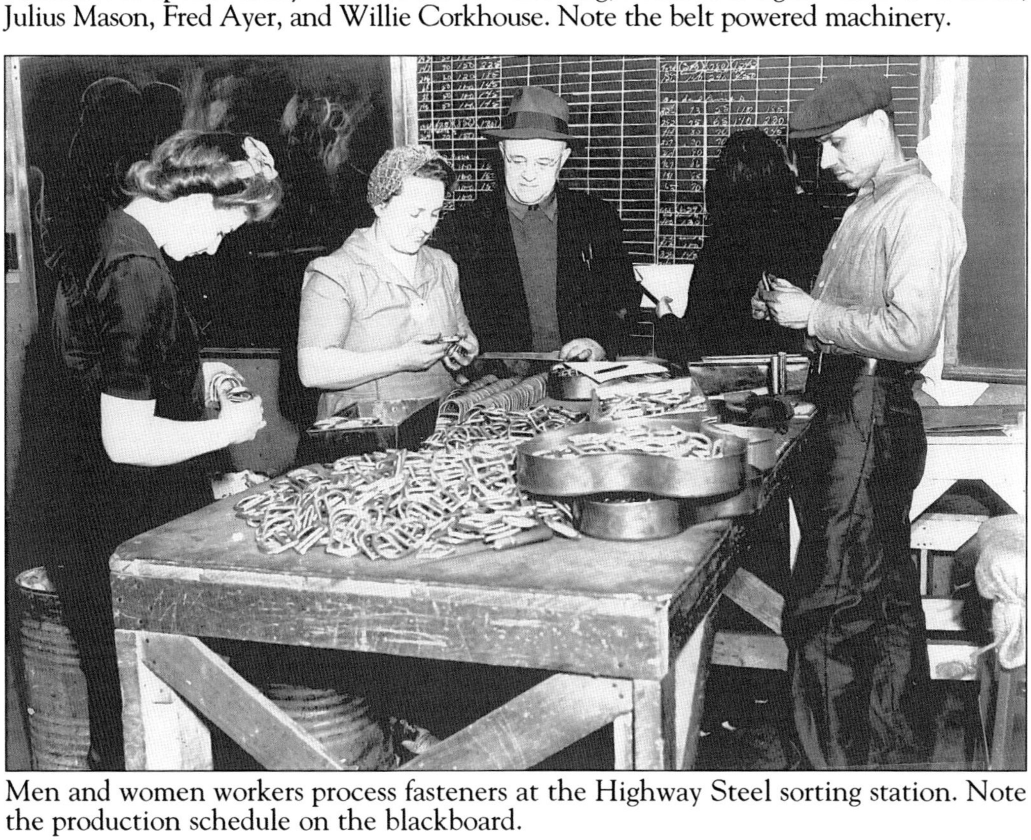

Men and women workers process fasteners at the Highway Steel sorting station. Note the production schedule on the blackboard.

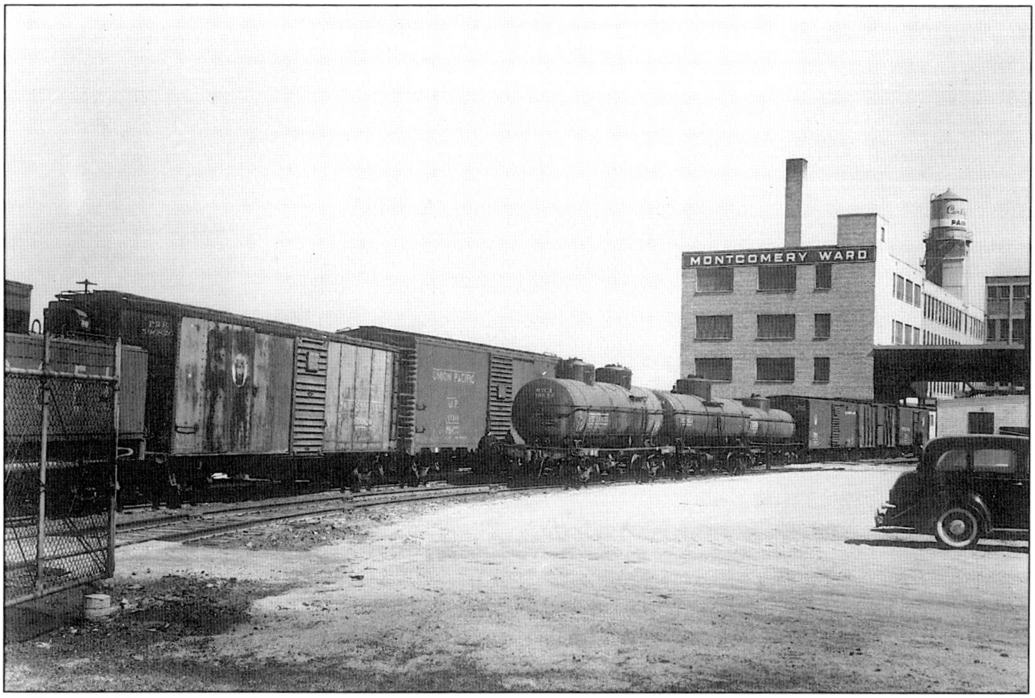

Off Twelfth Street, The Montgomery Ward paint factory employed hundreds of Chicago Heights residents and shipped millions of gallons of paint in the 1930s. It became Standard T Chemical Company in the 1970s and is now Ace Hardware Paint.

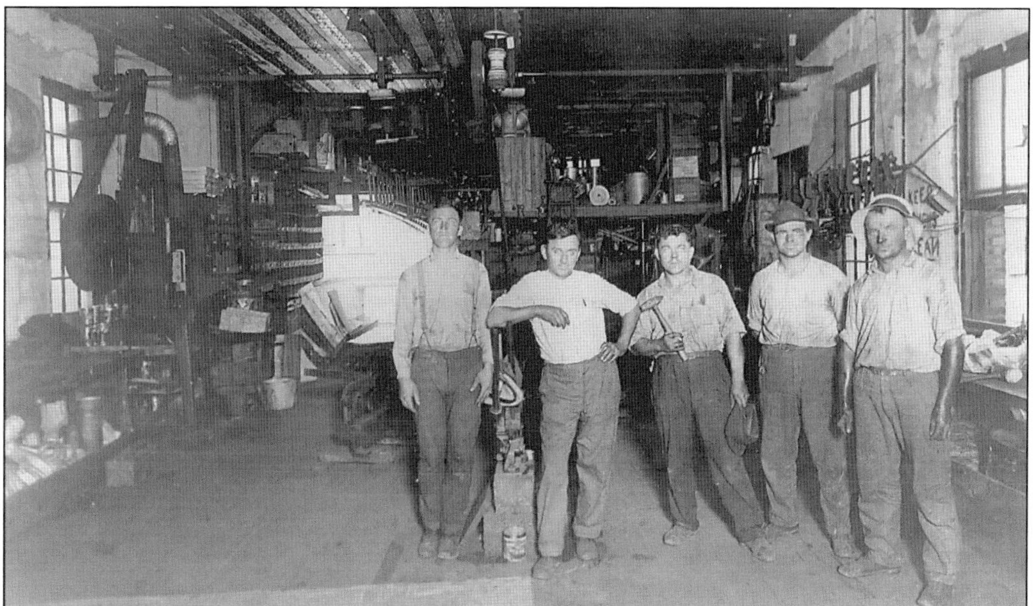

Workers pose inside the John Maier & Co. sheet metal works. The business has been in Chicago Heights for 98 years serving manufacturers and home owners

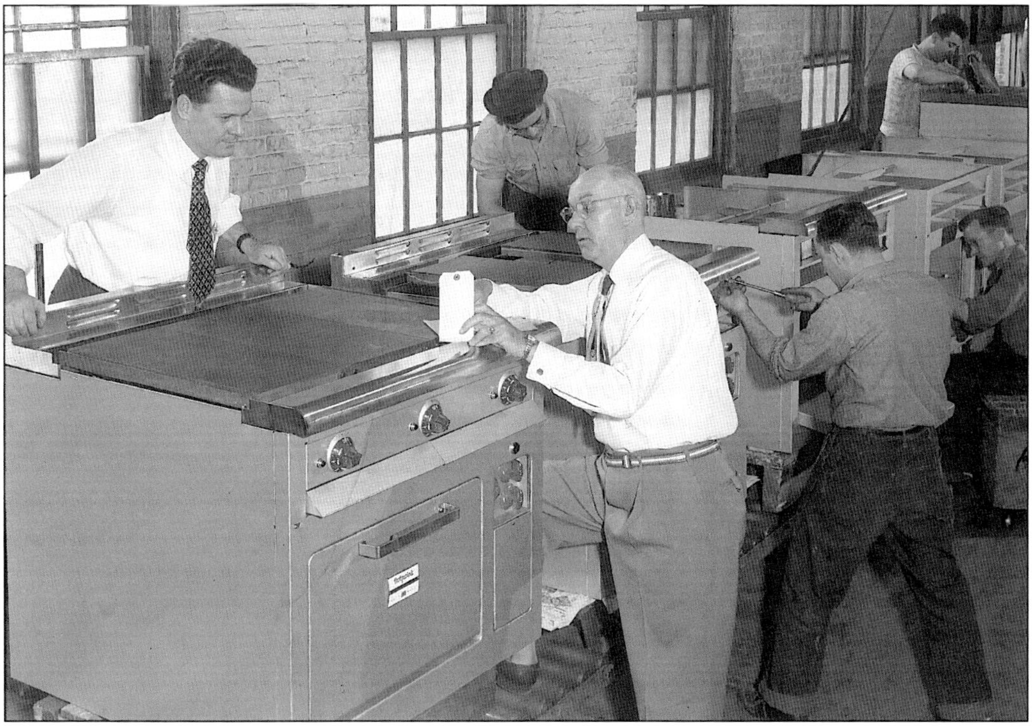

White-collar management officials inspect finished products in the General Electric Hotpoint Division at 14th and Arnold Streets, which claimed to be the world center of commercial cooking products used in the finest ocean liners, navy ships, and restaurants. Hotpoint came to Chicago Heights in the 1940s and folded in the 1970s.

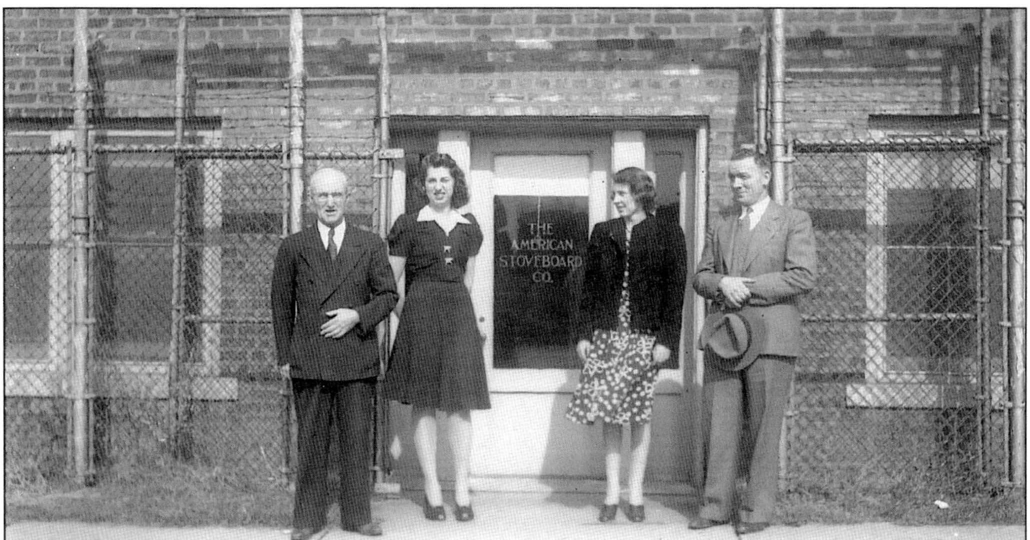

Henry E. Gunn (left) and George Zimmerman (right) stand with two unidentified women at the entrance to the American Stoveboard Company in the fall of 1942. The plant, located in Chicago Heights at the turn of the century, billed itself as the largest factory in the world dedicated exclusively to the manufacture of stoveboard.

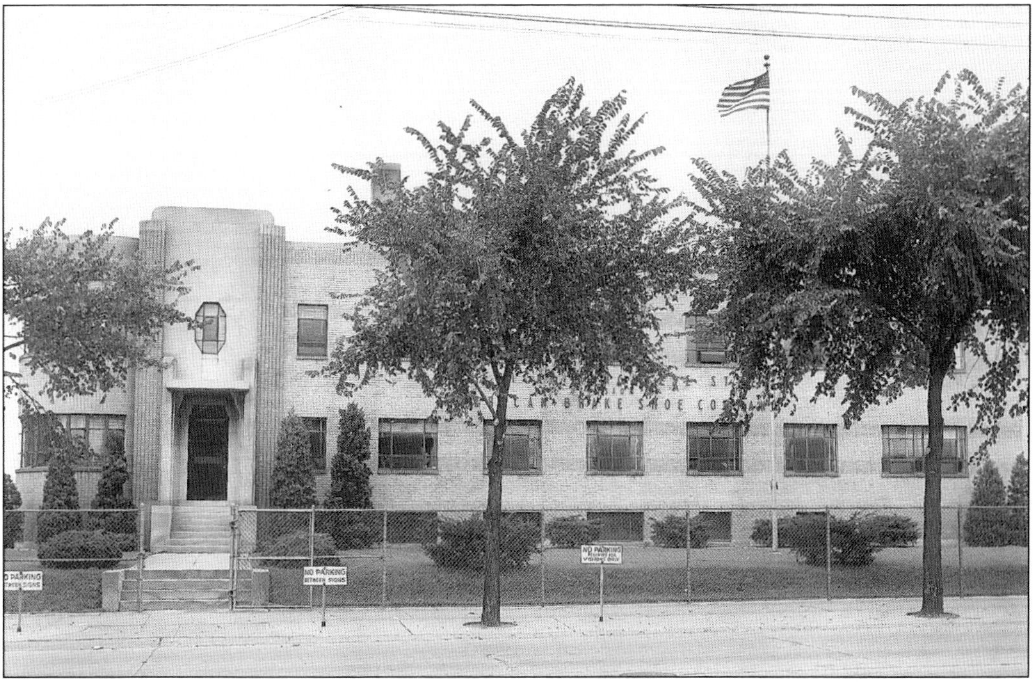

Pictured is the Art Deco front office of the American Manganese Steel Division of American Brake Shoe Company (AMSCO) located on the northwest corner of 14th and State. Before World War II, it was considered the largest manganese company in the world. Tradition has it that two generations of Italian Americans from the Marche region dominated the work force at AMSCO.

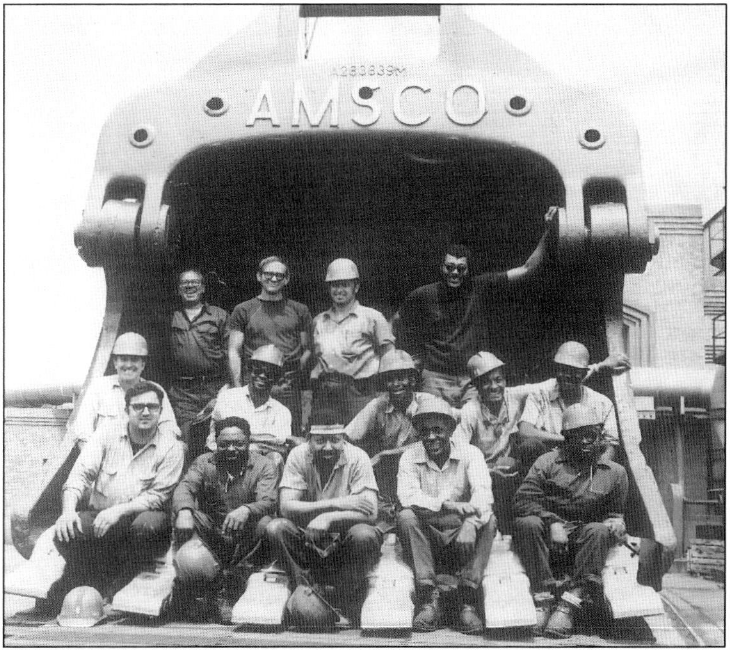

AMSCO workers pose inside the "Big Dipper"—the world's largest manganese mining scoop at 40 tons. The Dipper measured 12 by 11 by 13 feet. Among those pictured in this 1975 photo are Livio Planera, Al Flamini, Robert Stanley, Ben Gonzalez, and Frank LoBue. AMSCO closed in 1980.

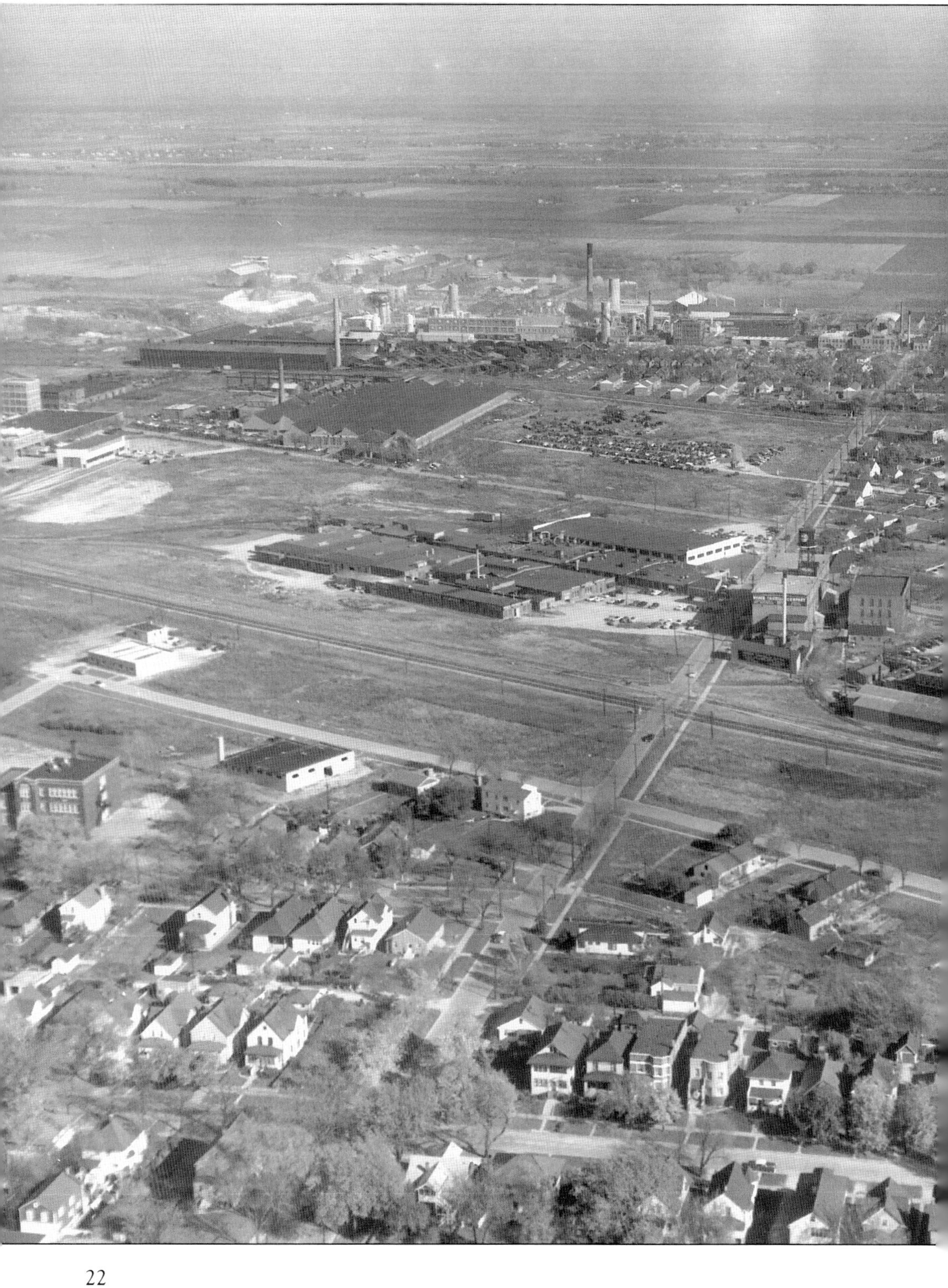

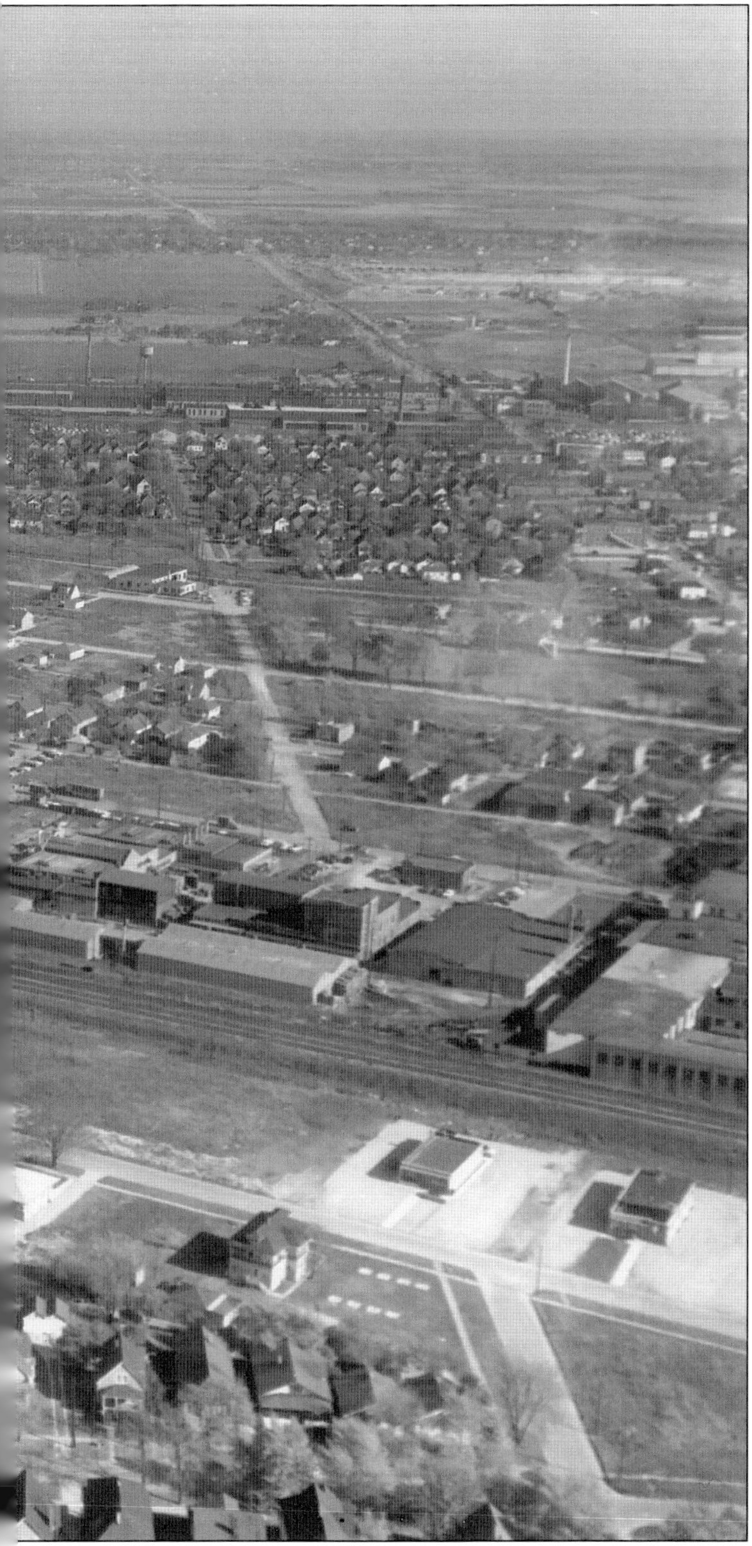

In this 1950s aerial view of the East Side industrial complex, we see Calumet Steel (left) and Victor Chemical (center background). In the foreground are the C&EI railway tracks and Wardway Paints.

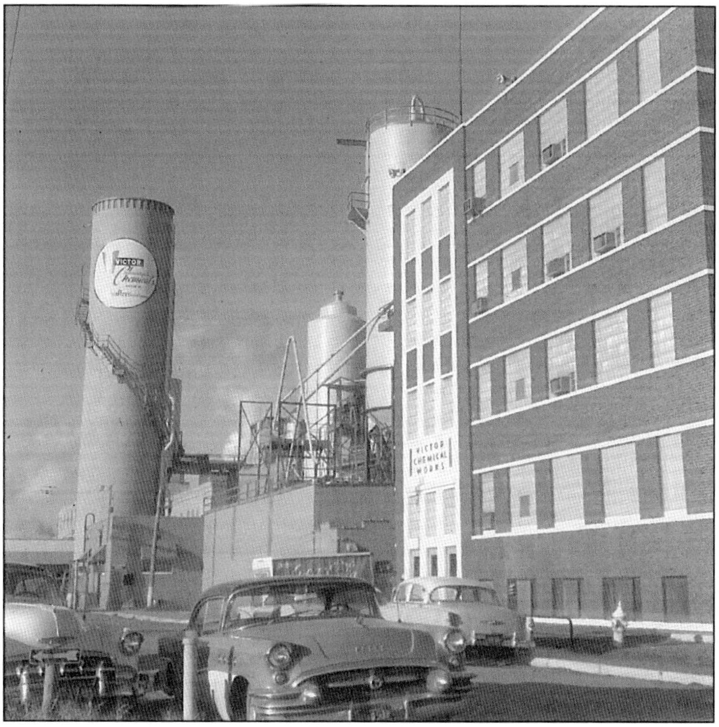

August Kochs founded Victor Chemical Works in 1902. The plant produced phosphate for the baking industry. It is still doing business as Rhodia, producing chemical compounds for baking, food processing, and tooth paste.

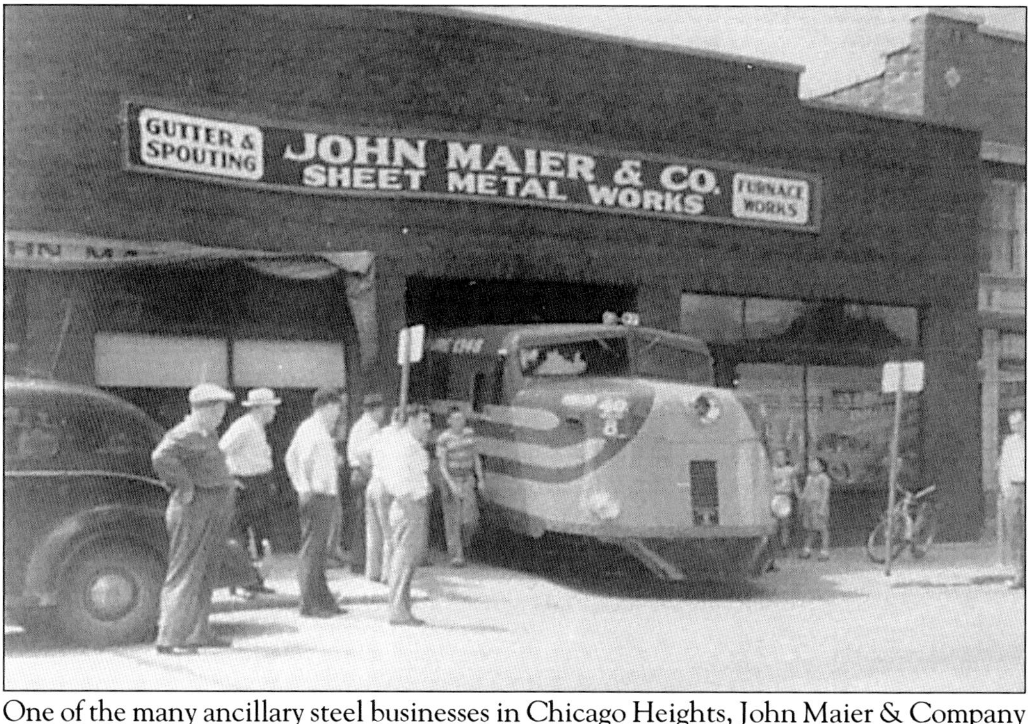

One of the many ancillary steel businesses in Chicago Heights, John Maier & Company sheet metal was located at 1640 Chicago Road in this 1950s photo. Here, the workers rolled out a parade float fashioned like a diesel locomotive.

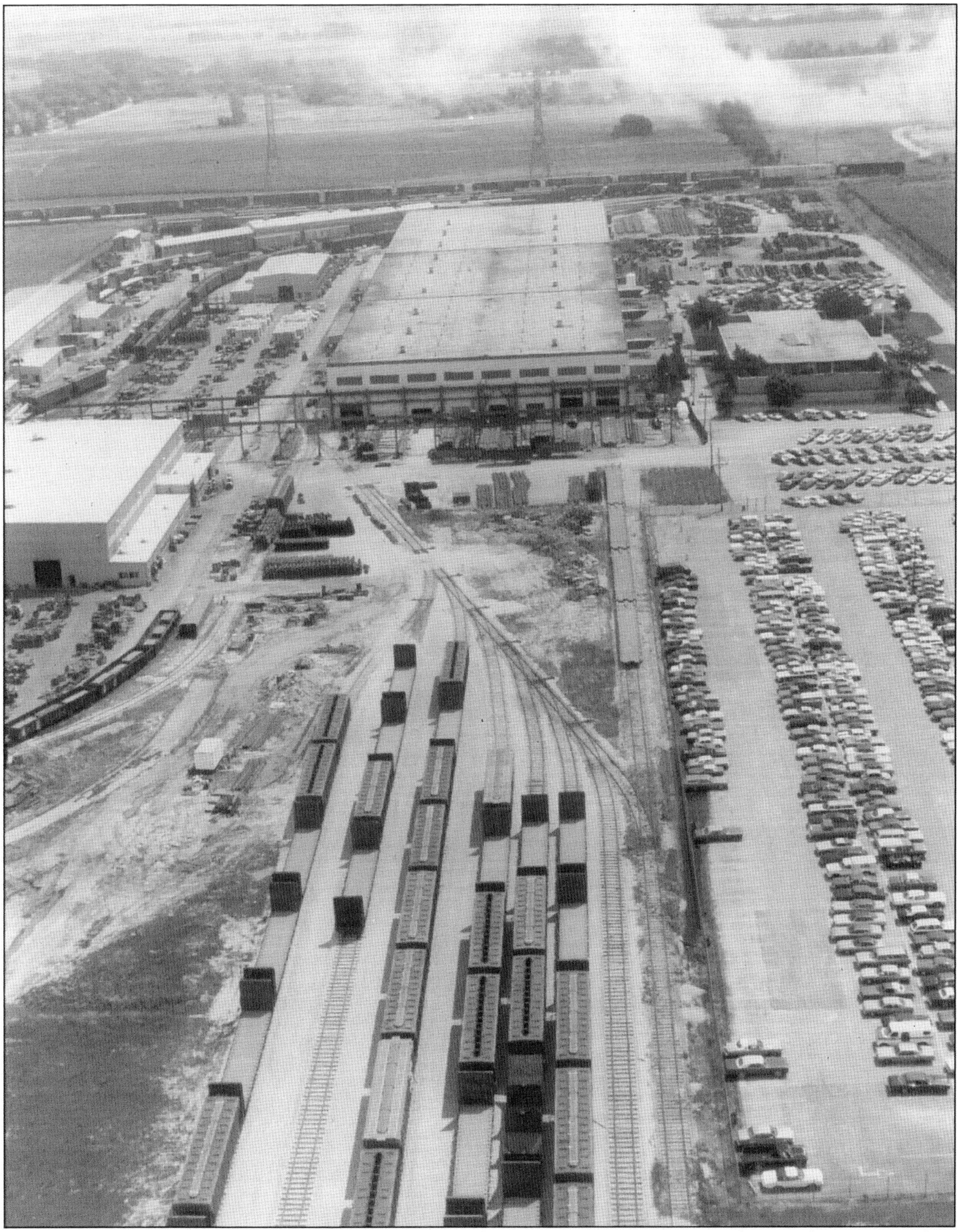

Here is an aerial view of Thrall Car Manufacturing Company in the early 1970s after a multi-million-dollar plant and office expansion program was completed in the late 1960s. The company produced more than 4,000 railroad cars per year at that time.

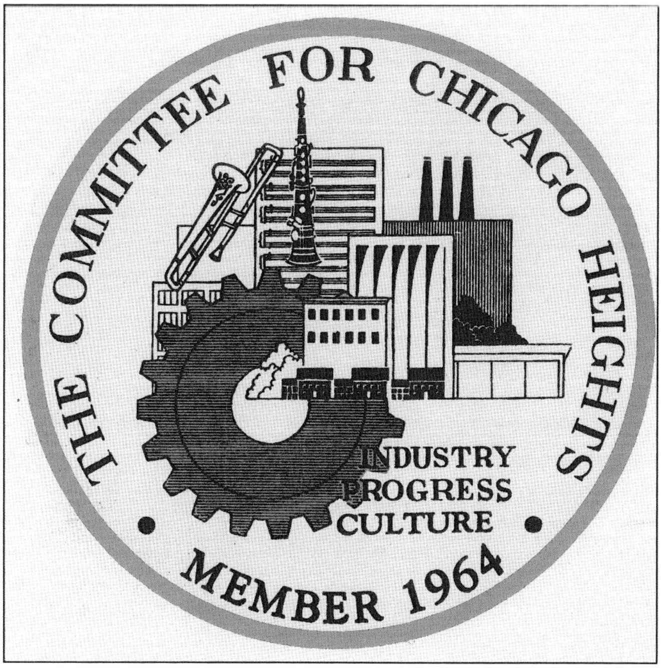

Led by Pierce Vandercook, the Committee for Chicago Heights spearheaded an economic development campaign in the 1950s and 1960s that allied the Chicago Heights Manufacturers Association with retail merchants. The group was credited with bringing Ford, Pennsalt, and other important industries to Chicago Heights. In 1958, the group sponsored "Culturama," an extravagant festival that featured humorist Herb Shriner.

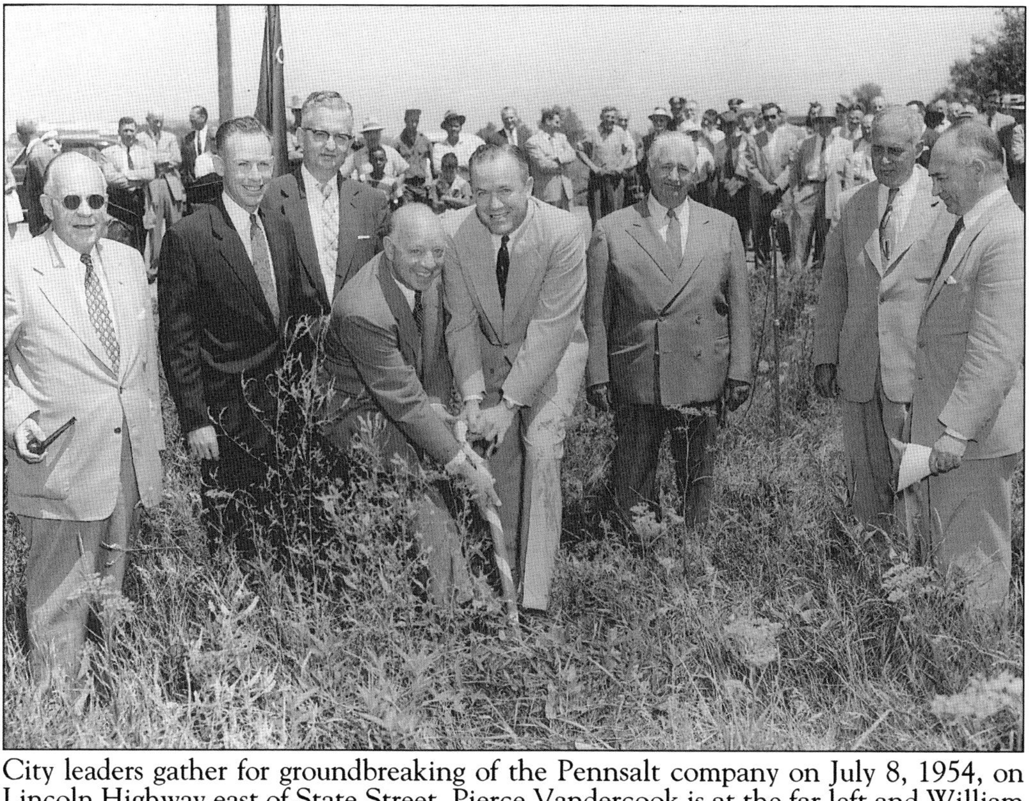

City leaders gather for groundbreaking of the Pennsalt company on July 8, 1954, on Lincoln Highway east of State Street. Pierce Vandercook is at the far left and William Thorsness is third from the left. Those at the right are Pennsalt executives.

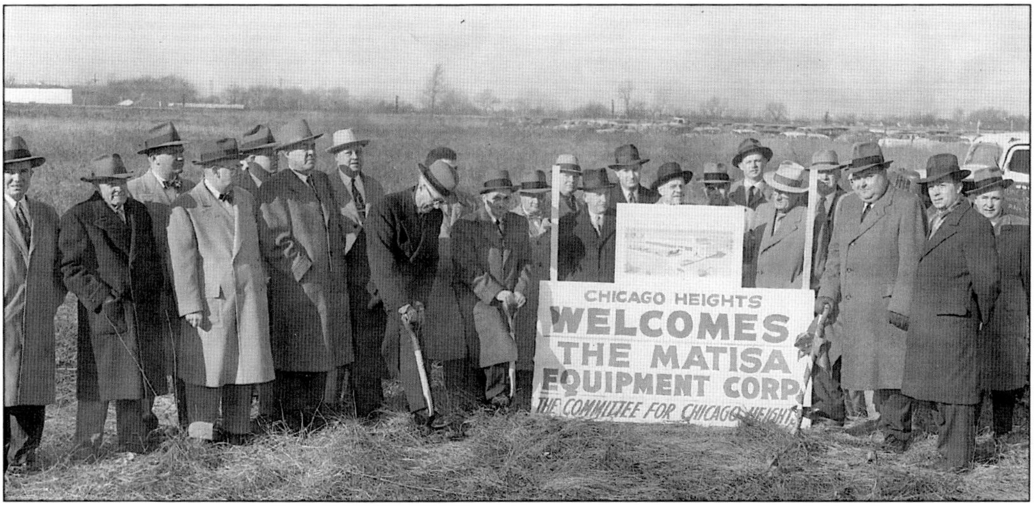

The Committee for Chicago Heights actively sought manufacturers to relocate in their city. Here, committee members and dignitaries break ground for the Matisa Equipment Company, which announced a purchase of land in January 1955. The *Star* headline read, "Rail Equipment Firm to Build Here."

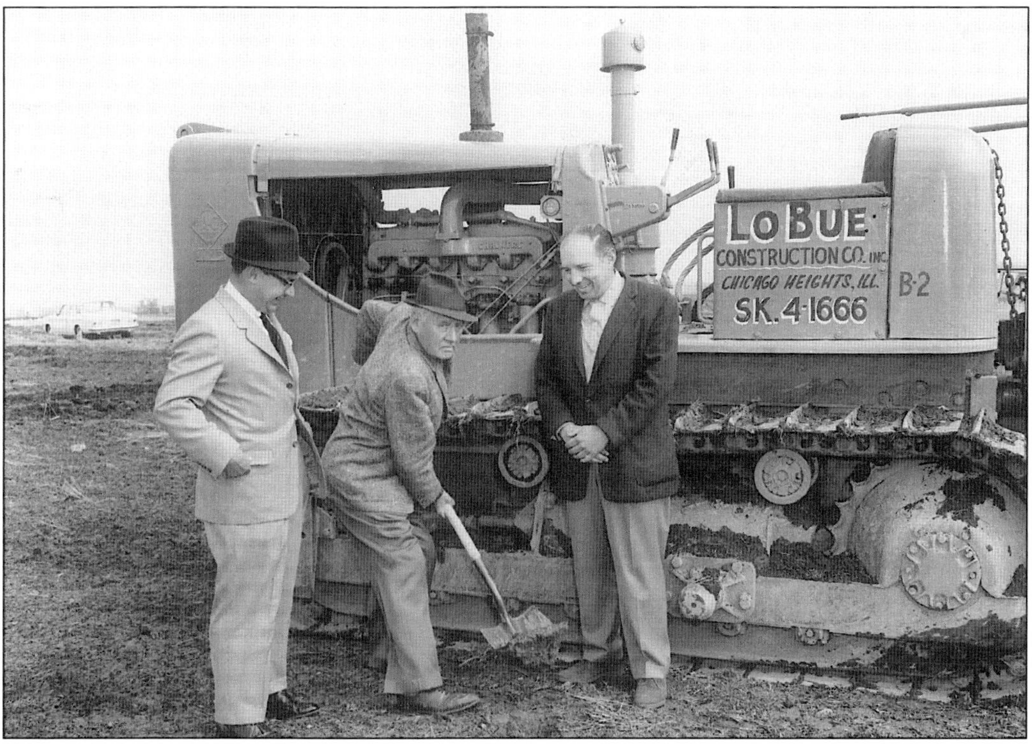

Ground was broken May 10, 1962, for a new expansion for Thrall Car Manufacturing Company. Presiding over the ceremonies were, from left to right, as follows: R.L Duchossois, president; Arthur J. Thrall, chairman of the board; and Jerry Thrall, executive vice president.

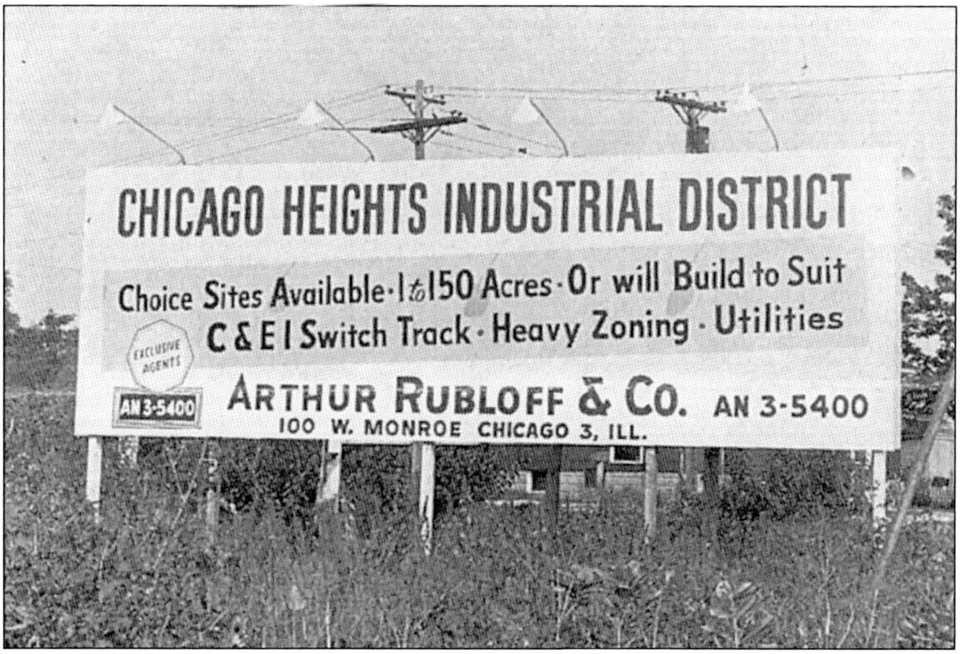

A sign of the times is pictured as the Committee for Chicago Heights worked with private relators to promote the State Street industrial area in the 1950s with remarkable success.

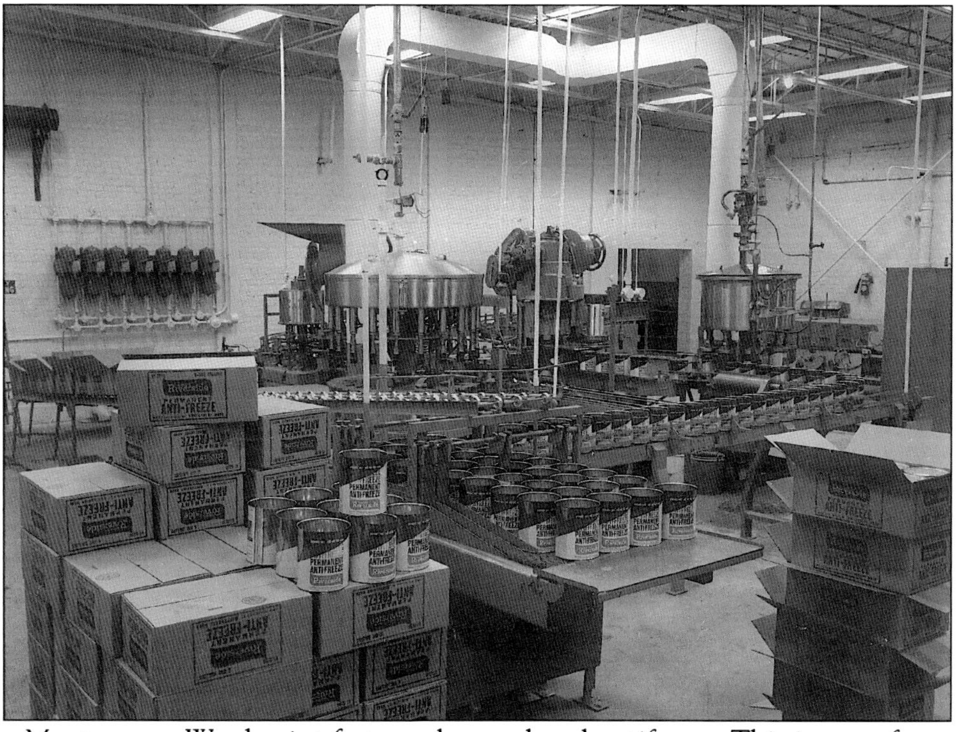

The Montgomery Ward paint factory also produced antifreeze. This is one of several assembly lines that operated in the plant.

Three

World War II

World War II changed America, and it changed Chicago Heights. The unified push of people, media, business, and social organizations to support the war effort was truly remarkable. Approximately 3,500 men and women served in the armed forces of whom 114 were killed, 86 were wounded, and 23 were missing. The war experience Americanized the second generation ethics, while veteran benefits for education and low-cost mortgages ultimately led them out of the old East Side and the Hill neighborhoods to the West Side and North End of Chicago Heights.

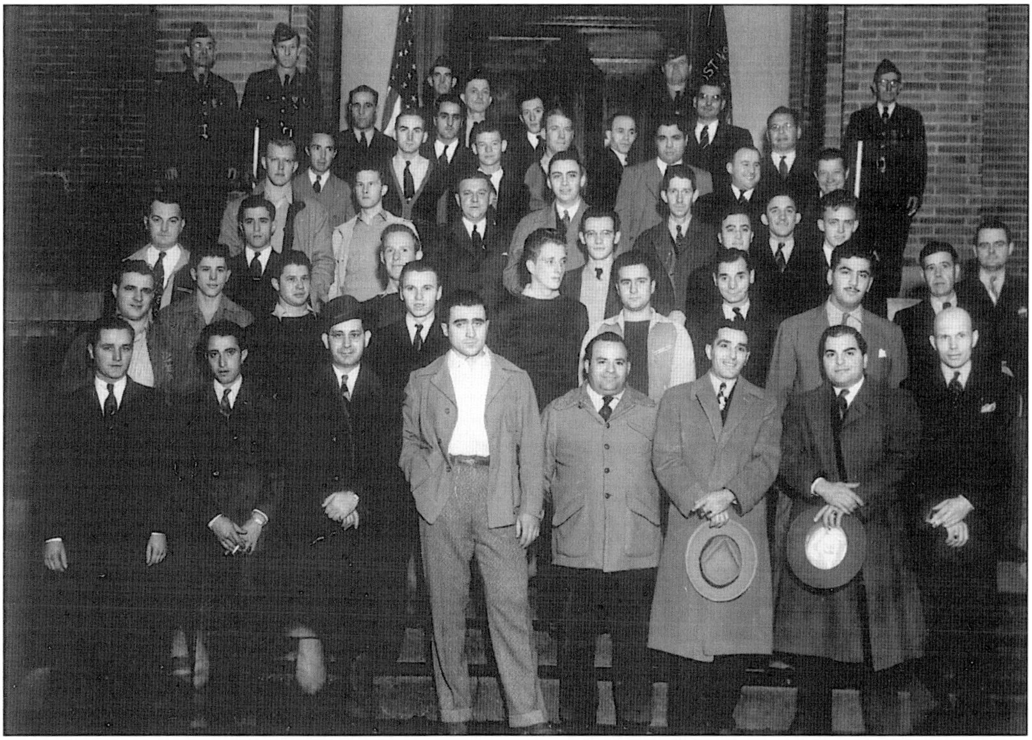

Young men pose on the library steps before departing for the Camp Grant Induction Center on October 15, 1942. Among those identified in this photo are Dom Pancrazio, John Martello, Theodore Acroupolos, Sanford Witter, and John Roberts.

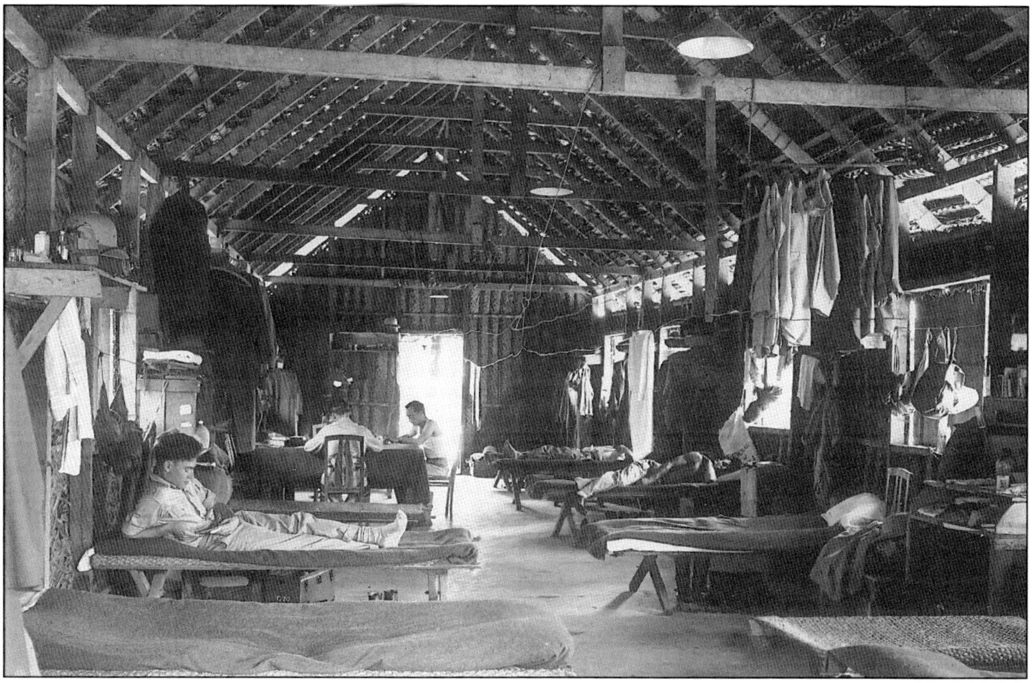

This typical army barracks was home to Joe Gannon, Jr. during part of his tour of duty during World War II. Many other Chicago Heights servicemen lived in similar conditions.

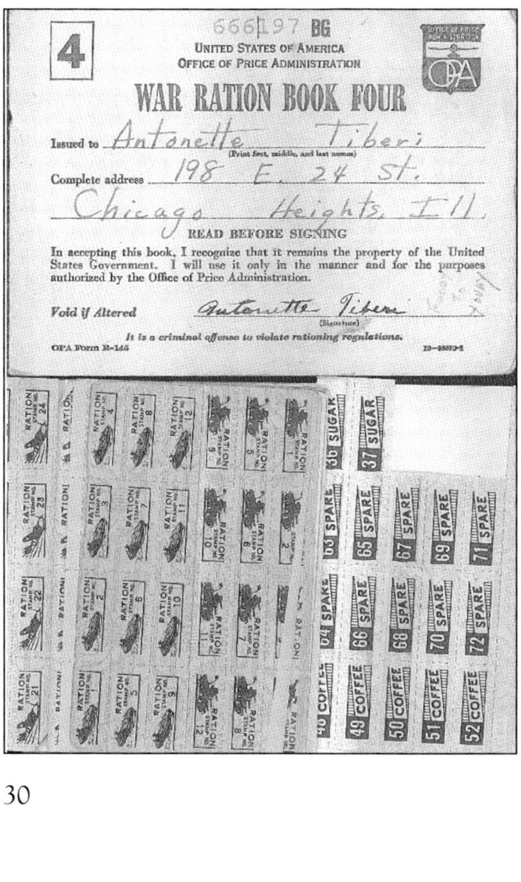

4

666197 BG

UNITED STATES OF AMERICA
OFFICE OF PRICE ADMINISTRATION

WAR RATION BOOK FOUR

Issued to Antonette Tiberi
(Print first, middle, and last names)

Complete address 198 E. 24 St.
Chicago Heights, Ill.

READ BEFORE SIGNING

In accepting this book, I recognize that it remains the property of the United States Government. I will use it only in the manner and for the purposes authorized by the Office of Price Administration.

Void if Altered Antonette Tiberi
(Signature)

It is a criminal offense to violate rationing regulations.

OPA Form R-145

Antonette Tiberi's War Ration Book contained stamps for coffee, sugar, and general merchandise. The OPA used ration stamps as a means of maintaining price levels and curbing black market trade in scarce food and commodities such as coffee, sugar, and gasoline.

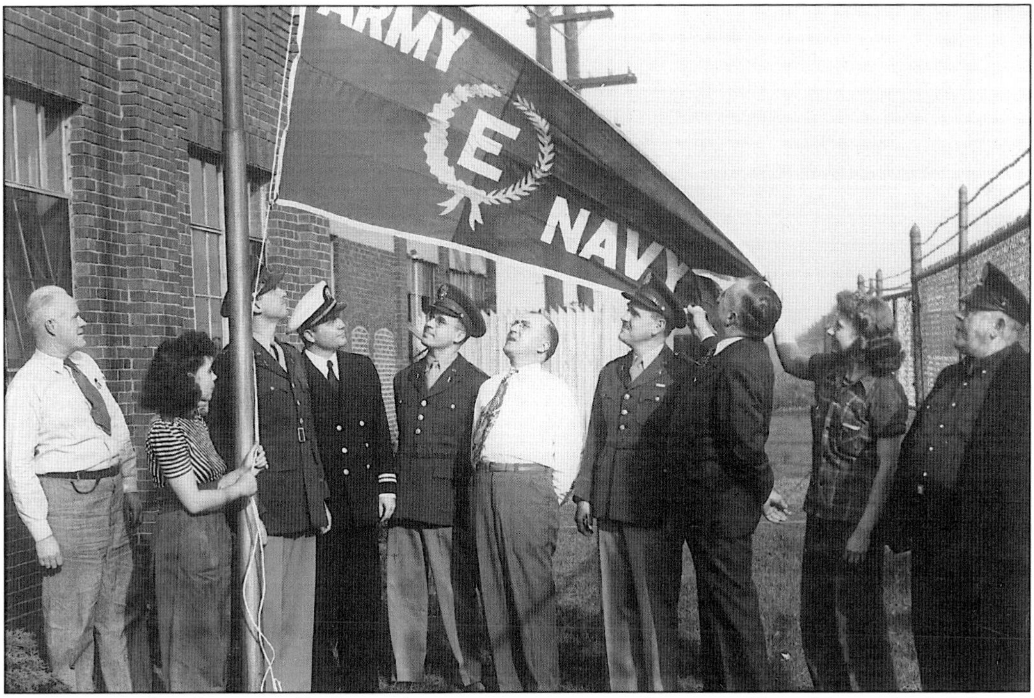

Business and industry pulled out the stops to support the war effort. Here, the Midwest Forging and Manufacturing company is being awarded the "E" pennant as well as 145 individual "E" pins for its efforts in the production of ammunition in 1943. Pictured from left to right are as follows: Louis Gatto, Frances Pascarella, Captain E.A. Kitch, Lieutenant H.A. Dellenback, Lieutenant K.L. Warren, Superintendent Nick Bardell, Major J.A. Roesch, President J.L. Hench, Isabel Palock, and Stefan Frecowski.

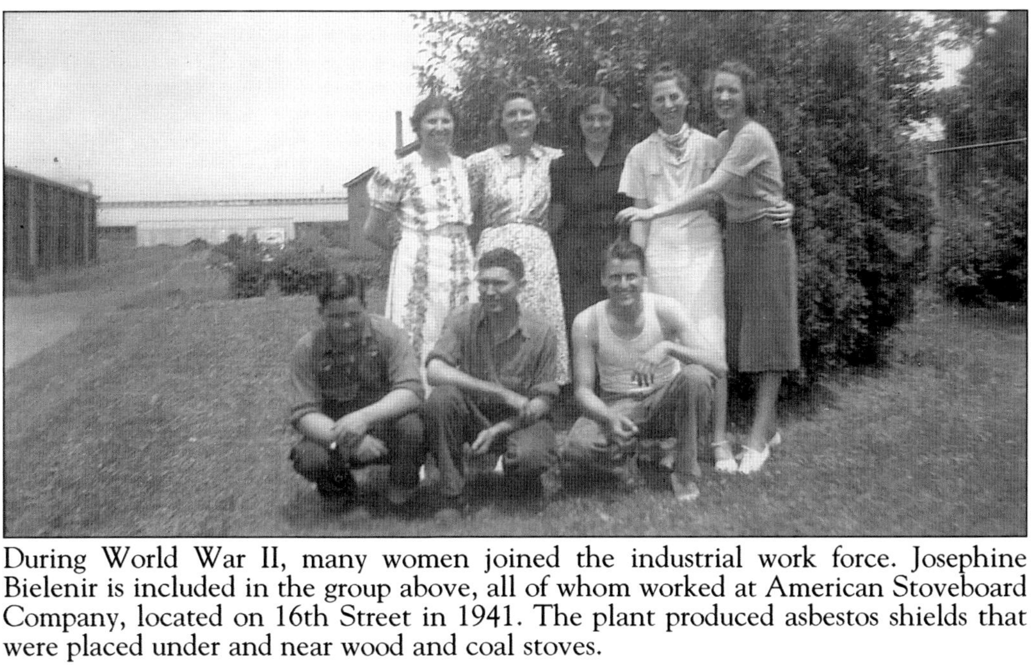

During World War II, many women joined the industrial work force. Josephine Bielenir is included in the group above, all of whom worked at American Stoveboard Company, located on 16th Street in 1941. The plant produced asbestos shields that were placed under and near wood and coal stoves.

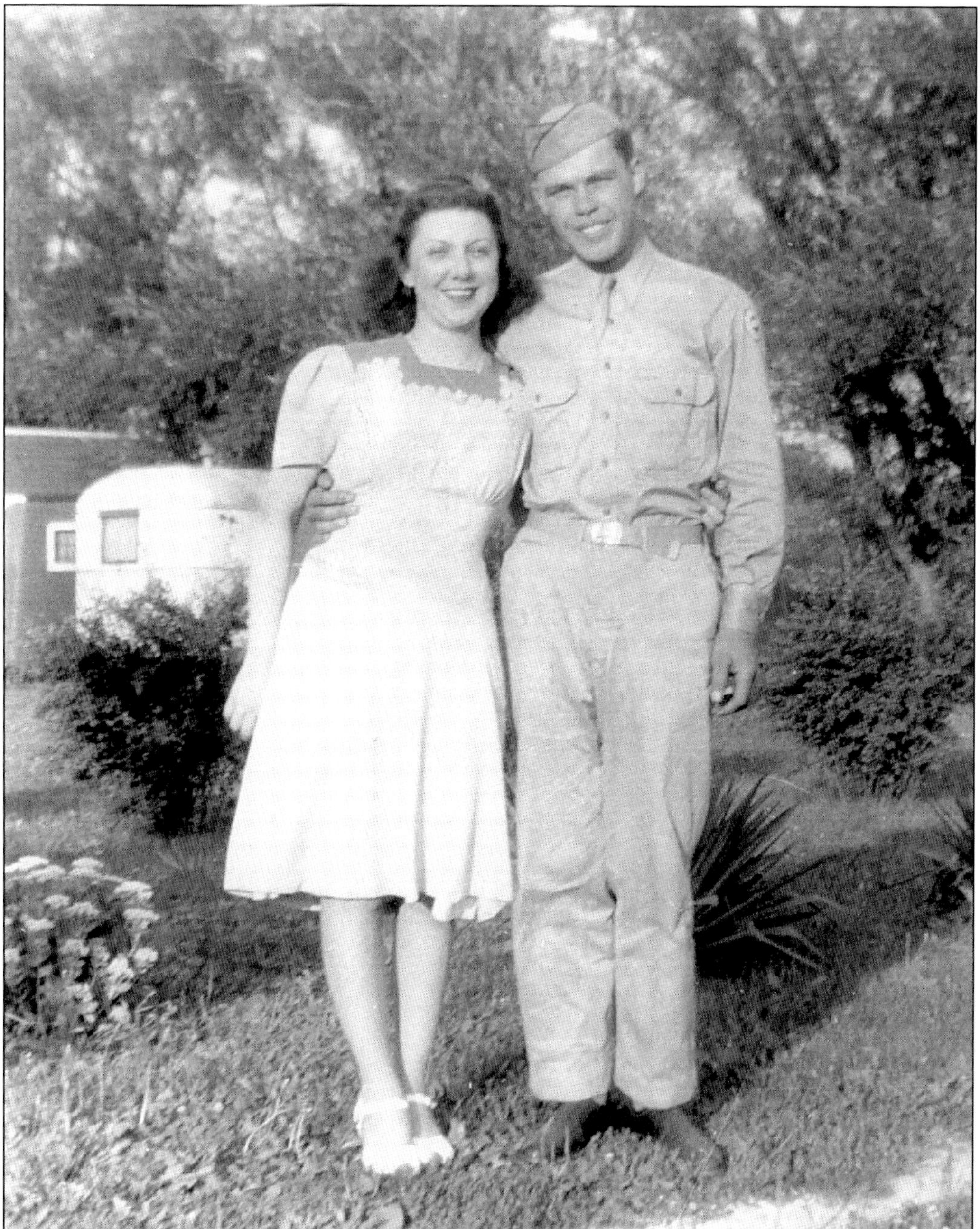

Typically during a leave from the military in 1942, friends, family, and sweethearts took photos to document the brief respite from the war. Sources were only able to identify the man in this photo as John Francher.

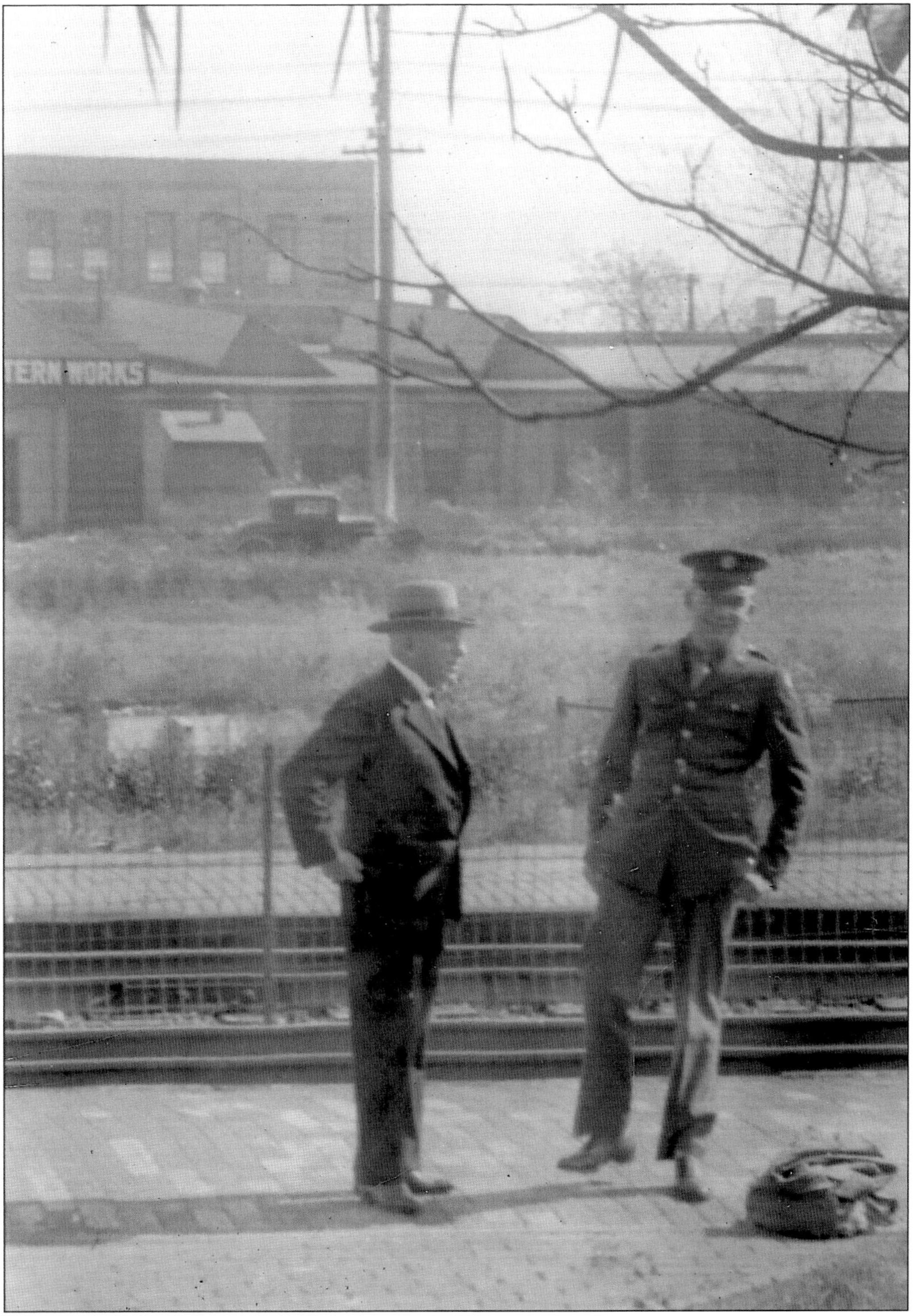

Mayor Joseph Gannon and his son wait at the C&EI station as Joe Junior's leave comes to an end.

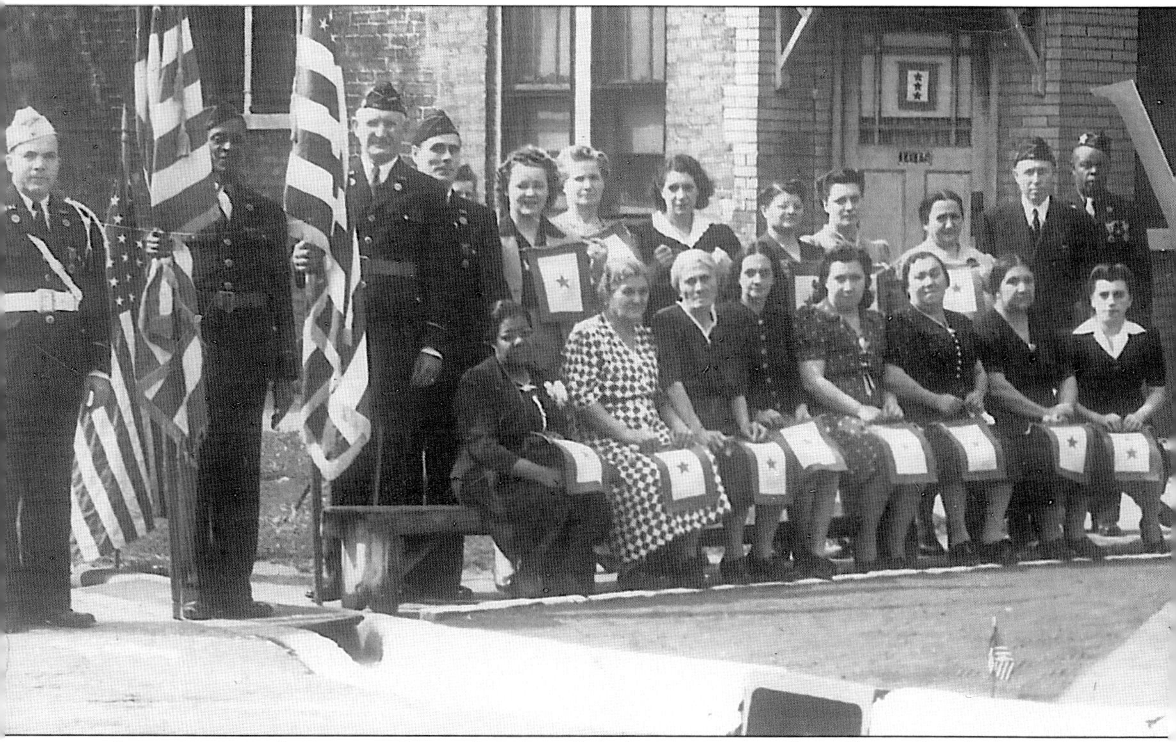

An interracial group of mothers and relatives attend a flagpole dedication in honor of neighborhood servicemen. Members of the American Legion Posts # 410 (Franklin Dennison Post—African-American) and #131 participated in the ceremony at Butler and 16th in September 1942. Some of the surnames of

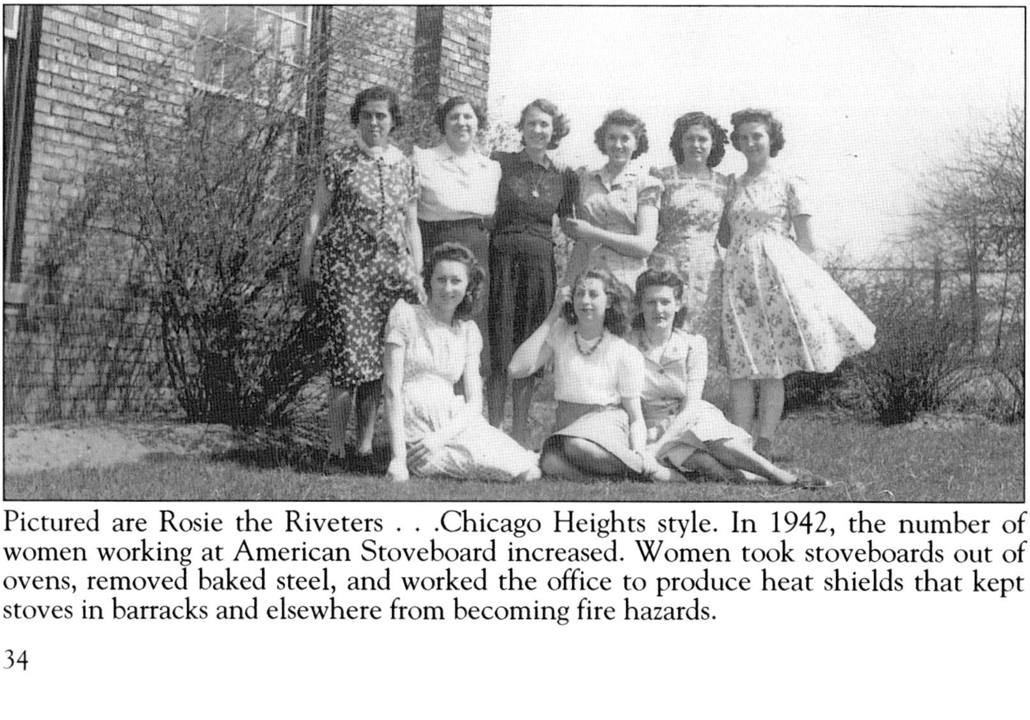

Pictured are Rosie the Riveters . . .Chicago Heights style. In 1942, the number of women working at American Stoveboard increased. Women took stoveboards out of ovens, removed baked steel, and worked the office to produce heat shields that kept stoves in barracks and elsewhere from becoming fire hazards.

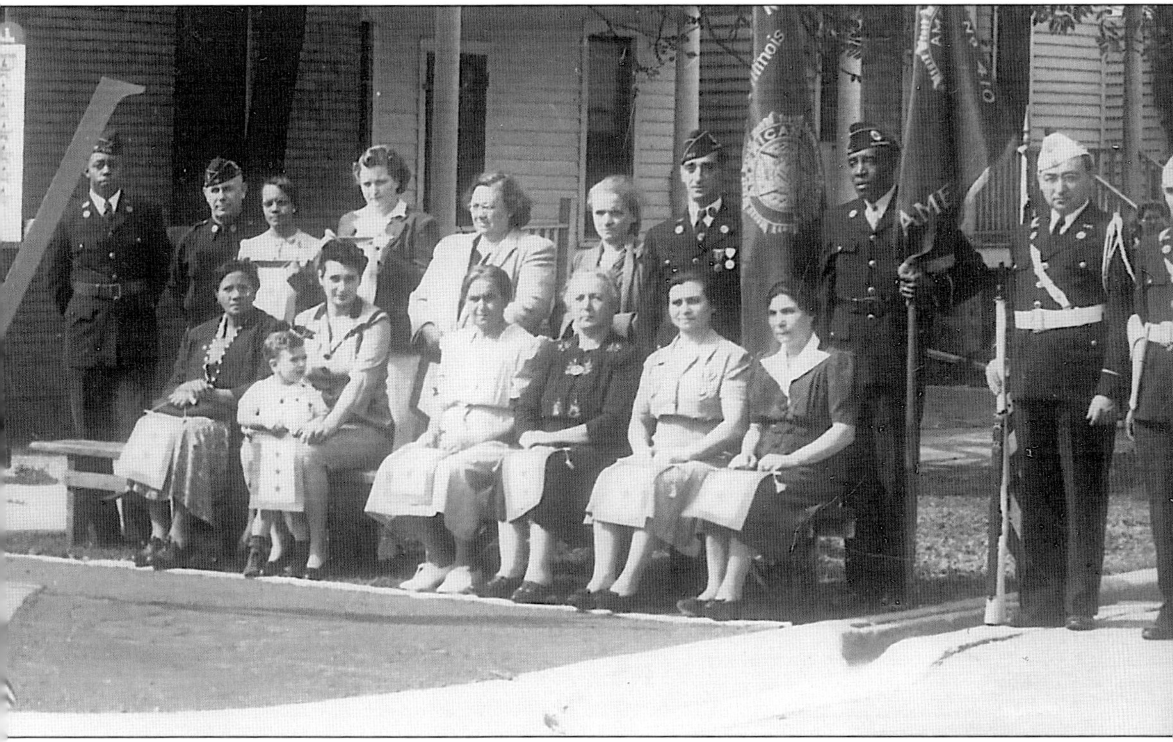

those pictured are as follows: Jack, Perozzi, Prospero, Shugar, Firrantello, Firrantello, Gentile, Guidera,Webb, Amato, Capeletti, Patrizi, Capacasa, Pizzimenti, Kwasek, Marousek, Marino, George, Saculla, Tribo, Williams, Windhorst, Wojcieszak, Marconi.

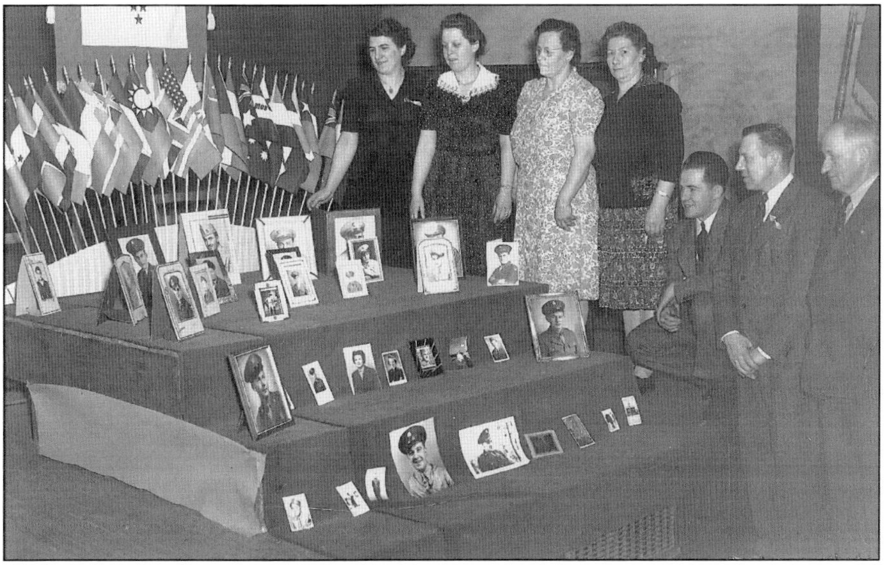

Committee members from the Polish Falcons admire a display honoring local servicemen and women during World War II. Home-front activities, war bond sales, and conservation efforts drew overwhelming support from the media and the people of Chicago Heights.

Killed in the Service of Their Country

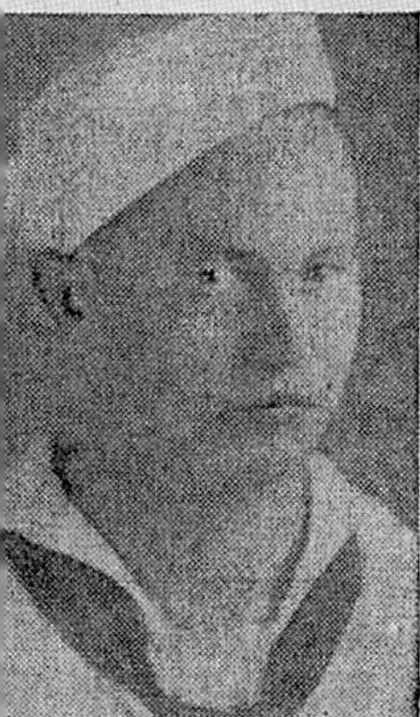

AMAN FIRST CLASS STAN- ley Bury died September 3, 1942, near Carolla, N. C. His ents, Mr. and Mrs. Joseph Bury, e at 1430 Portland avenue.

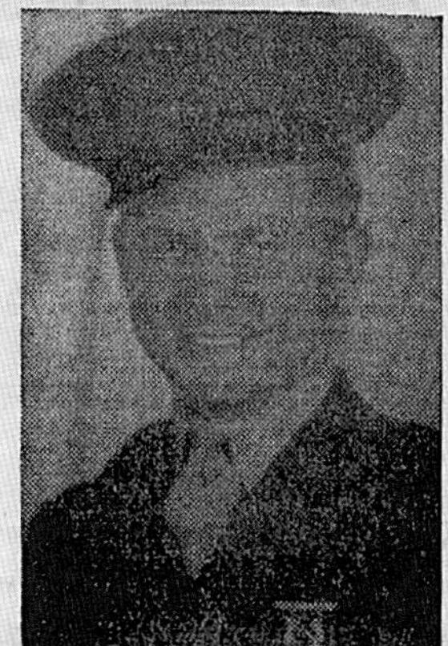

PRIVATE FIRST CLASS JOHN Nykaza died May 24, 1945, on Okinawa. He was nineteen years old. His parents are Mr. and Mrs. Nick Nykaza, Route 2, Chicago Heights.

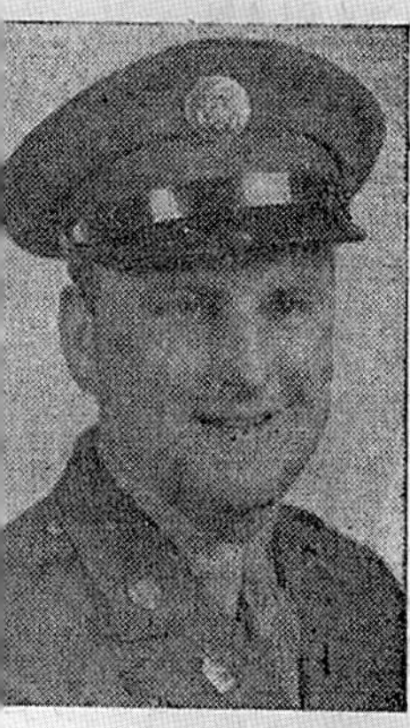

RGEANT JAMES NODUS DIED April 29, 1945, on Okinawa. His father, Joseph Nauduzas, ides at 1442 Green street. His e, Mrs. Bertha Nodus, lives at West Twenty-first street.

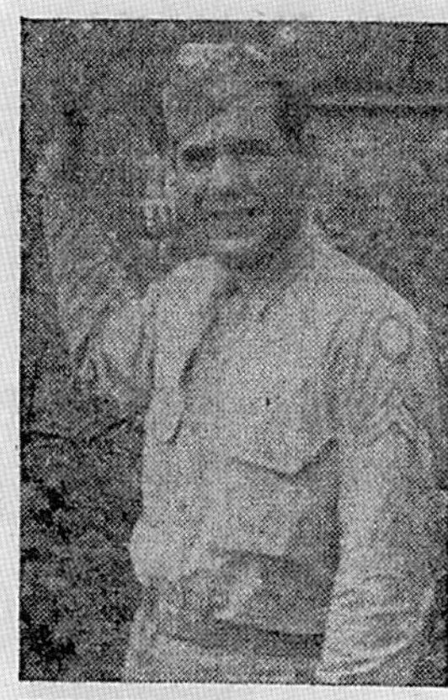

PRIVATE FIRST CLASS ARmondo S. Cioe died May 31, 1945, on Mindanao island in the Philippines. He was twenty-one years old. His parents, Mr. and Mrs. Dominic Cioe, live at 121 East Twenty-fourth street.

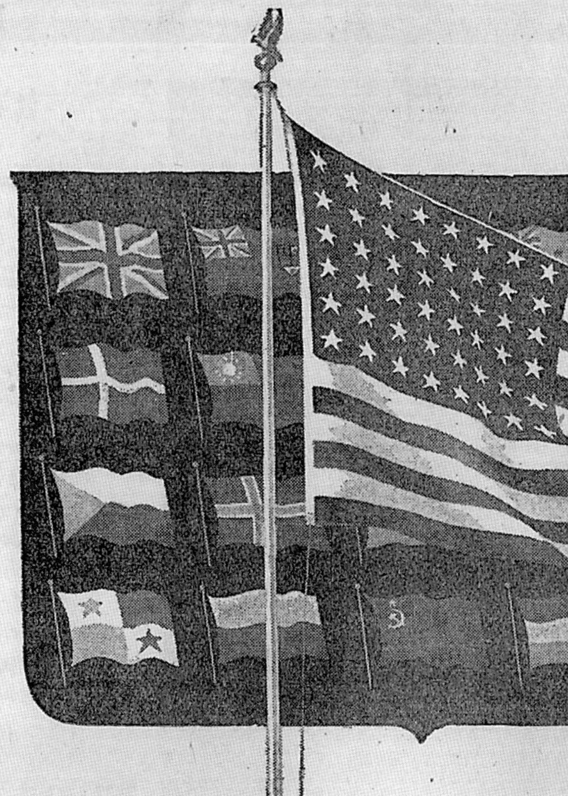

On these pages appears the
service men reported killed, m
wounded during the closing
These are in addition to casualti

Missing in Action

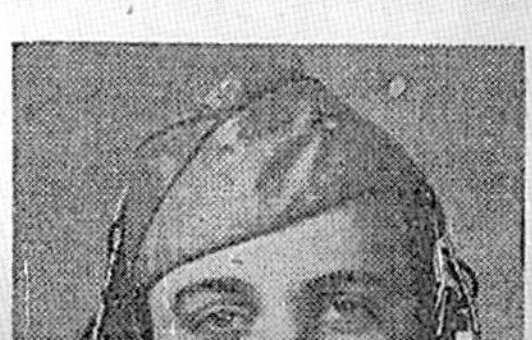

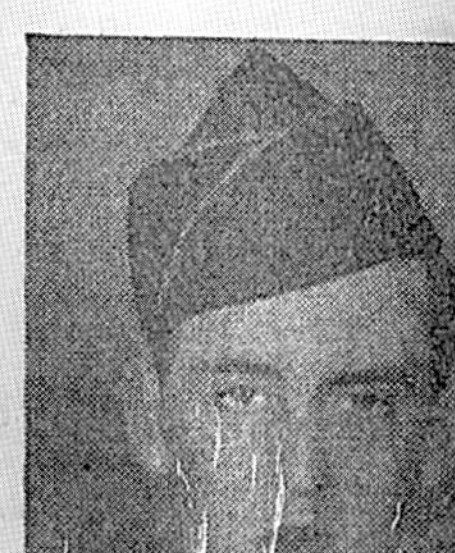

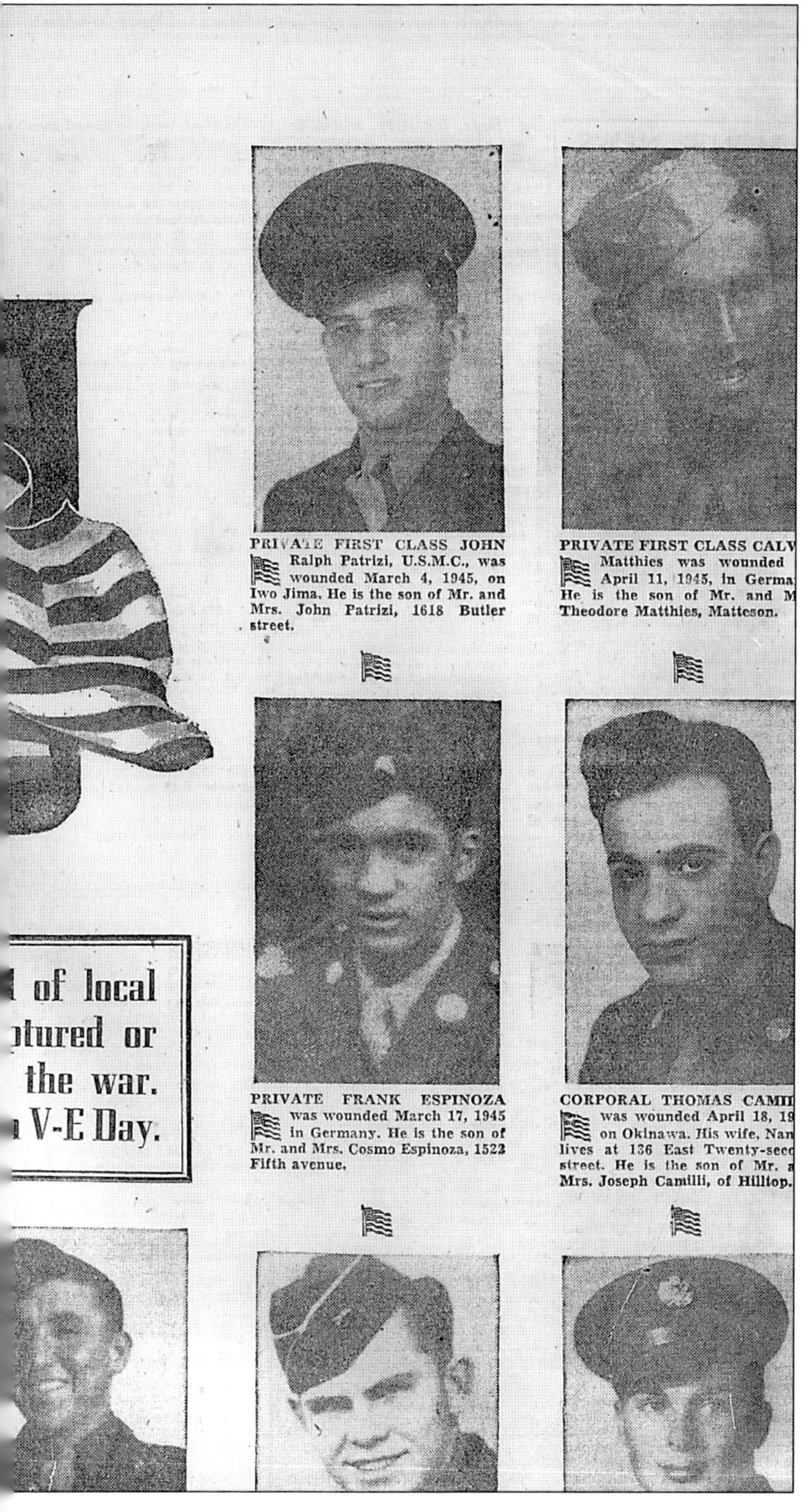
of local
ptured or
the war.
V-E Day.

PRIVATE FIRST CLASS JOHN Ralph Patrizi, U.S.M.C., was wounded March 4, 1945, on Iwo Jima. He is the son of Mr. and Mrs. John Patrizi, 1618 Butler street.

PRIVATE FIRST CLASS CALV Matthies was wounded April 11, 1945, in Germa He is the son of Mr. and M Theodore Matthies, Matteson.

PRIVATE FRANK ESPINOZA was wounded March 17, 1945 in Germany. He is the son of Mr. and Mrs. Cosmo Espinoza, 1522 Fifth avenue.

CORPORAL THOMAS CAMII was wounded April 18, 19 on Okinawa. His wife, Nan lives at 136 East Twenty-seco street. He is the son of Mr. a Mrs. Joseph Camilli, of Hilltop.

Throughout World War II, the *Star* acted as a cheerleader in giving generous support to the war effort, especially in honoring local servicemen. This August 16, 1945, tribute to the men killed, missing, captured, or wounded in the closing weeks of the war is only a small sample of the newspaper's and the community's devotion to the cause.

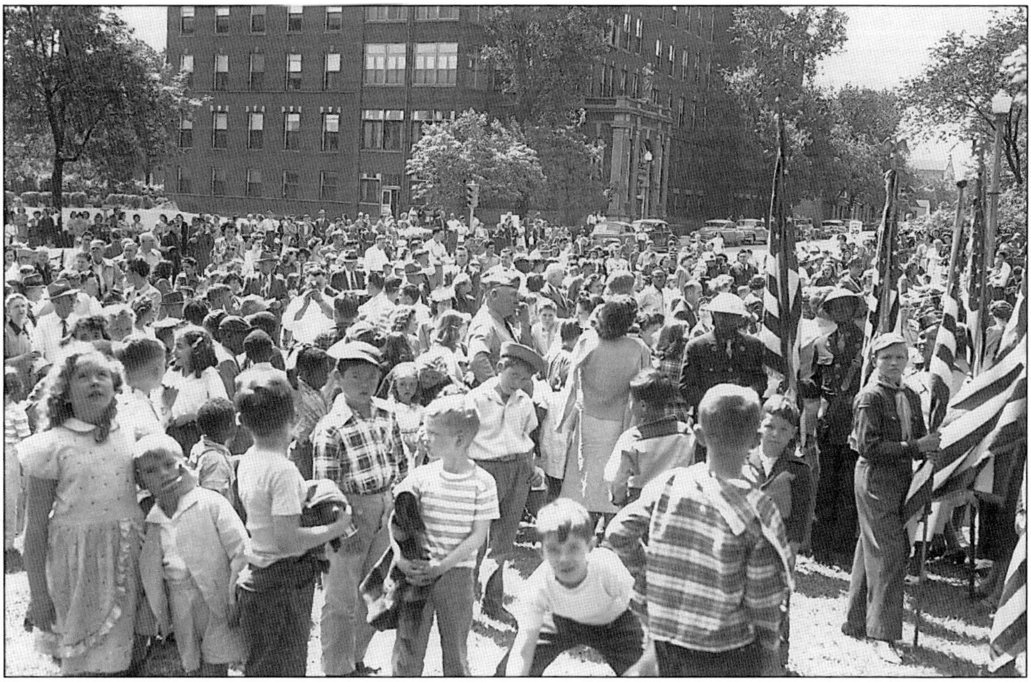

Ceremonies on Memorial Day at the Mound drew large crowds of young people and veterans in the 1950s. The patriotism inspired by the World War II experience, had a deep impact on the culture of Chicago Heights lasting for at least two generations after the war.

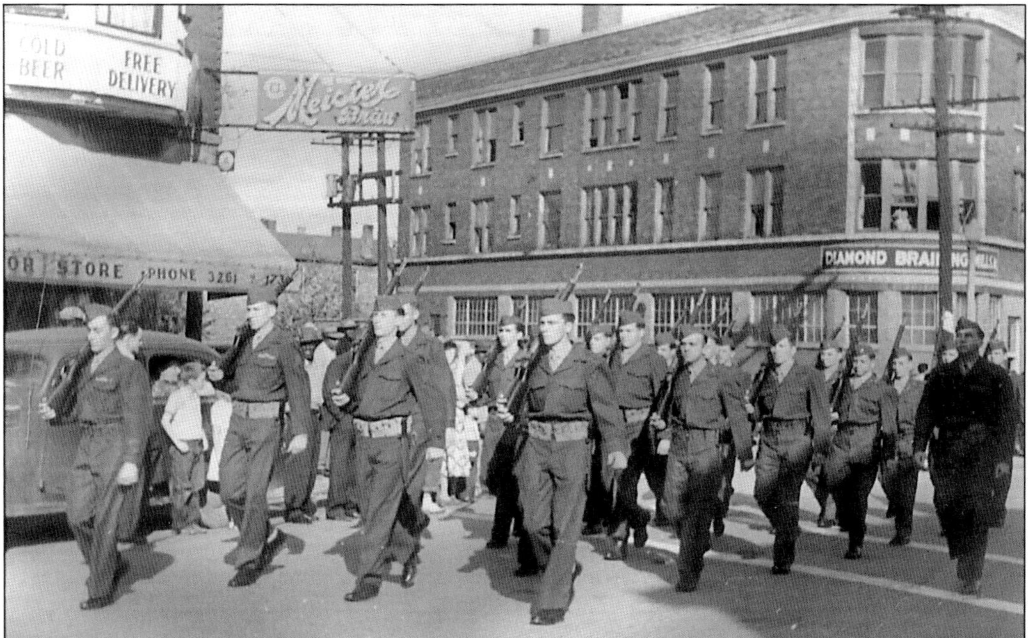

Above is a picture of a 1949 parade as it marches west on 16th Street past the Diamond Braiding Mills.

Four

ILLINOIS STREET

Gone but not forgotten, Illinois Street was a two-block span from Chicago Road to Halsted that included a furniture store, Sallo's, Garden City Creamery, Sears, Rio Theatre, Wirth Fur, Palanca Tailoring, Chicago Heights Lunch, Einhorn's Tap, Ace Hardware, Coppotelli's Music Store, K&H Sporting Goods, Cities Service Gas Station, Karmelkorn, Lincoln Theatre, Liberty Restaurant, Carrier Electric, EZ Snack, Illinois Grill, Solomon Brothers Tobacco, Duke's Barbershop, Leon's Men's Wear, Foley Travel, the Victoria Hotel, and Walgreen's. From 1900 to the 1970s, this strip constituted about half of Chicago Heights' bustling business district. Since many of the two-story buildings had apartments above the stores, the business district was also a neighborhood with hotels, theaters, and all-night restaurants. In the 1970s, detailed downtown renewal plans were aborted after the building of the parking lot (Exhibition Center), city hall, and the police station.

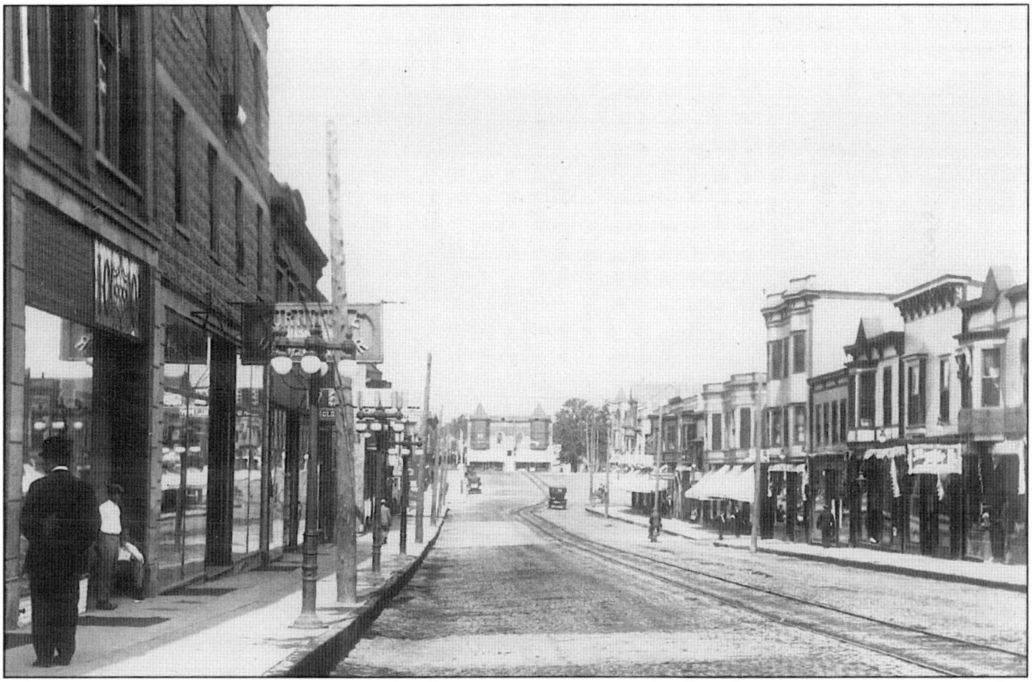

This 1915 view of Illinois Street looking west reveals the brick streets, streetcar tracks, "antique" lighting, and few automobiles.

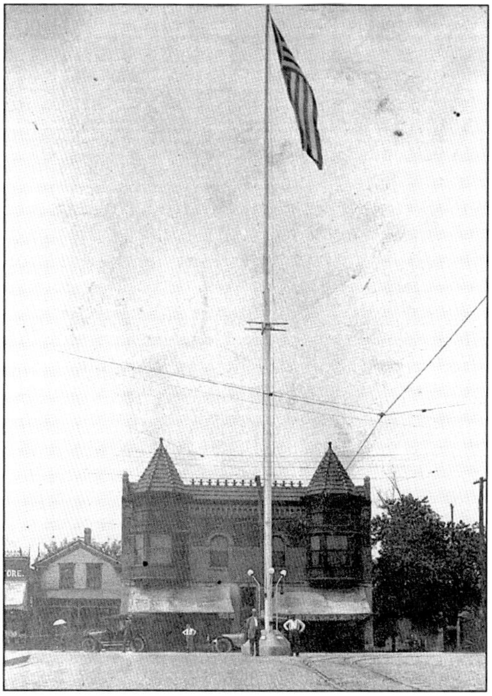

While looking west on Illinois Street in the 1920s, note the streetcar tracks and the municipal flagpole. Soon after this photo was taken, the Lincoln-Dixie Theater was erected to the right of the building pictured in the center of the photo.

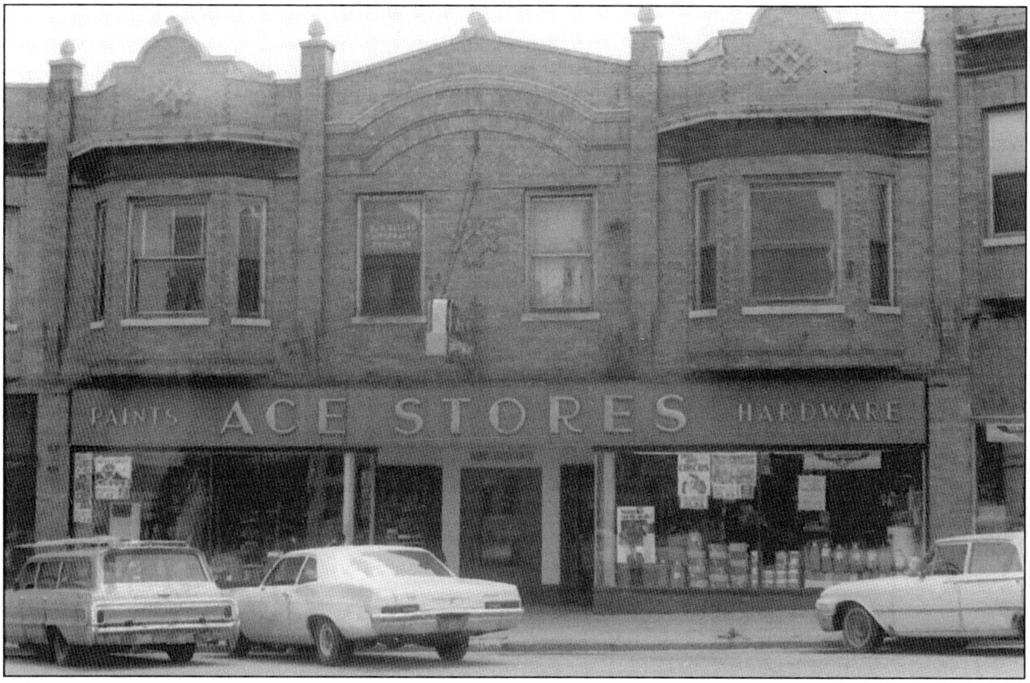

The Ace Hardware store at 14 East Illinois Street in the early 1960s featured apartments with bay windows on the second floor. Though diagonal parking helped to maximize capacity, downtown Chicago Heights was so busy that it strangled itself due to a lack of parking. This allowed newer retailers in places like Park Forest Plaza and Lincoln Mall to attract some of the bigger stores like Sears, Wards, and Goldblatts.

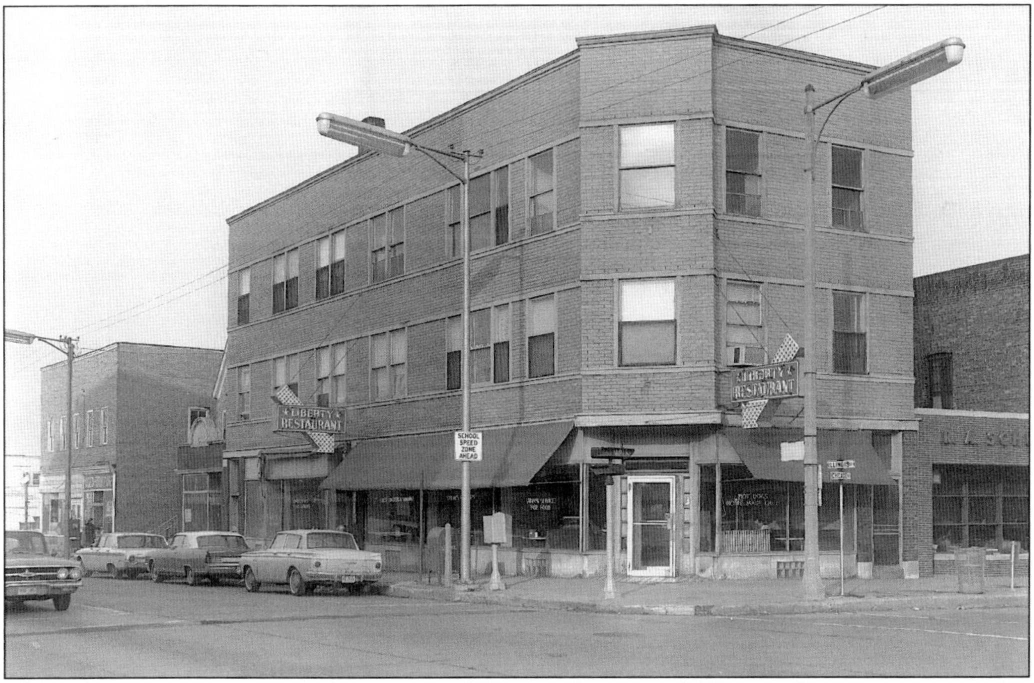

The Liberty Restaurant, at the corner of Illinois Street and Chicago Road, was a popular eatery from the 1950s to the mid-1970s. Open twenty-four hours a day, the Liberty was famous for its hot dogs and homemade chili. This 1960s photo illustrates the eclectic character of the building with residential apartments above the restaurant.

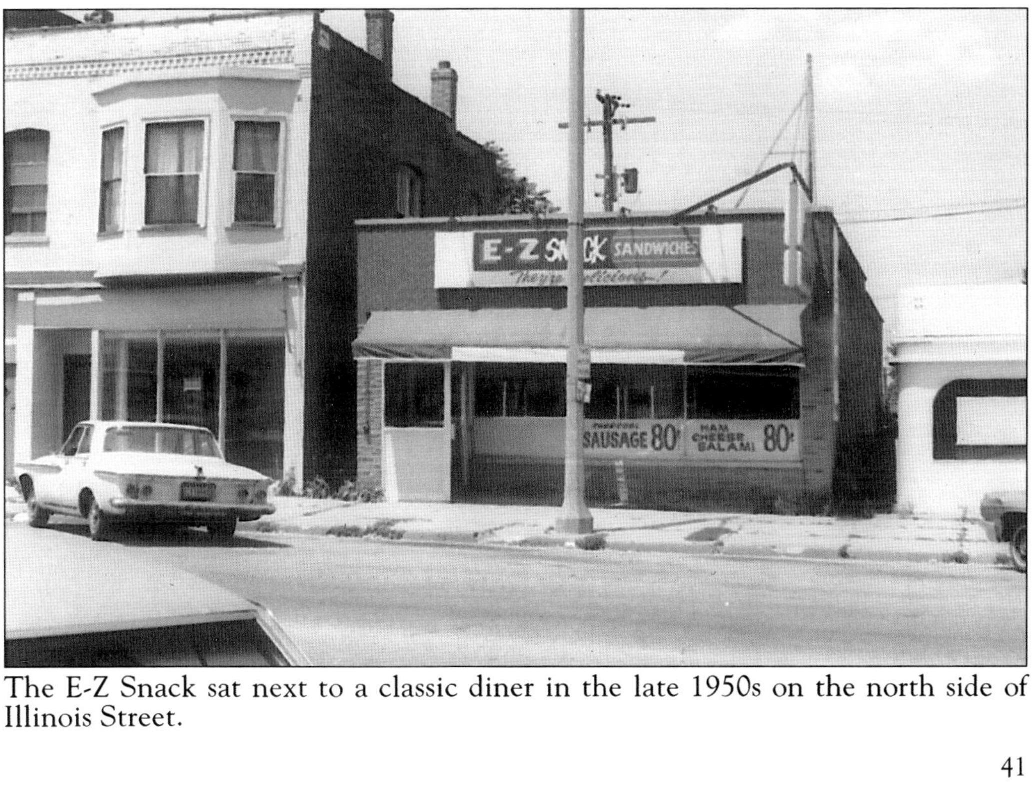

The E-Z Snack sat next to a classic diner in the late 1950s on the north side of Illinois Street.

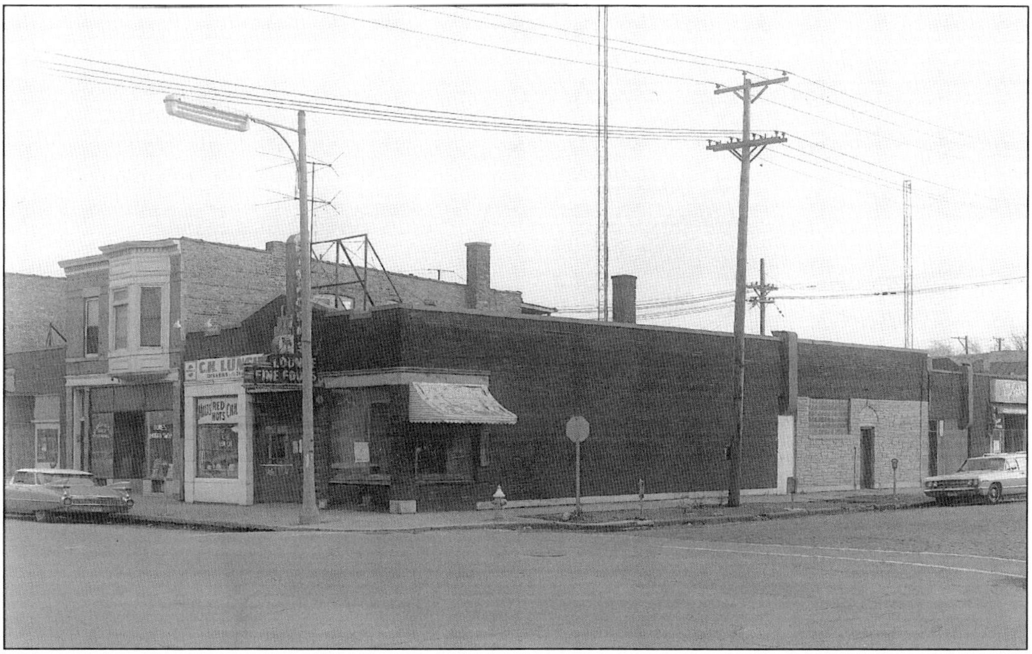

Chicago Heights Lunch and the more elegant Einhorn's restaurant stood side-by-side to serve shoppers and downtown workers. Note the high finned Cadillac and the second floor residential apartments.

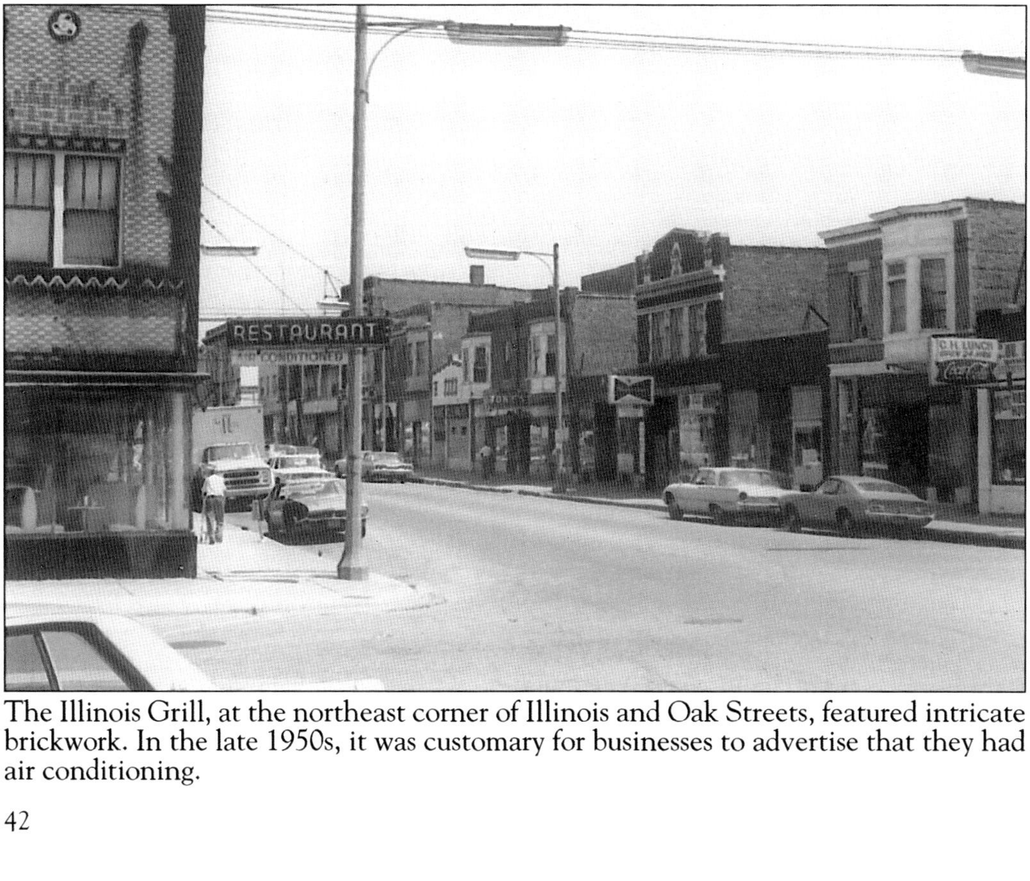

The Illinois Grill, at the northeast corner of Illinois and Oak Streets, featured intricate brickwork. In the late 1950s, it was customary for businesses to advertise that they had air conditioning.

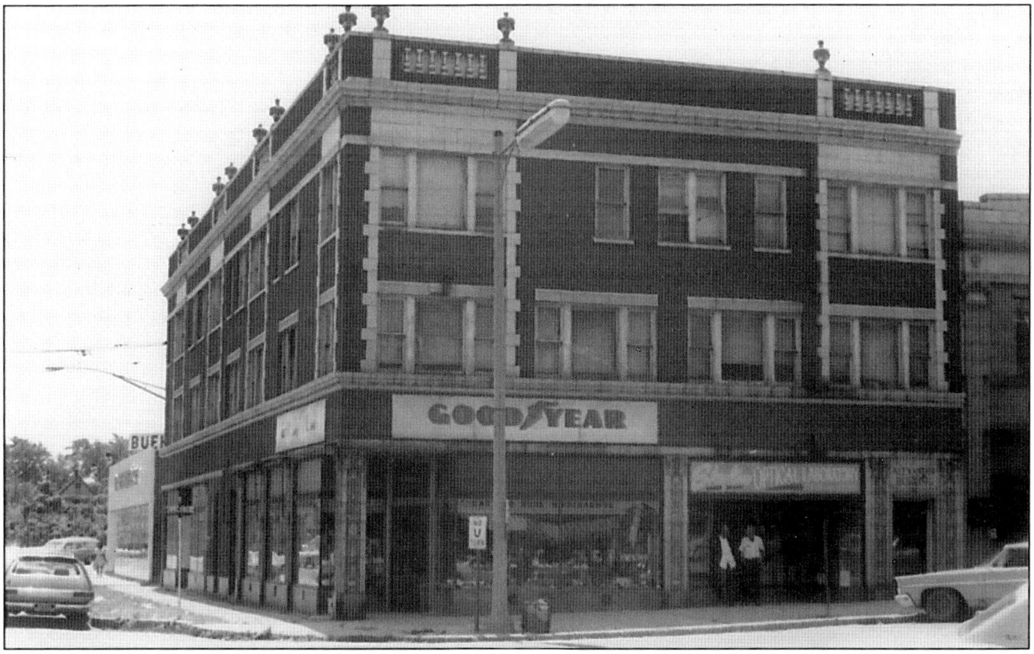

The terra-cotta Alexander building at the southwest corner of Illinois and Oak Streets was constructed by DiCicco Contractors. Though once used as the South Suburban bus terminal, in the 1960s this structure housed the Goodyear Tire Store. To the left is Buehler's Meat Market and Grocery and, to the right is Skyline Optical Laboratory.

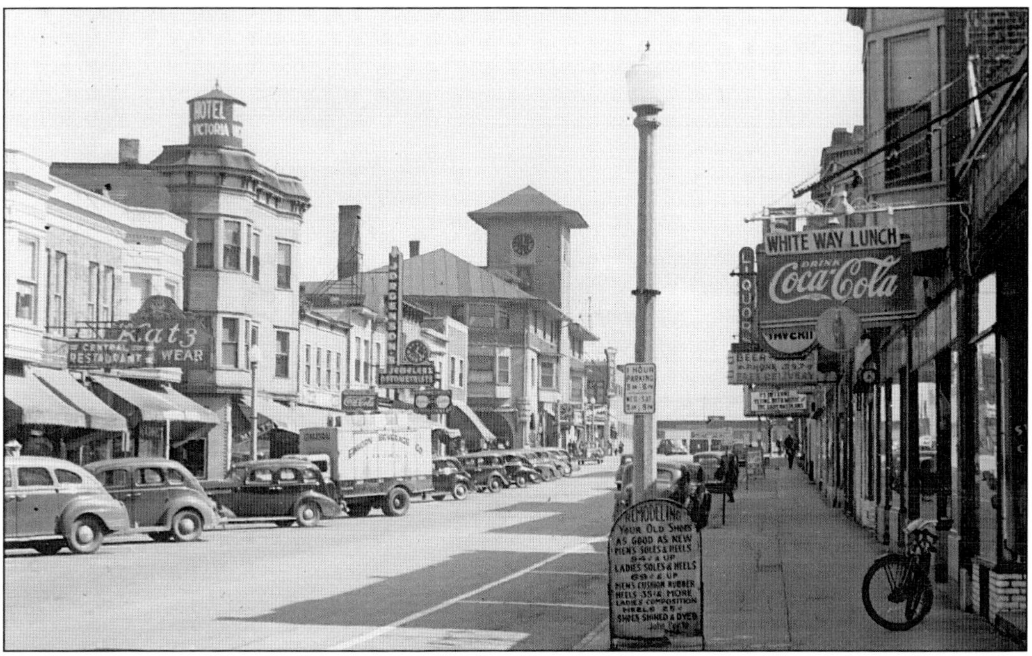

Looking east on Illinois Street reveals the Central Restaurant, Katz Men's Wear, the Einhorn Beverage Company truck, Jorgenson Jewelry, the Victoria Hotel (designed by Louis Sullivan), and the White Way Lunch. Note the street lights and water tower.

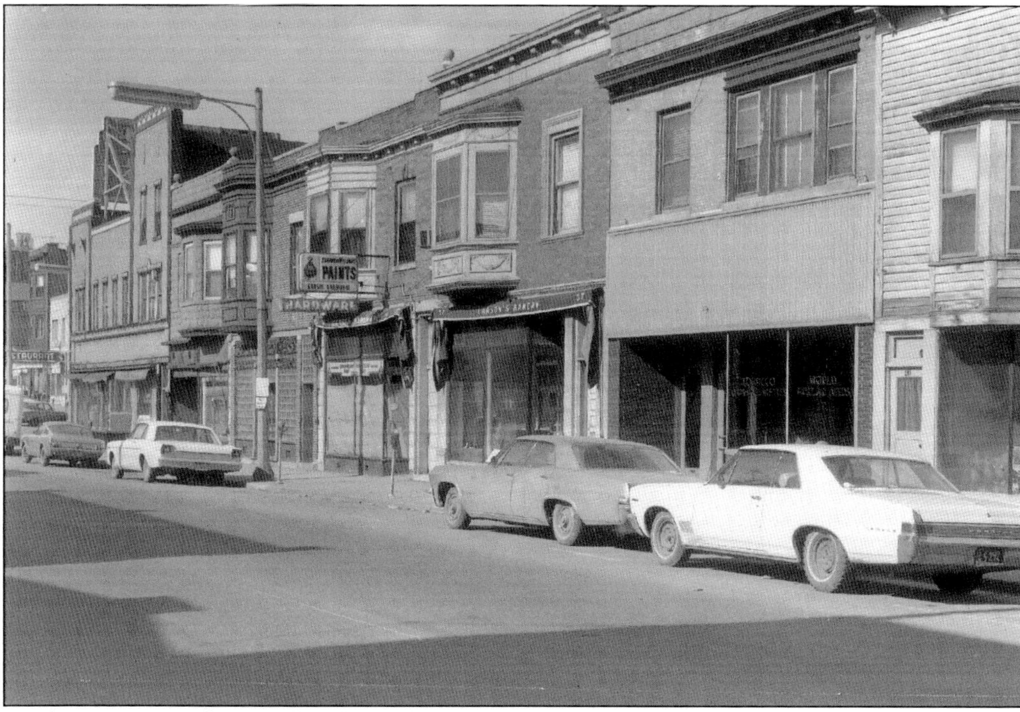

Looking west at the north side of Illinois Street is the Illinois Grill, Gansen Hardware, and Larson's Bakery. The lighting on Illinois Street resembled that on the Loop's State Street. When it was installed in 1949, the merchants used the slogan "Daylight shopping after dark will now be yours on upper Illinois Street." Above the Illinois Grill was a giant billboard.

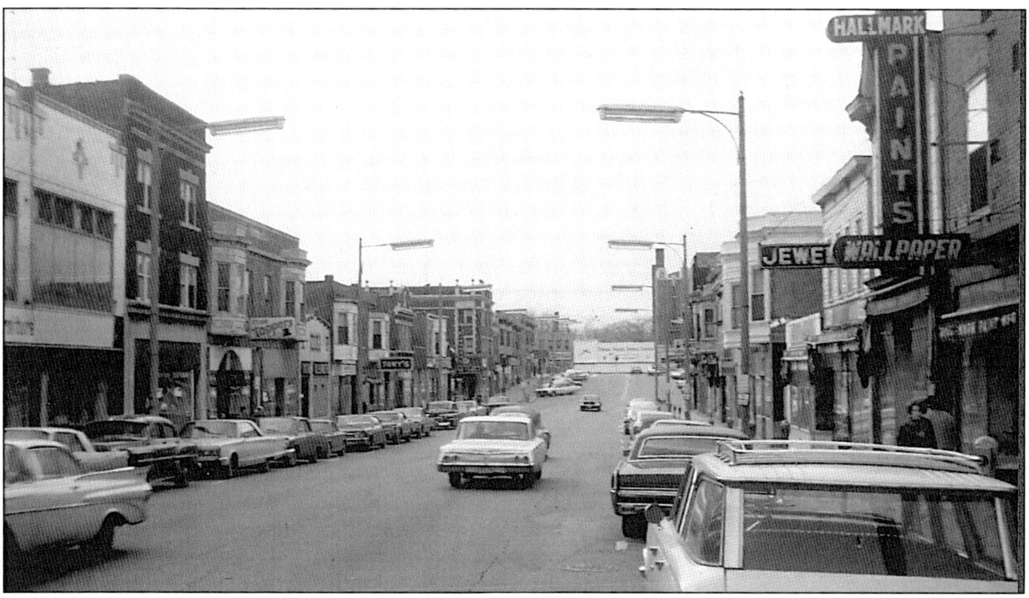

Pictured is a view looking west on Illinois Street in 1967.

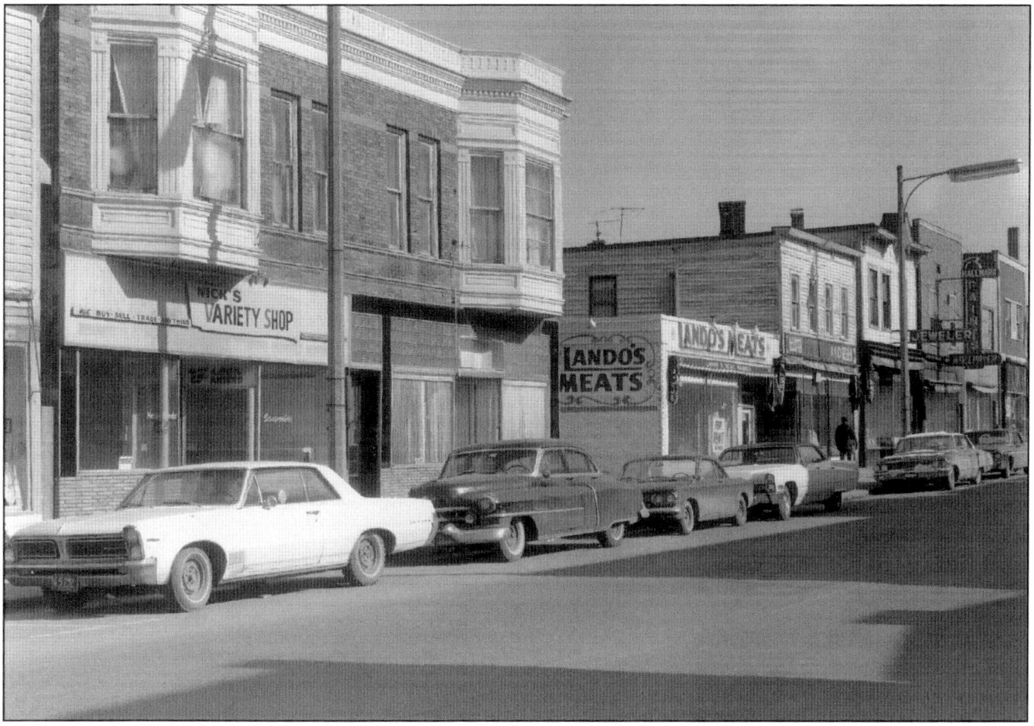

The North side of Illinois Street featured Lando's Meats and Nick Guzzino's Barbershop. Nick spent 53 years serving as barber to area men and boys.

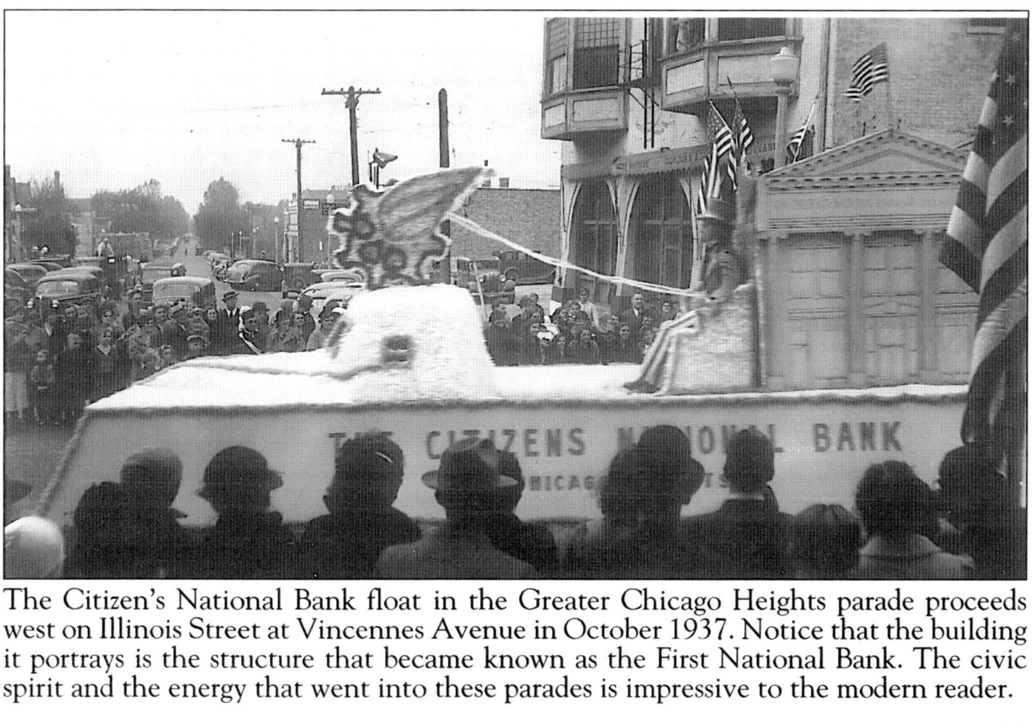

The Citizen's National Bank float in the Greater Chicago Heights parade proceeds west on Illinois Street at Vincennes Avenue in October 1937. Notice that the building it portrays is the structure that became known as the First National Bank. The civic spirit and the energy that went into these parades is impressive to the modern reader.

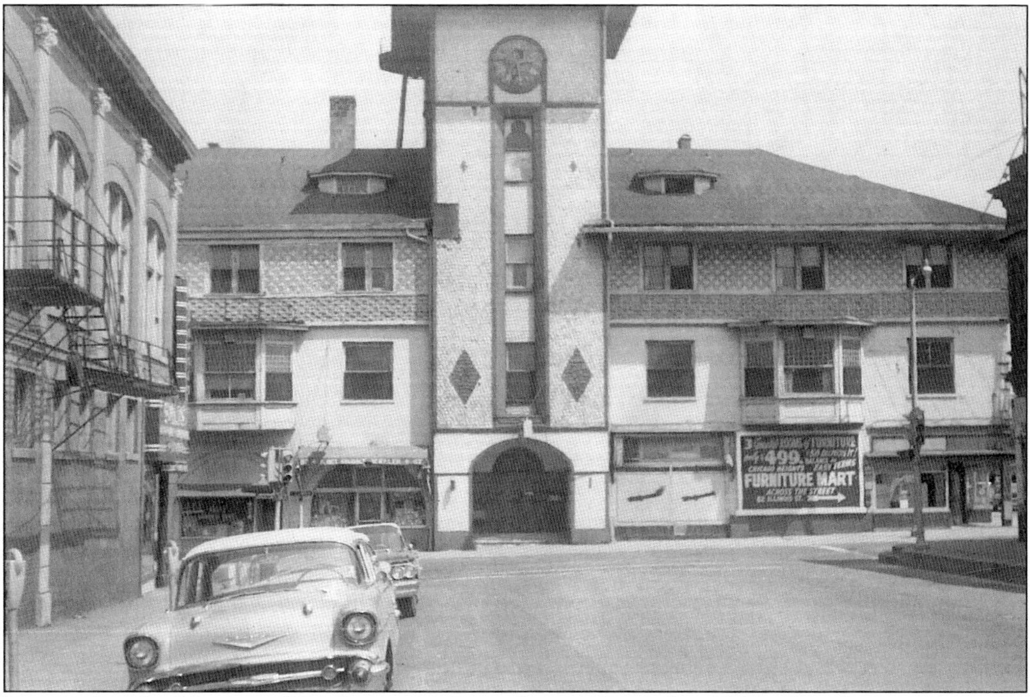

Pictured is the Victoria Hotel as seen from the south in the 1950s. Its placement in the 1890s apparently did not line up with the positioning of Halsted Street, creating an S-curve where it crossed Illinois Street.

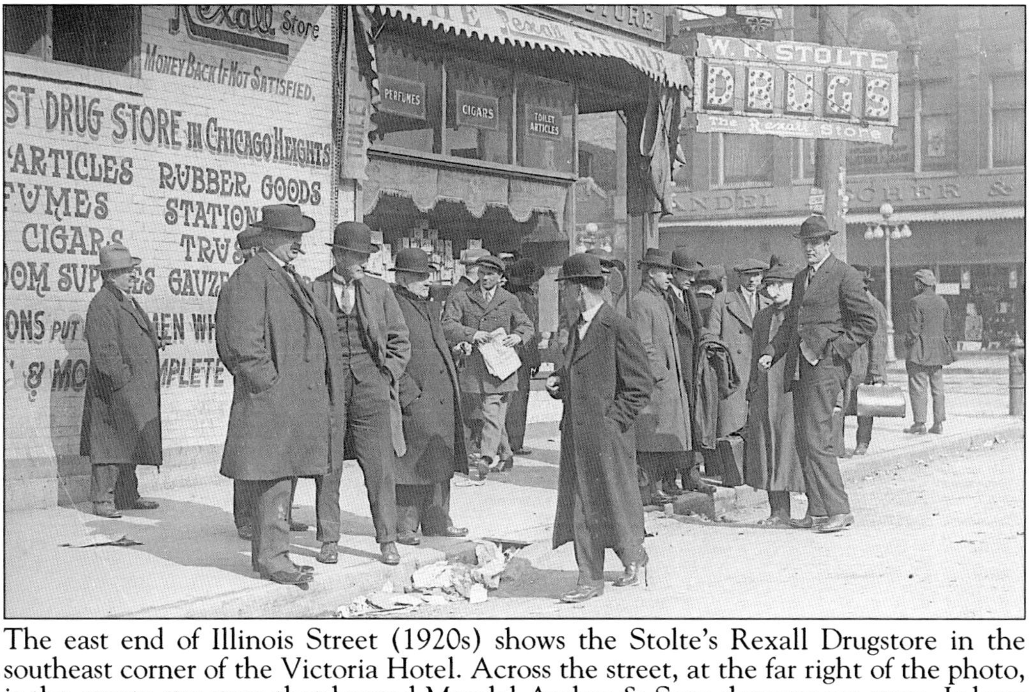

The east end of Illinois Street (1920s) shows the Stolte's Rexall Drugstore in the southeast corner of the Victoria Hotel. Across the street, at the far right of the photo, is the ornate structure that housed Mandel Ascher & Sons department store. It later became a Montgomery Ward store.

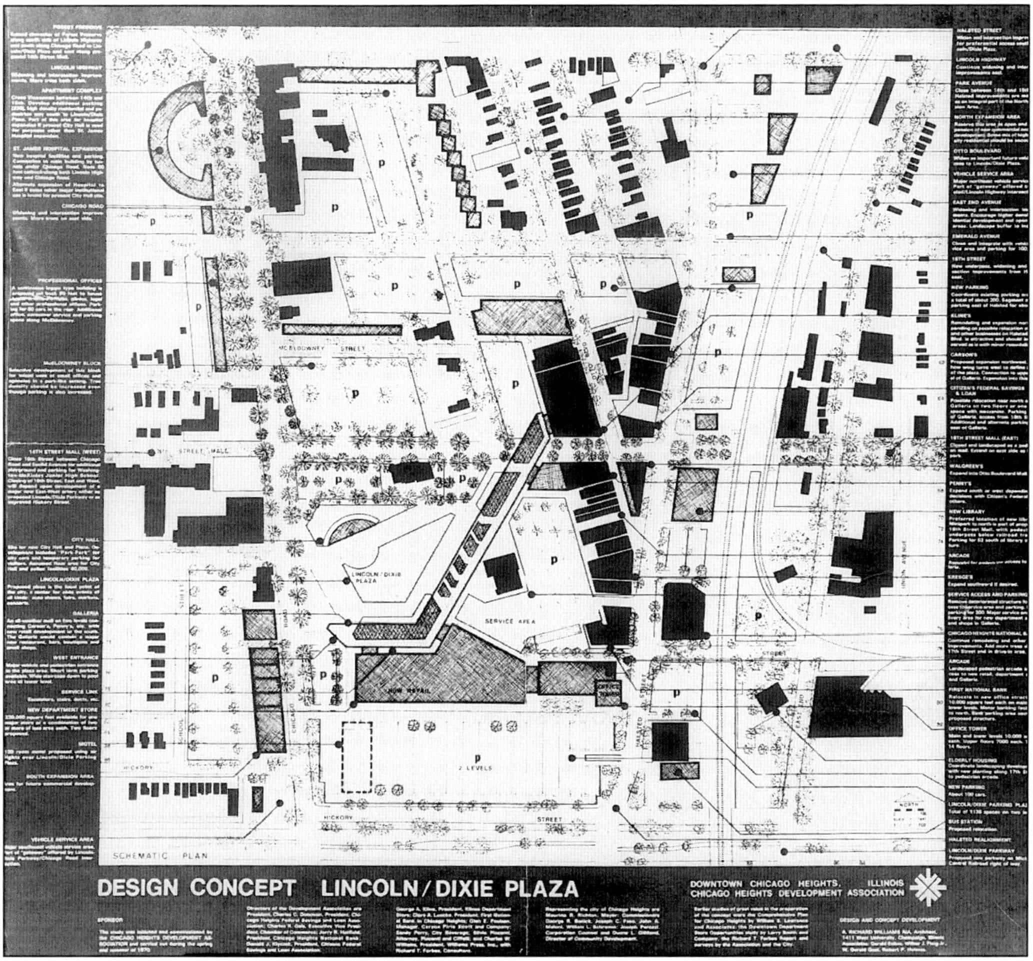

This 1970 Design Concept for the Lincoln/Dixie Plaza envisioned a retail mall running along old Illinois Street next to a two-level parking structure with a motel at the west end and a high-rise office building at the east end. City hall was to sit where it is now, at about 16th and Chicago Road, but facing eastward toward the Lincoln/Dixie Plaza. The plan also included a galleria running diagonally from Illinois Street to the Carson's building. The new library was to have gone on an expanded version of the old site on Depot Court and Halsted. St. James Hospital expansion was planned for the area across Chicago Road from the original structure, which is now occupied by the Recreational Center and the library. Sixteenth Street was to be converted into a tree-lined pedestrian mall. A full-size copy of this plan is available in the Chicago Heights Library.

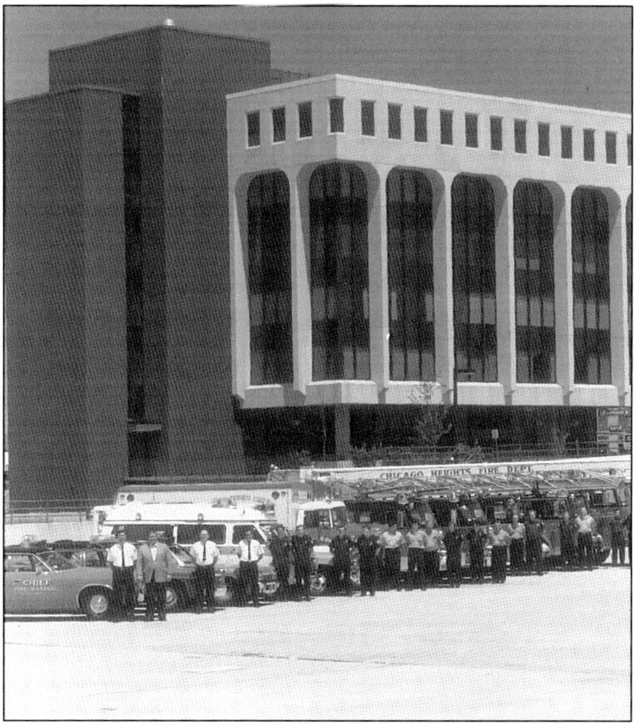

Chief Julio Narcisi and Commissioner John Gliottoni pose with firefighters in front of the newly completed First National Bank Building at Halsted and Illinois. The hook and ladder truck attests to the department's readiness to handle emergencies in high-rise buildings.

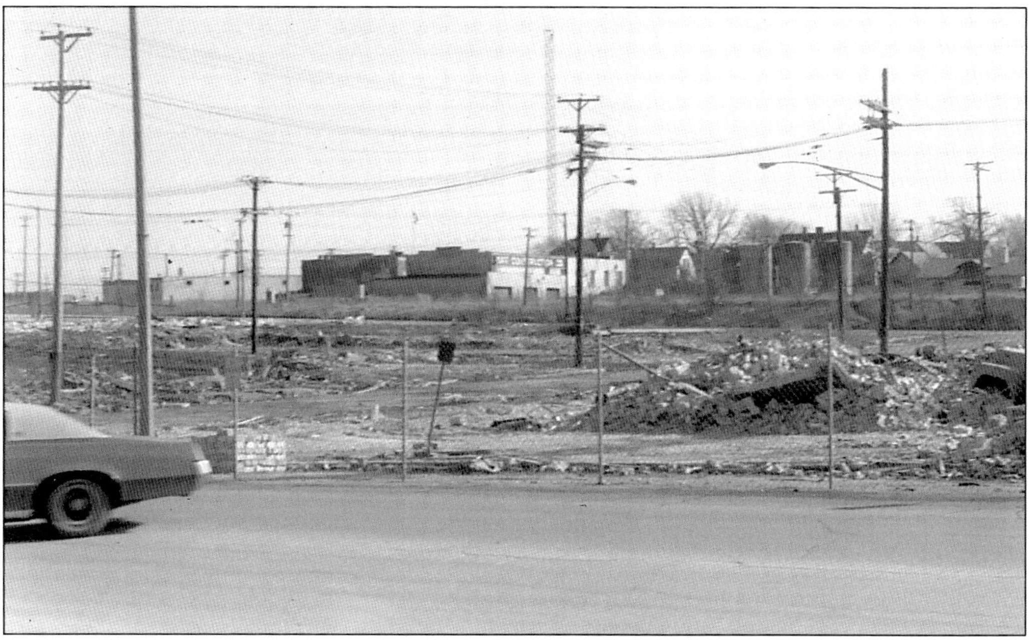

The urban renewal program of the 1970s featured the demolition of dozens of commercial buildings along Illinois Street. The plan was to build a multi-level parking lot (now the Exhibition Center) and then erect a mall along what was the north side of Illinois Street. City leaders abandoned that project in the mid-1970s leaving only the parking lot and the First National Bank highrise.

Five

HALSTED STREET

Running at a right angle to Illinois Street from the spot where the Victoria Hotel was built, Halsted Street continued the parade of businesses north to 15th Street and over to Otto Boulevard. According to the 1941 City Directory, the major establishments going from south to north on the east side of the Halsted Street were Montgomery Ward, Thomas Hotel, Chicago Heights National Bank, Zalman Furniture, J.C. Penney (1940s), Jordan's, McEldowney Insurance, the library, the post office, Western Auto, Gregory's, Chicago Heights Tire, Friedlander Furniture, Bowl Aire, Western Union, Railway Express, and Asher Used Cars. Going north on the west side of Halsted were the Victoria Hotel, Walgreen's, Wald Men's Wear, Kappmeyer Stationery, Miller's Men's Wear, Sallo's Millinery, Joy Candy, Kiddie Shop, Cohen's Men's Wear, Citizen's National Bank (later First National), Main Lunch, Harry Yaseen Jewelry, R&S Shoes, Ladies Shop, Ames Dress Shop, Woolworth, Kresge, Father and Son Shoes, Waddington Meats, Mauropoulos Barber Shop, Jewel Store, city hall, Barwig Pharmacy, Brass Rail Tavern, Rex Theatre, Citizen's Federal, L&R Shoes, Kline's, Panici Barbershop, A&P Supermarket, and Wright Service Station. The smaller territory, the smaller population, the fact that all public school students went to Washington Junion High and all Chicago Heights students attended Bloom, as well as the stability of the downtown business district, all combined to produce a strong sense of community in the 1950s.

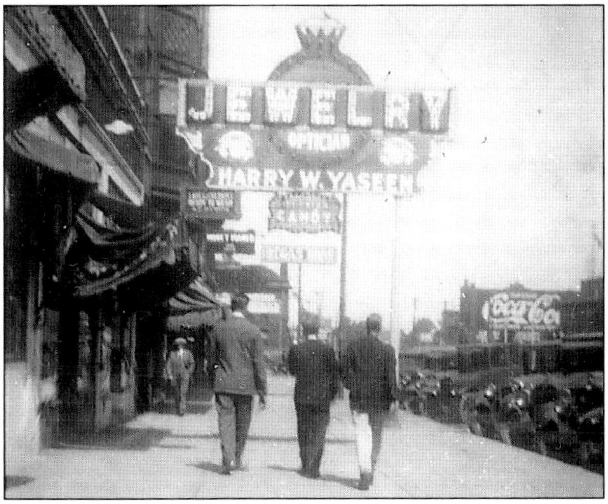

A stroll north on Halsted Street in the period from 1900 to the 1970s offered expansive opportunities for commerce, business, banking, entertainment, services, and shopping for residents and employees who worked in Chicago Heights and lived within a 20-mile radius.

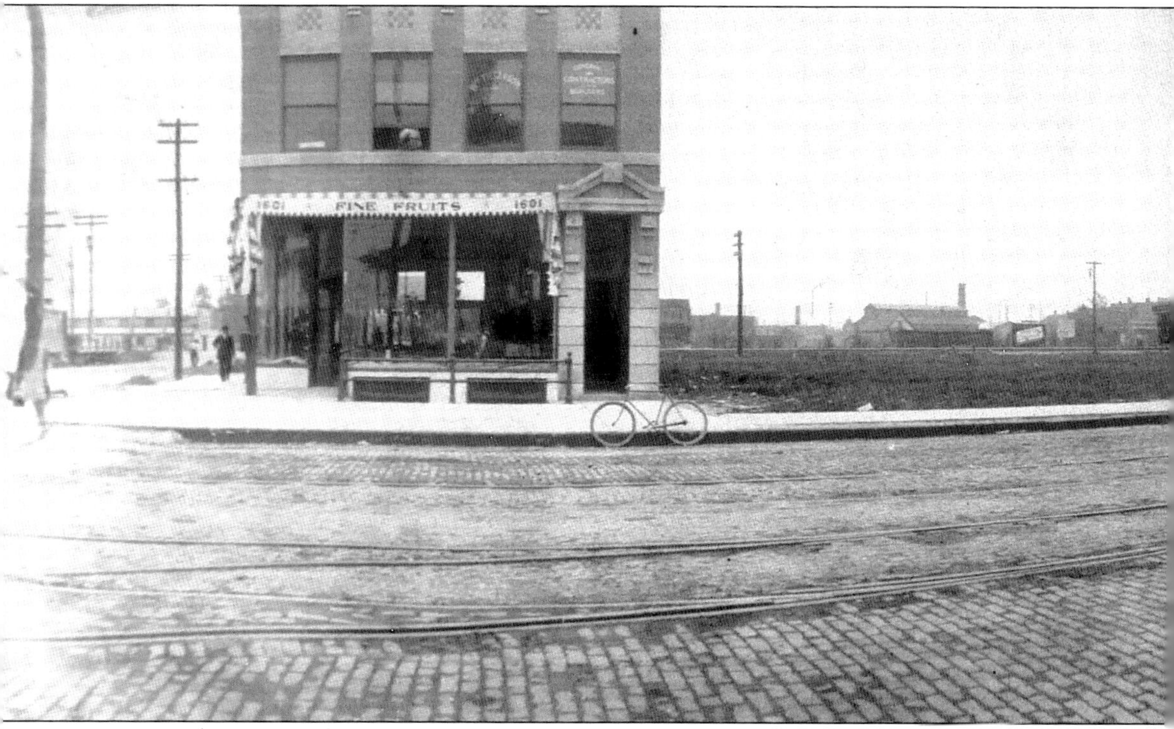

Pictured is a view looking east and south along Halsted Street at 16th Street before the 1911 construction of the post office. Visible toward the center of the photo

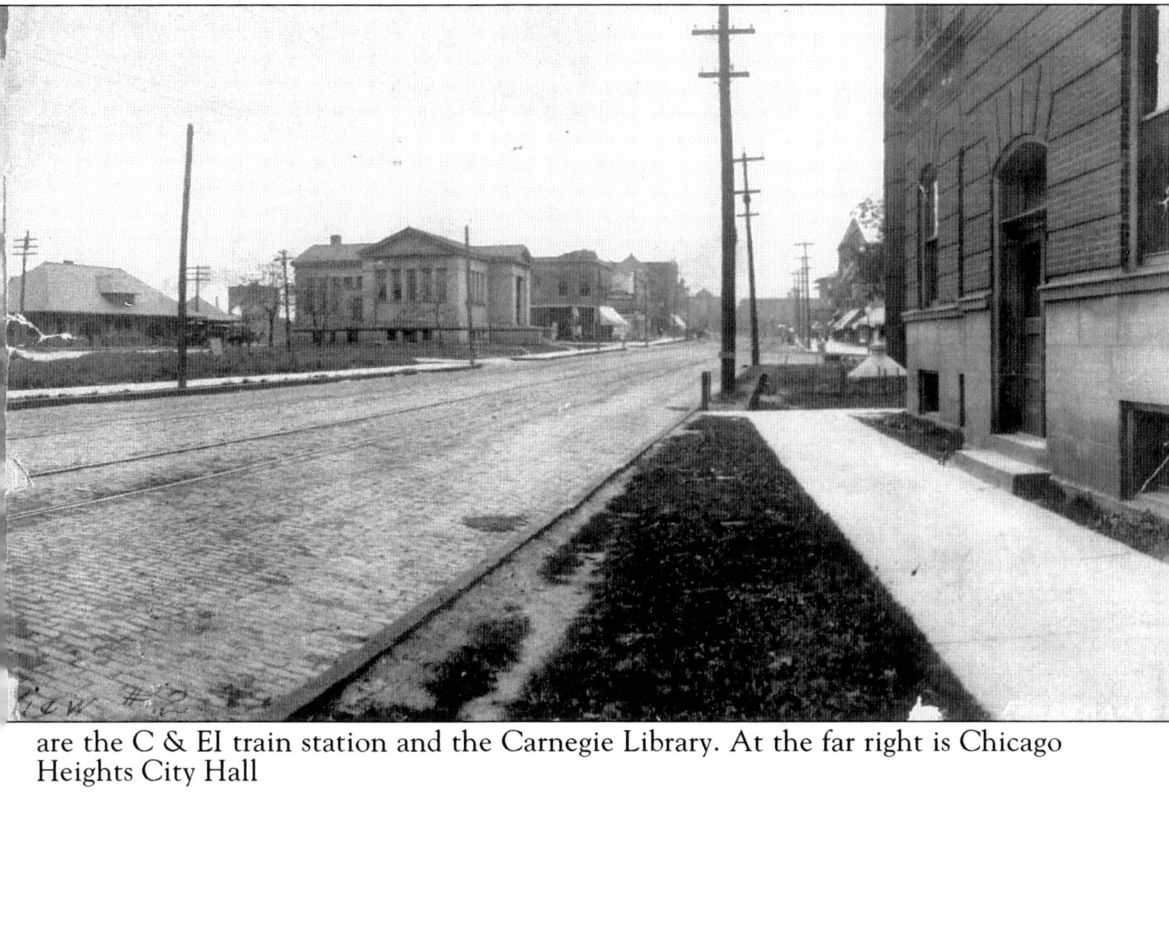

are the C & EI train station and the Carnegie Library. At the far right is Chicago Heights City Hall

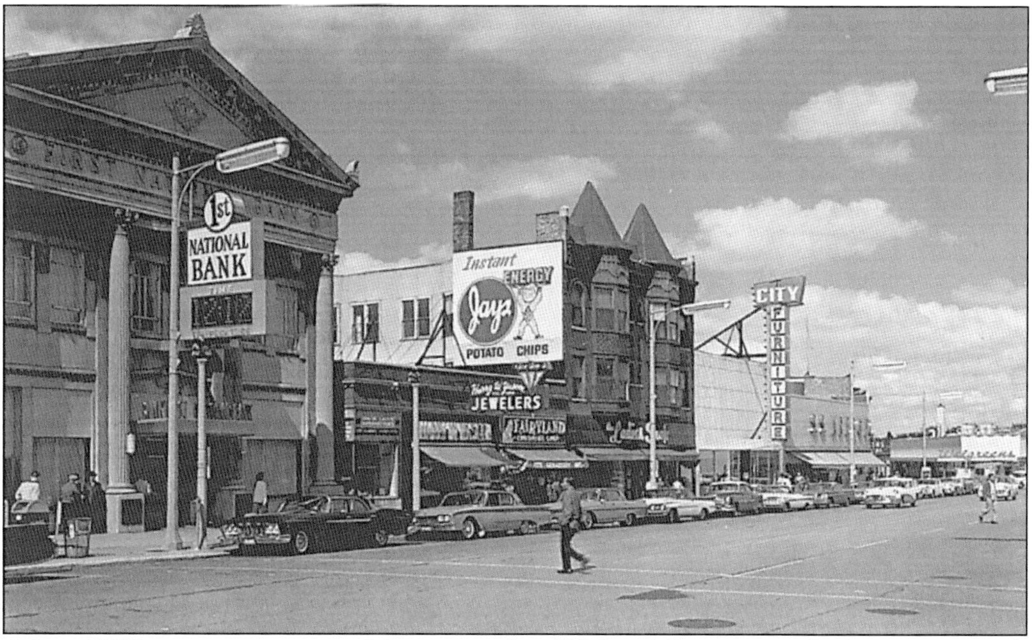

A late 1950s noontime view of the west side of Halsted Street reveals the commercial heart of Chicago Heights—anchored by the temple-like First National Bank.

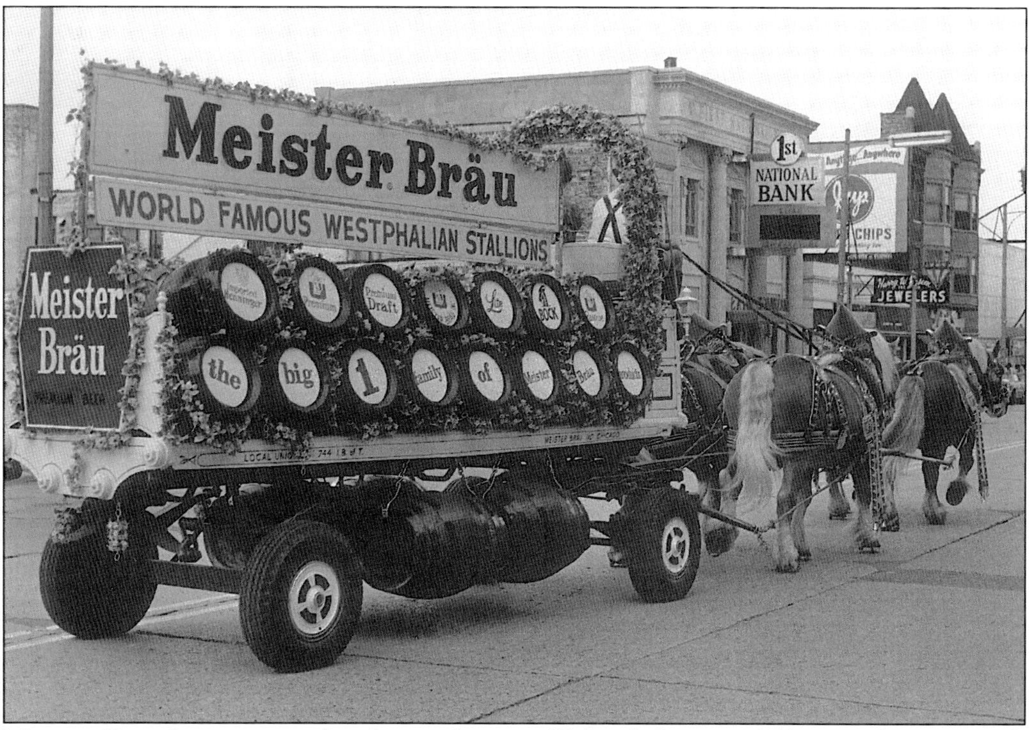

Meister Brau beer wagon heads north in a Halsted Street 1950s parade past such commercial Chicago Heights icons as the First National Bank, Harry Yaseen Jewelry, and the Ladies Shop.

The Chicago Heights National Bank building was made of terra cotta, produced by the city's Northwestern Terra Cotta Company. It was a focal point of downtown activity at 17th and Halsted Streets from the 1920s to the 1970s. Built in 1926, the building is an outstanding example of monumental classical architecture. The Chicago Heights Historic Preservation Committee declared it a landmark in 1997.

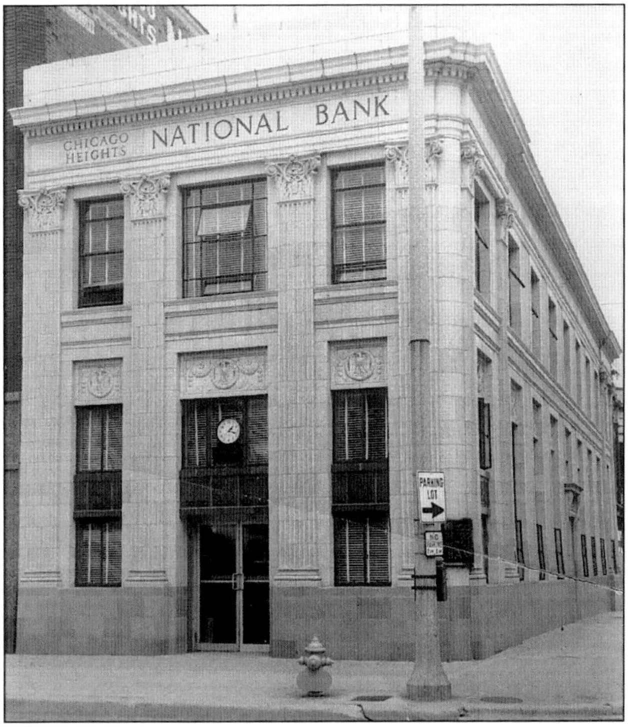

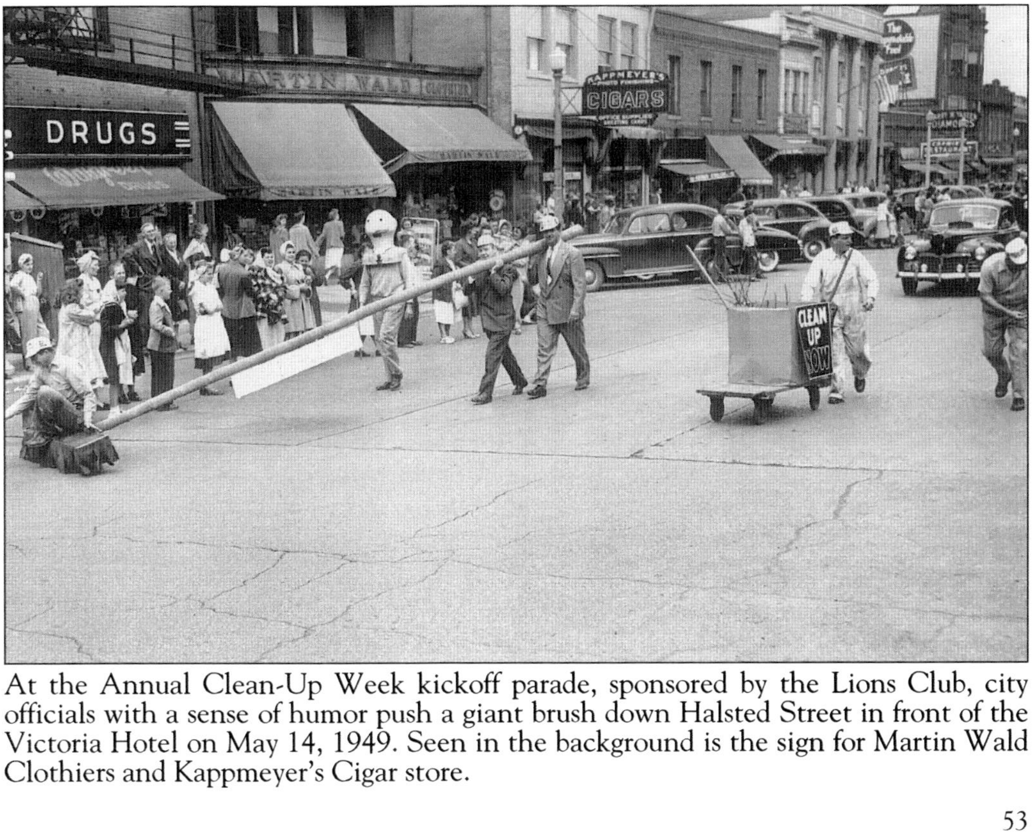

At the Annual Clean-Up Week kickoff parade, sponsored by the Lions Club, city officials with a sense of humor push a giant brush down Halsted Street in front of the Victoria Hotel on May 14, 1949. Seen in the background is the sign for Martin Wald Clothiers and Kappmeyer's Cigar store.

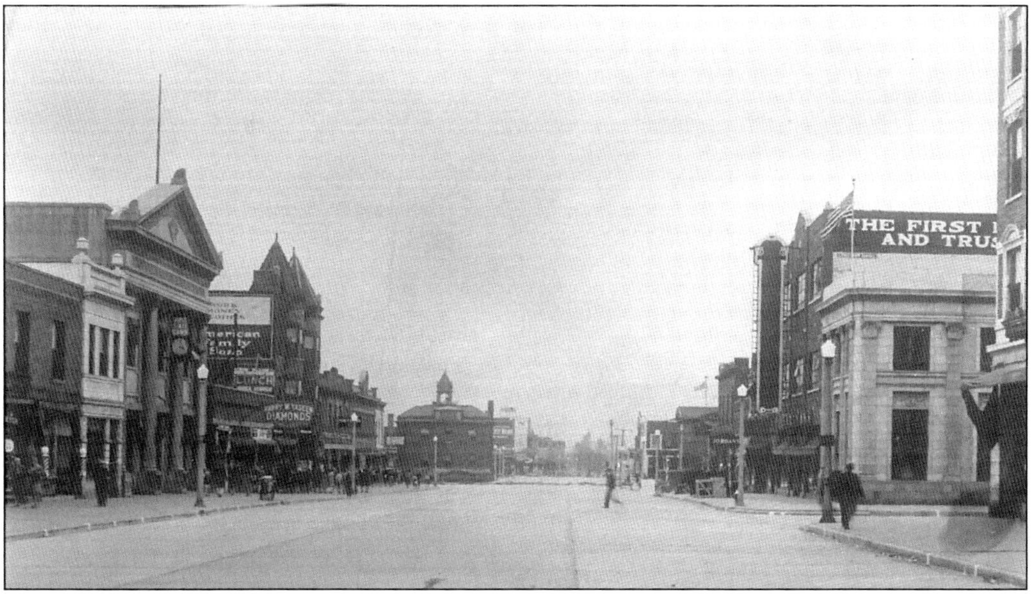

Pictured is a view looking north on Halsted Street from Illinois Street. At the far right is the Thomas Hotel. In the left-center of the photo is city hall.

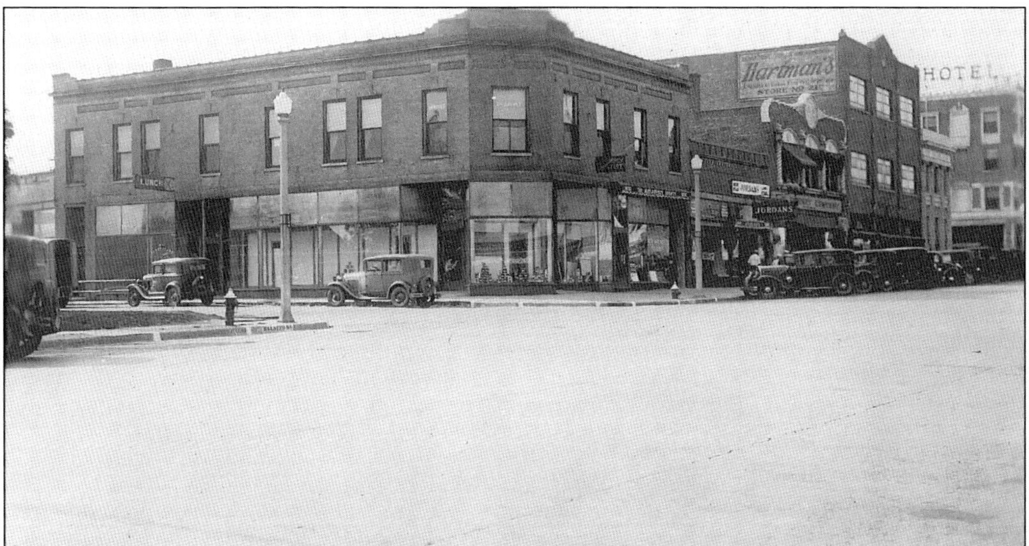

Pictured above is a 1920s view of Depot Court and the Thomas Hotel looking southeast from city hall on Halsted.

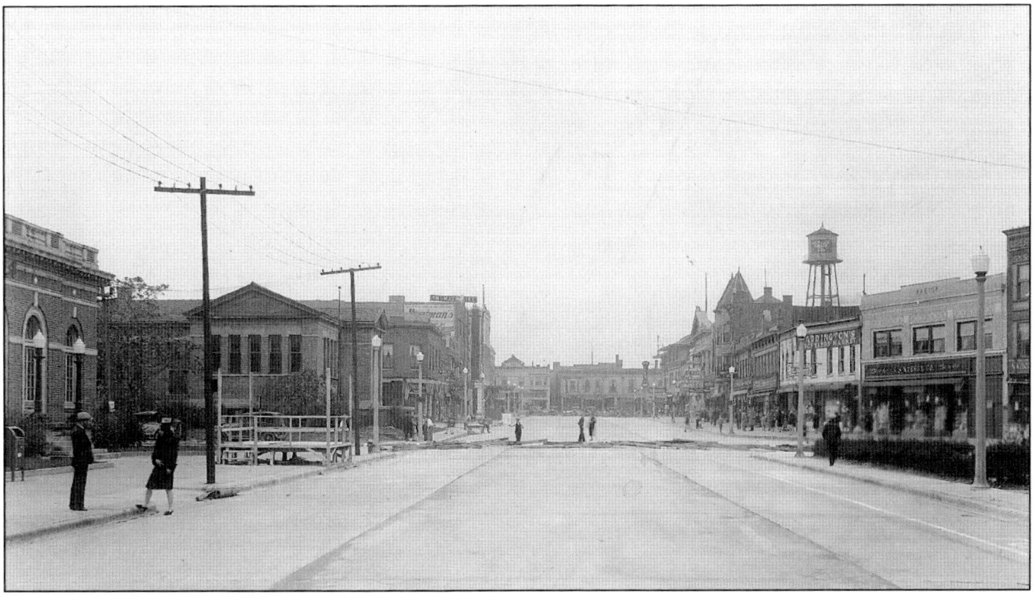

Looking south on Halsted from 16th Street before a 1930s parade reveals (left to right) the post office, the library, the Thomas Hotel, the Victoria Hotel, the First National Bank, Waddington's Stock Yards Market, and Kresge's Dollar Store.

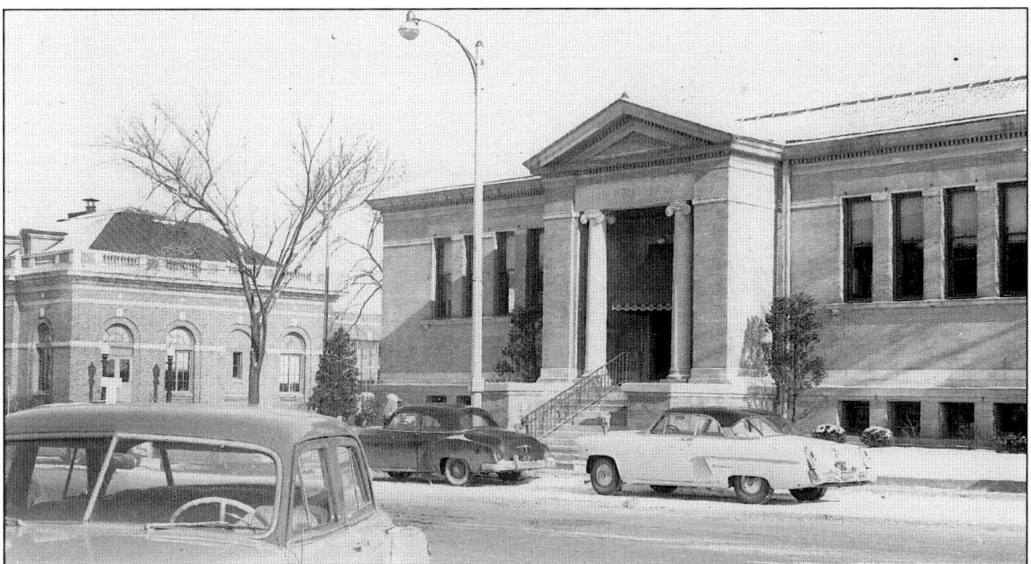

The Chicago Heights Public Library, the U.S. Post Office, and the train/bus station east of the library made an ideal town center; it was the heart of the city until the 1970s.

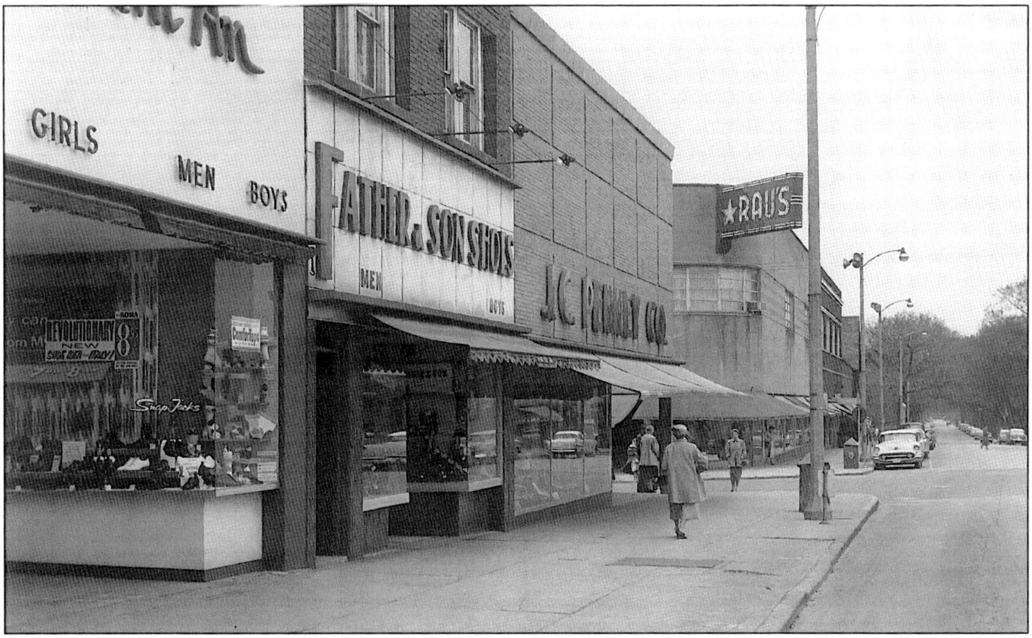

Looking north on Otto Boulevard 1950s, one realizes the prominence and modern look of the Rau Store. The presence of two successful shoe stores next door to each other is another indication of the strength of the retail market in downtown Chicago Heights.

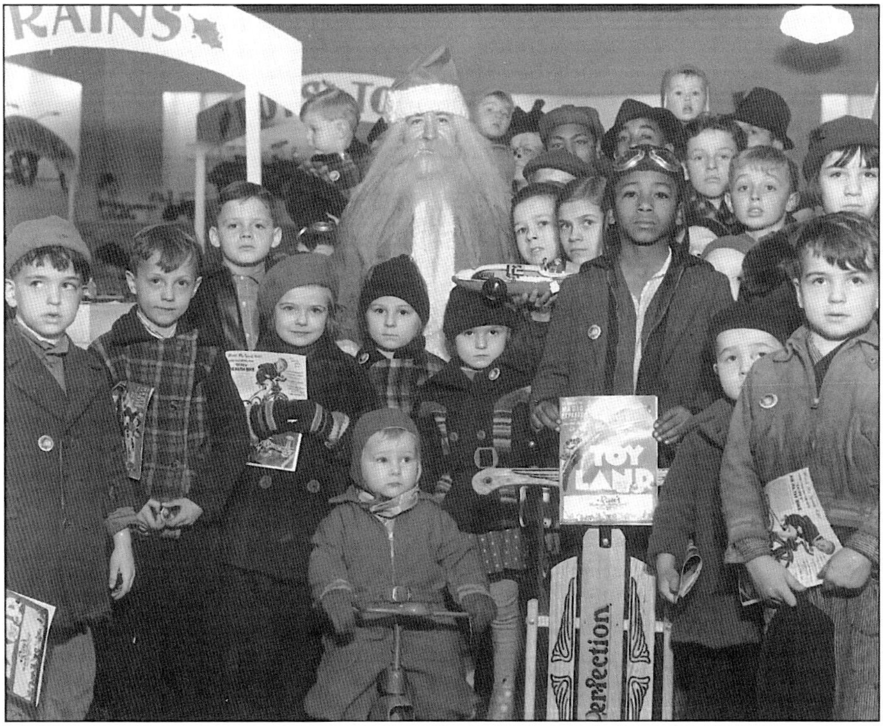

Chicago Heights kids pose with Santa in Rau's Toyland this 1940s photograph. This was the era of Lionel trains, Perfection sleds, and Monarch bikes.

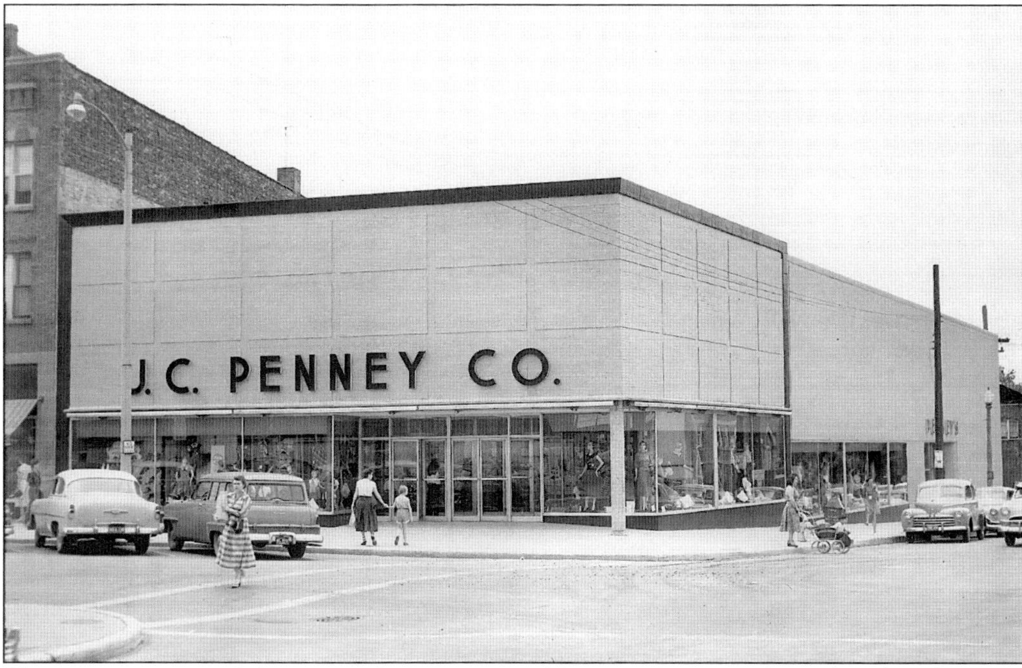

The construction of the new J.C. Penney Building on Otto Boulevard and 16th Street in 1953 was the occasion for a personal visit by Mr. J.C. Penney himself. Considered a large store when it was built, this structure was deemed too small for profitable retailing only 25 years later.

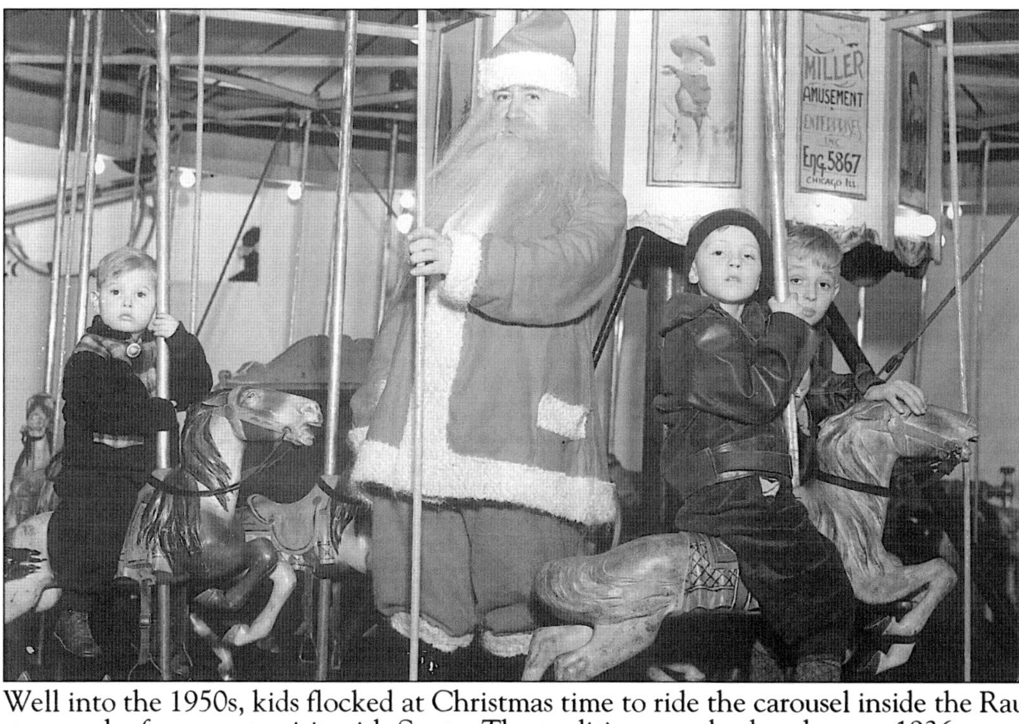

Well into the 1950s, kids flocked at Christmas time to ride the carousel inside the Rau store and, of course, to visit with Santa. The tradition goes back at least to 1936.

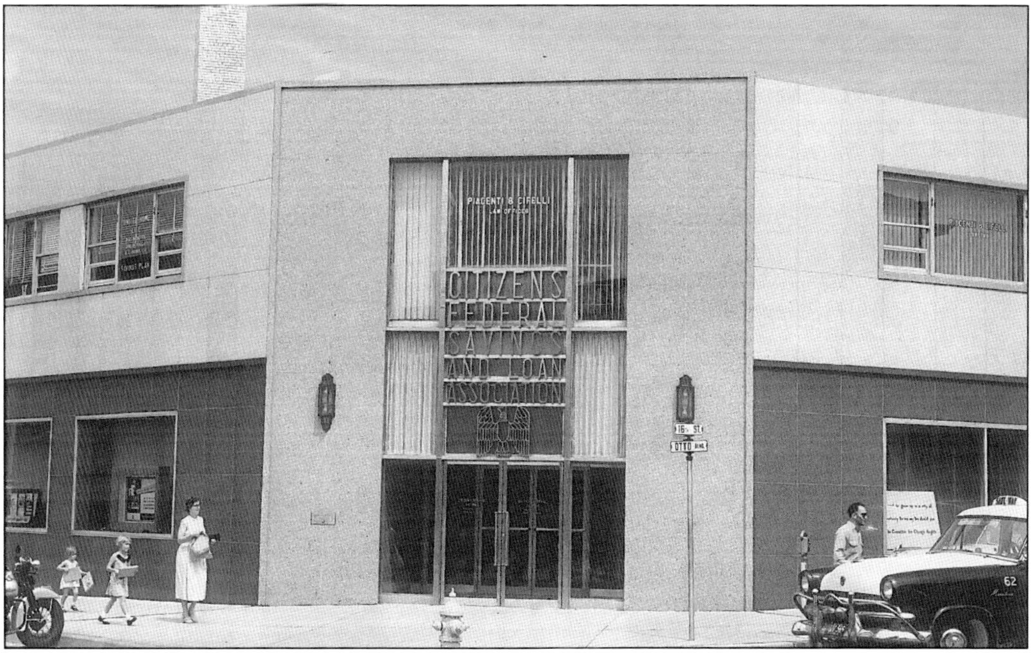

The Citizens Federal Savings and Loan Association was first organized in January 1914 as the Polish Citizens' Building and Loan Association on the East Side. Led by members of the Klyczek family, the enterprise prospered. In 1954, they moved into this new building erected on the old site of the Hood Building and the Washington Theatre in the heart of downtown Chicago Heights at 16th and Otto Boulevard. Second floor office space was rented to the prominent law firm of Piacenti and Cifelli as well as United Home Life insurance agents Joe Berger and A. E. Giannetti.

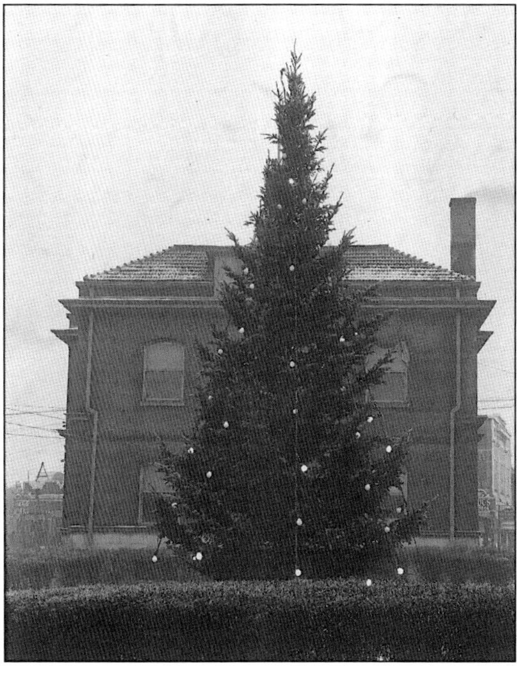

The old downtown was a favorite shopping destination during the holidays. This tree stood on the south lawn of city hall where it could be enjoyed by Halsted Street shoppers. North, beyond city hall, was Barwig Drugs at 16th and Halsted, the Rex Theatre, and Kline's Department Store in the late 1940s and early 1950s.

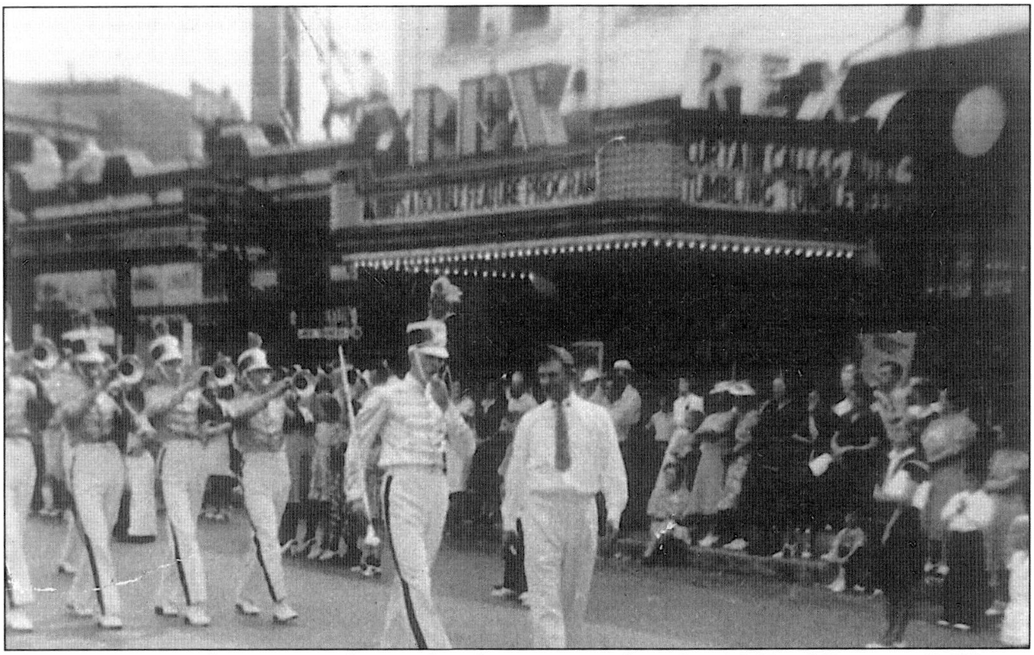

The Rex movie theater at 1544 Halsted was opened in the 1940s. "Curtain Call" was one of the features playing when this 1950s photo was taken.

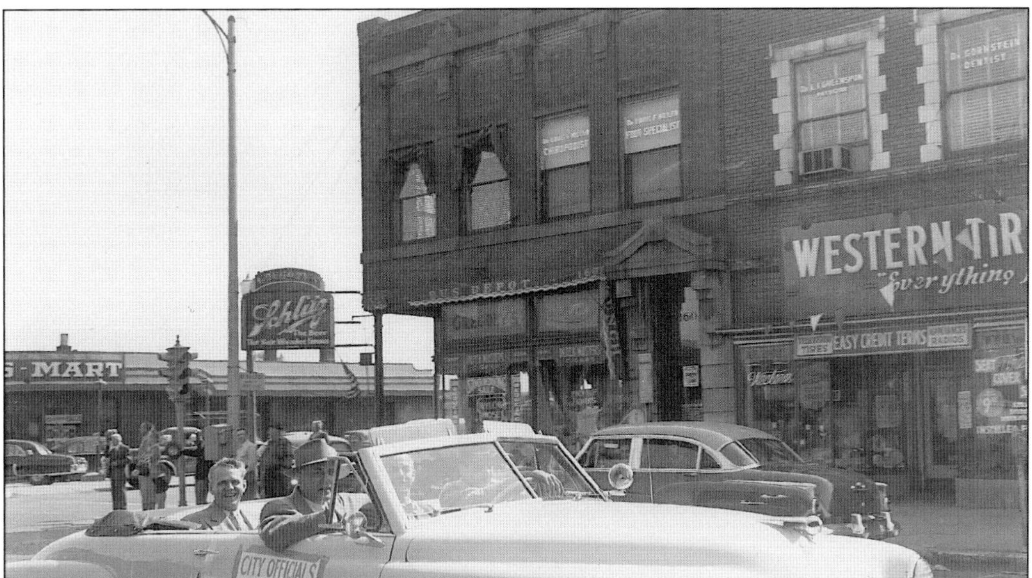

This Decoration Day parade photo, taken in 1953, reveals a microcosm of downtown commerce at the corner of 16th and Halsted. Gregory's Depot featured a bar, packaged liquors, Dutch Master cigars, and nylon hose. The Western Tire and Auto Store offered easy credit on radios, TVs, appliances, and tires. Foot specialist Louis F. Miller, dentist Dr. Gornstein, and physician L. I. Greenspan all practiced their professions on the second floor. City officials include Commissioner Louis Marks (driver), Andy Foley (front seat), Mayor Carl McGehee, and Commissioner George Brooke (rear).

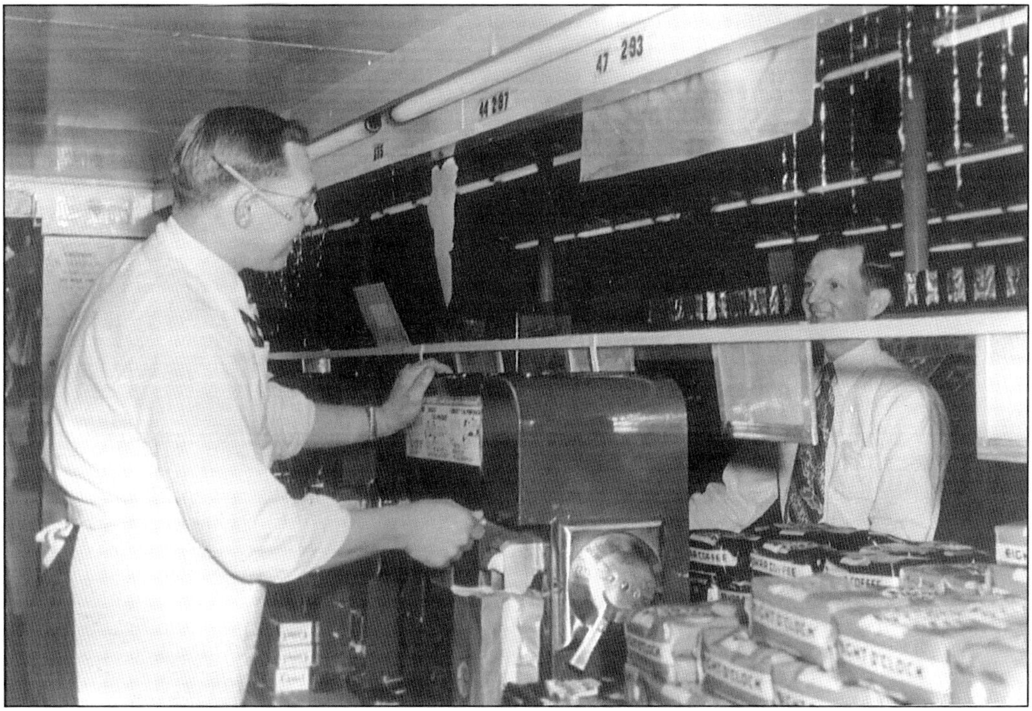

Senior manager Francis Farabaugh is pictured above in this 1950s photo grinding coffee—the product around which the A & P national chain originated. Mr. Farabaugh was a local, respected businessman involved in his community.

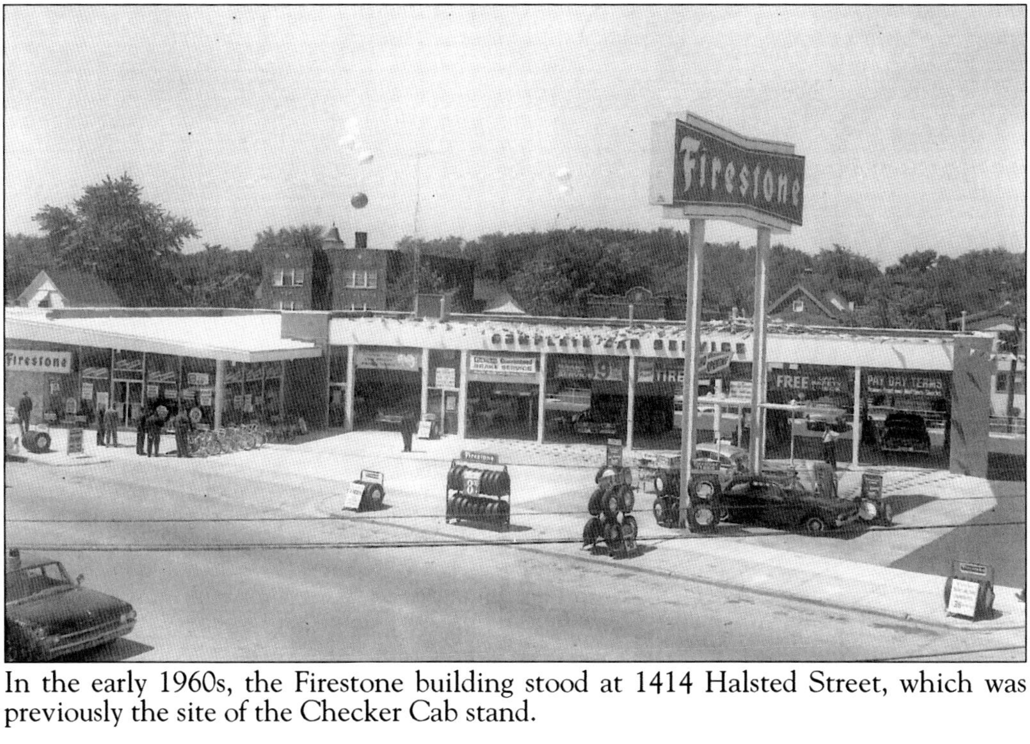

In the early 1960s, the Firestone building stood at 1414 Halsted Street, which was previously the site of the Checker Cab stand.

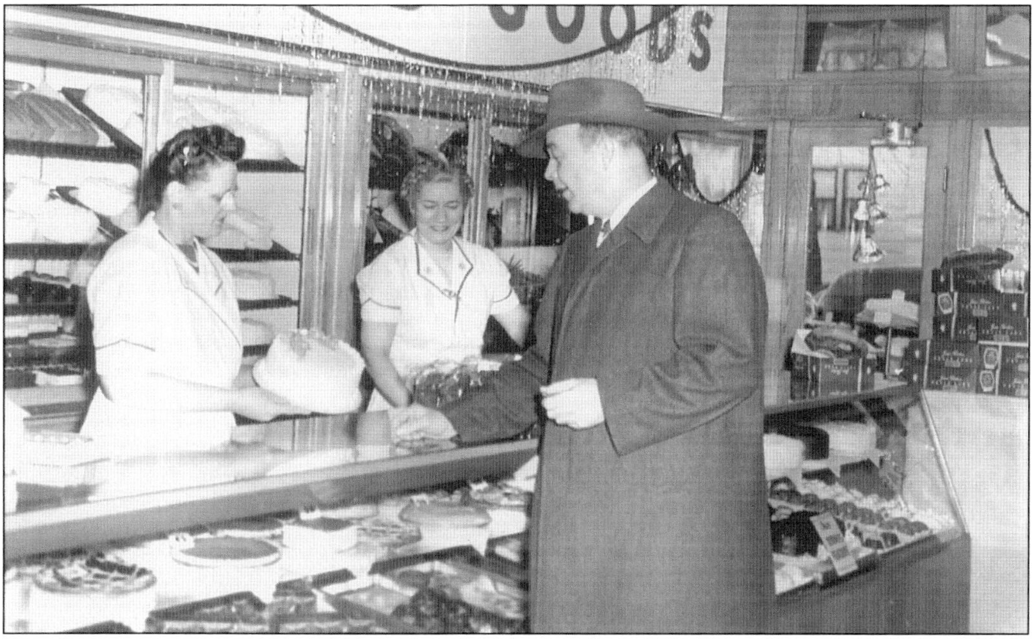

Betsy Rossi and Marquette Newquist serve a customer at Christmas time in the newly updated bakery section of the 1950s A&P Supermarket at 1516 Halsted Street. The expansion and improvement of the chain stores destroyed the mom-and-pop corner groceries during that period.

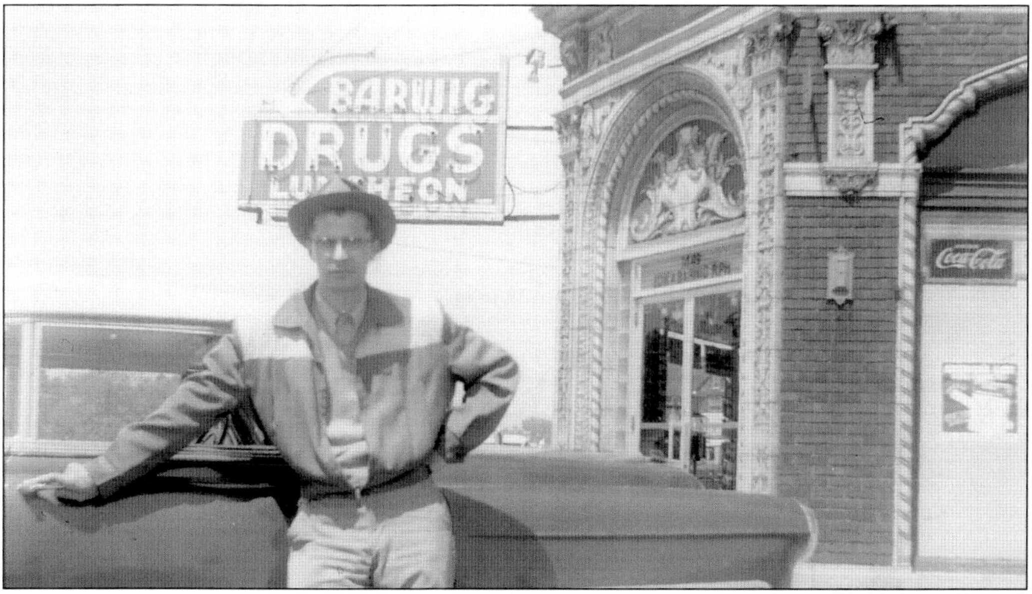

Edward Hoertline poses with his 1950s Chevy in front of the Flat Iron Building when it was occupied by Edward Barwig's Drugstore. As was customary in those days, this drugstore included a soda fountain and short-order food service.

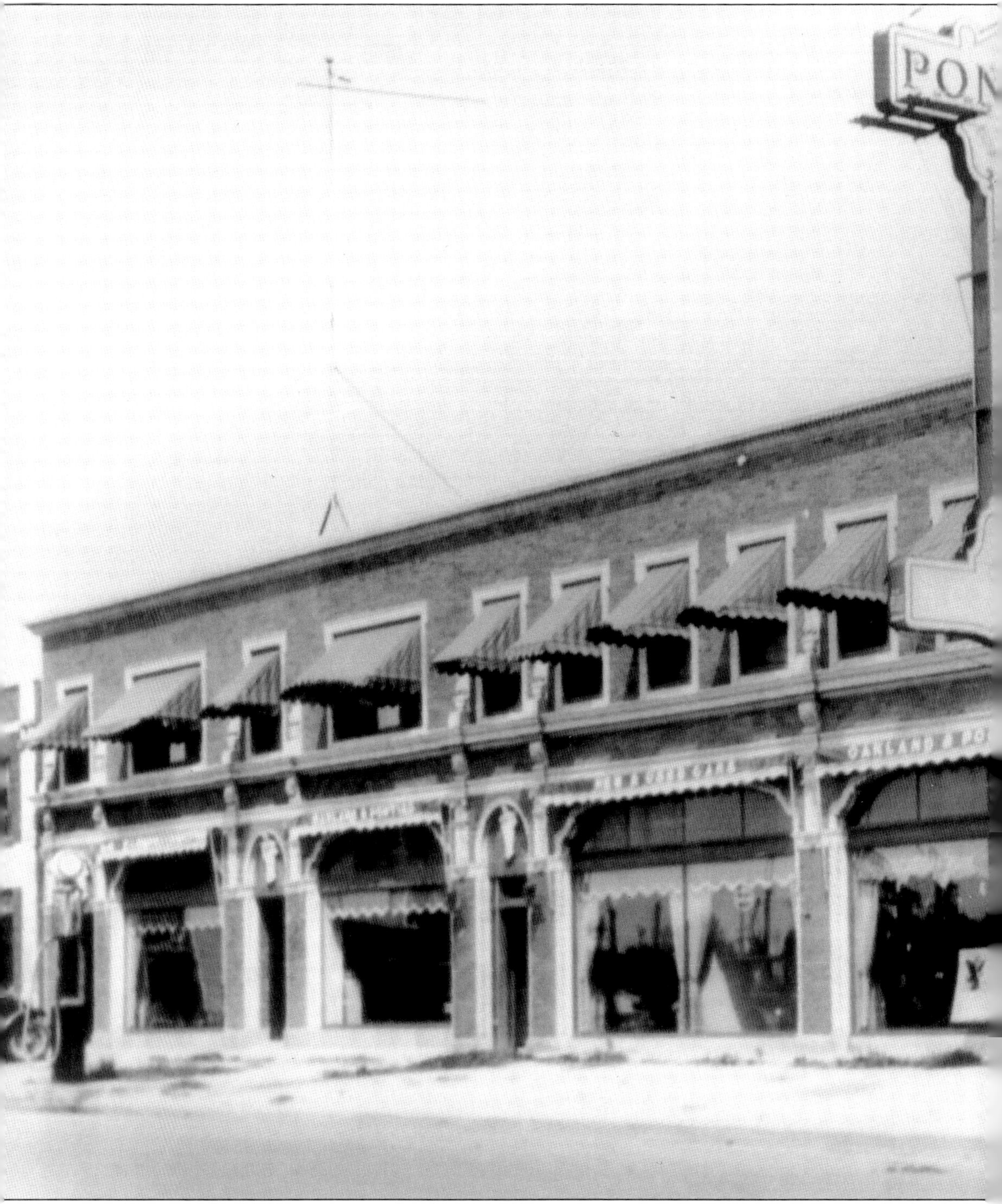

In the 1930s, the Flatiron Building, at 1449 Emerald, housed an auto dealership. Built in 1925 by the DiCicco Construction Company, the structure was handsomely adorned with terra-cotta trim produced in Chicago Heights. The awnings protected both the showroom and the apartments from the afternoon sunset. This building

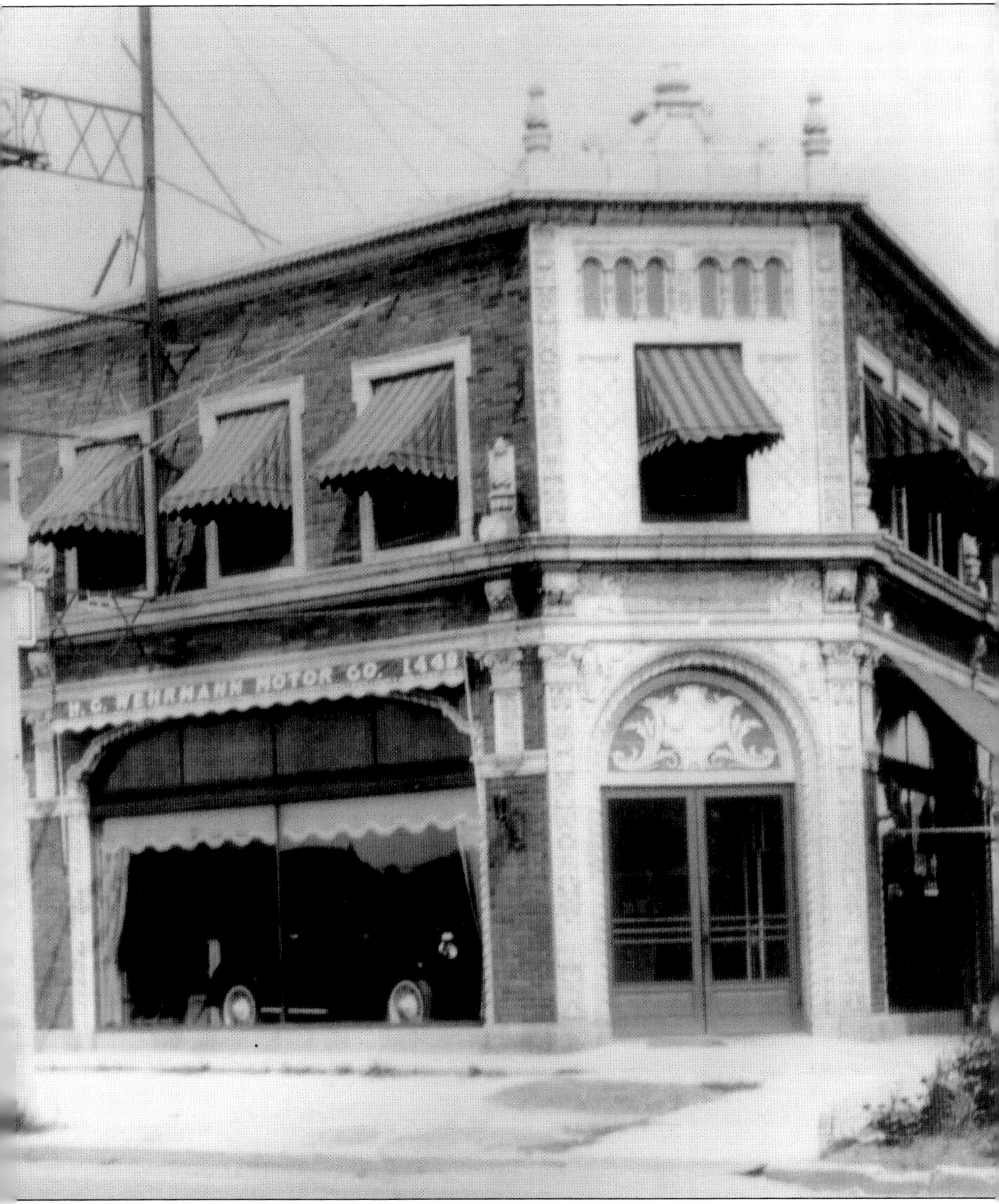

has the distinction of being one of the few downtown Chicago Heights structures to survive the failed urban renewal of the 1970s. The Historic Preservation Committee has desiginated the Flat Iron Building a landmark and plans to house a historic transportation museum in the restored structure.

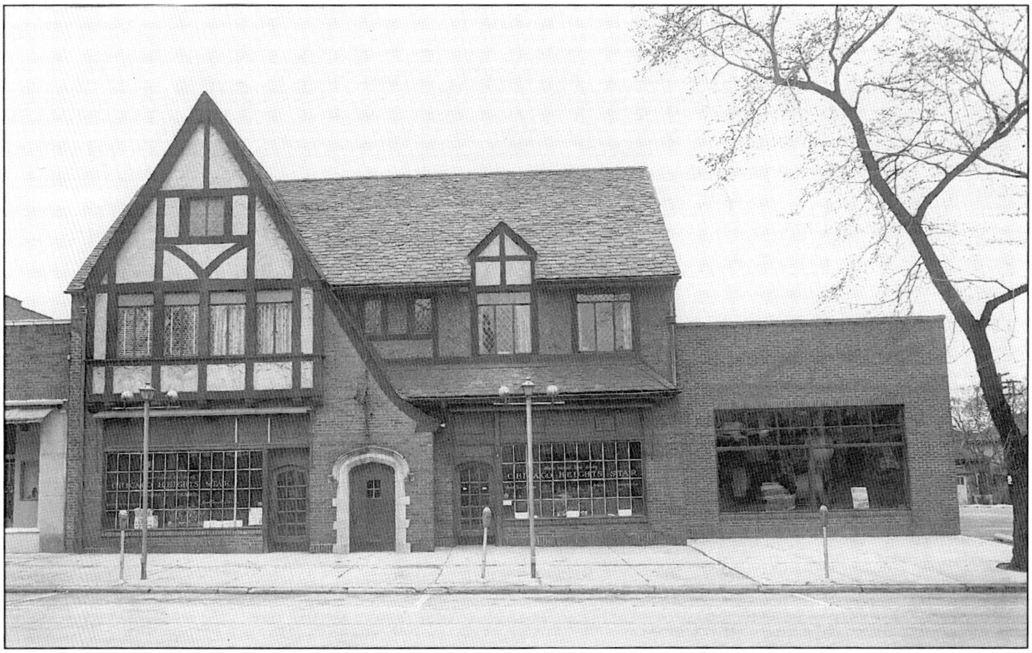

This Tudor-style building on Otto Boulevard was built in 1928. It housed the editorial offices and print shop of the *Chicago Heights Star,* which was owned by the Williams family. From 1901 to the mid-1990s, the publication was a major community institution chronicling the city's political, social, and business history.

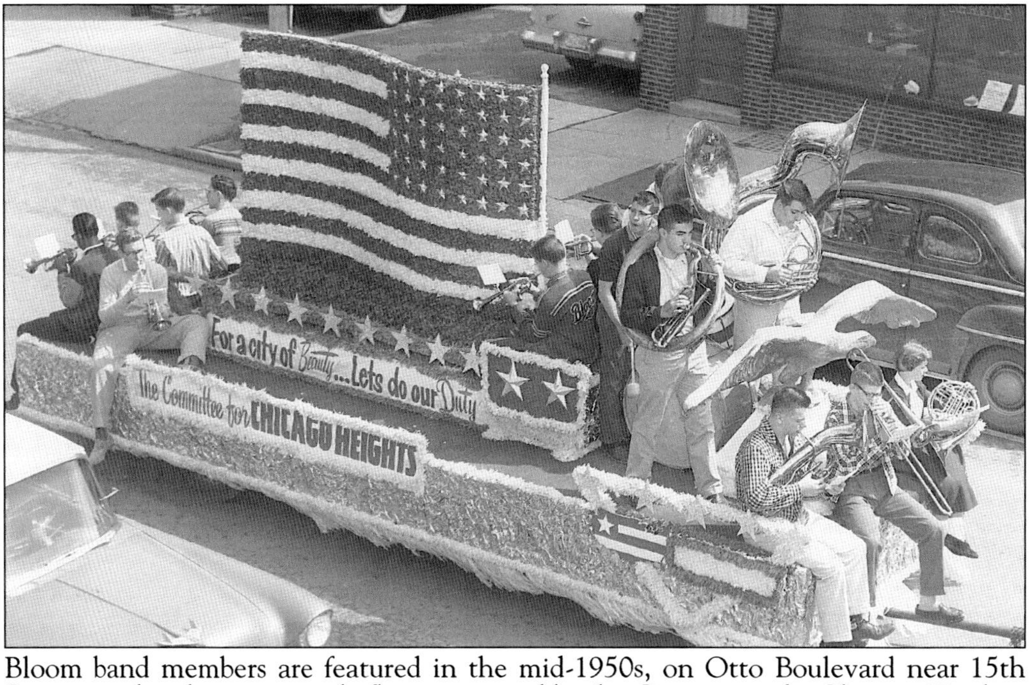

Bloom band members are featured in the mid-1950s, on Otto Boulevard near 15th Street, on the clean-up parade float sponsored by the Committee for Chicago Heights. "For a City of Beauty…Let's do our Duty," read the slogan on the float.

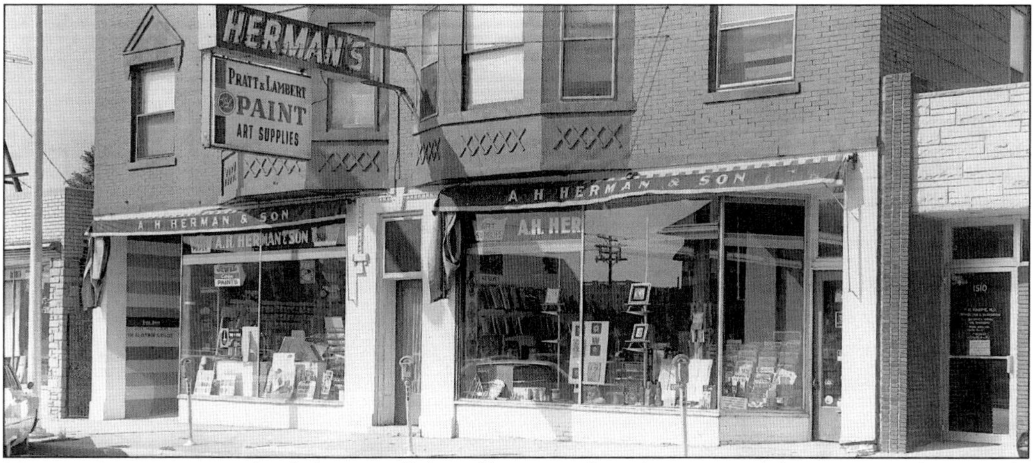

Herman's was typical of the small locally-owned and managed businesses that made downtown Chicago Heights so successful.

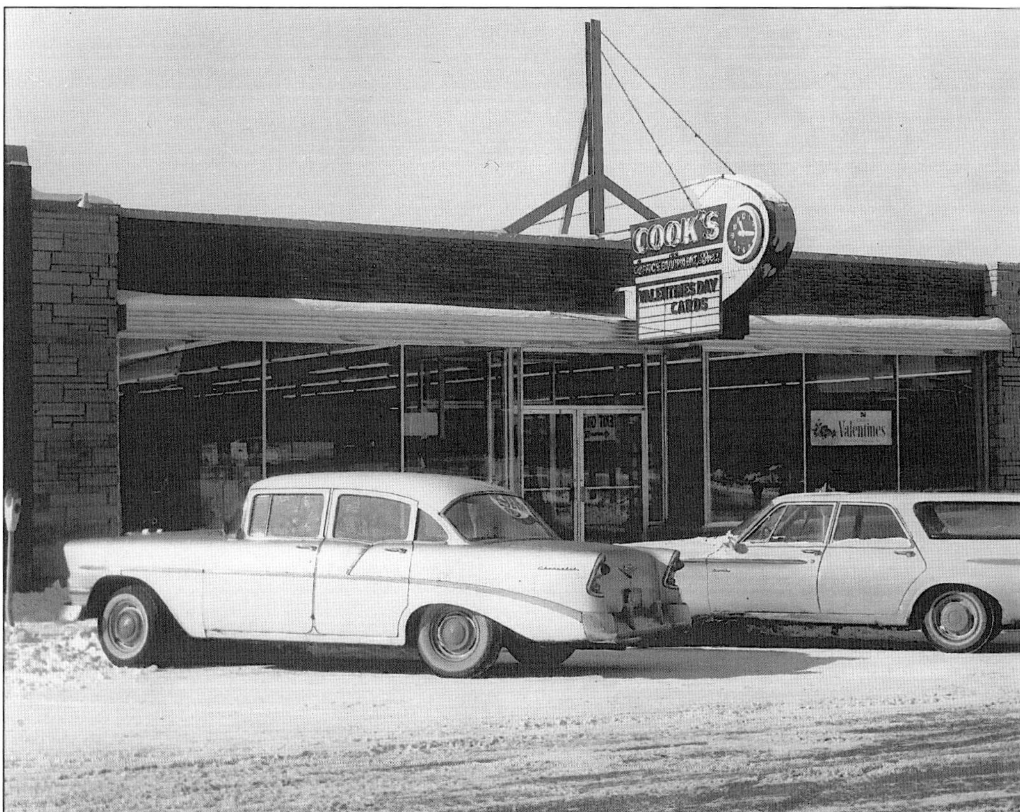

The 1950s headquarters for Cook's Office Supply was located at 1644 Vincennes Avenue. Cook's is one of the dwindling number of businesses that have endured in Chicago Heights for over 50 years.

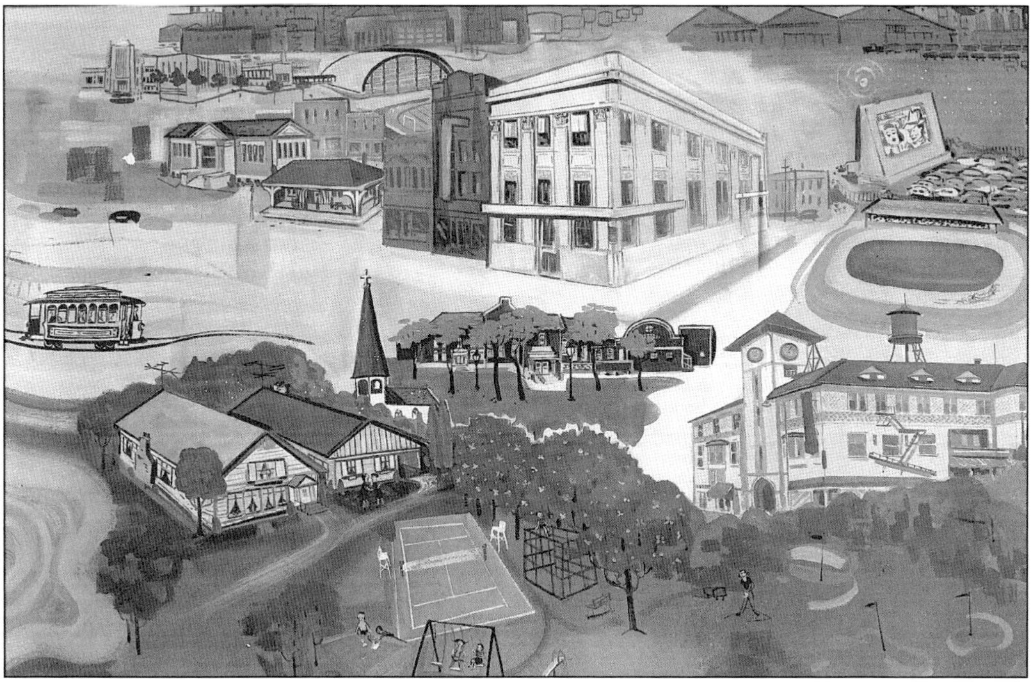

Above is a 1960s sketch, prepared for the Committee for Chicago Heights, which highlights major architectural features of Chicago Heights including Bloom High School, the Victoria Hotel, the public library, schools, churches, nearby race tracks, drive-in movies, and the old streetcars.

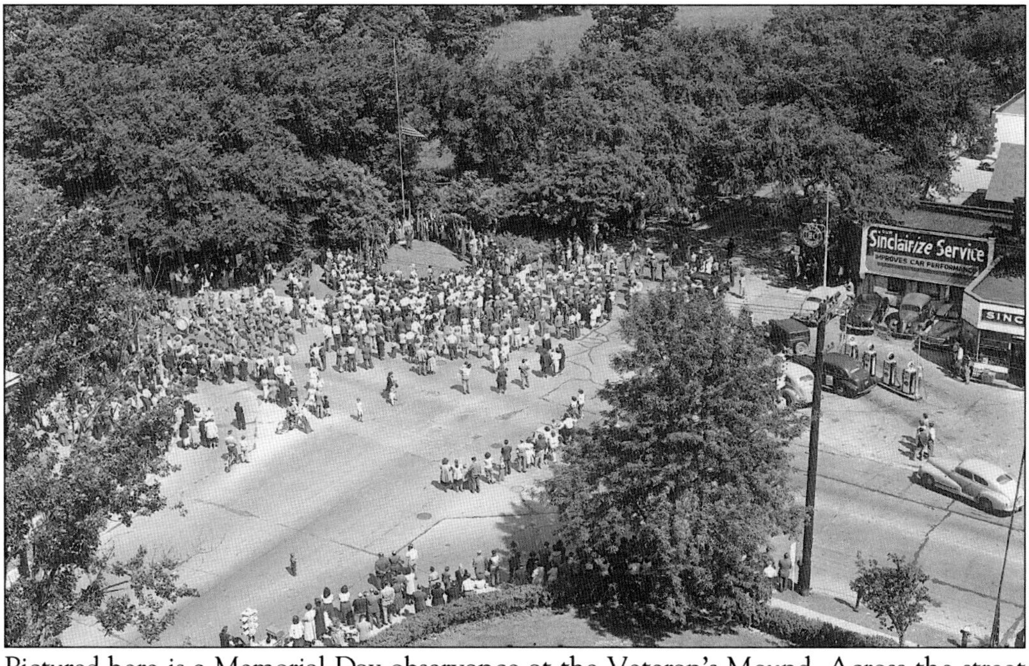

Pictured here is a Memorial Day observance at the Veteran's Mound. Across the street was Louis Dandurand's gas station offering "Sinclairize Service." East of the station were the "Eskimo" ice cream parlor and the Charles E. Hofmann Florist Shop.

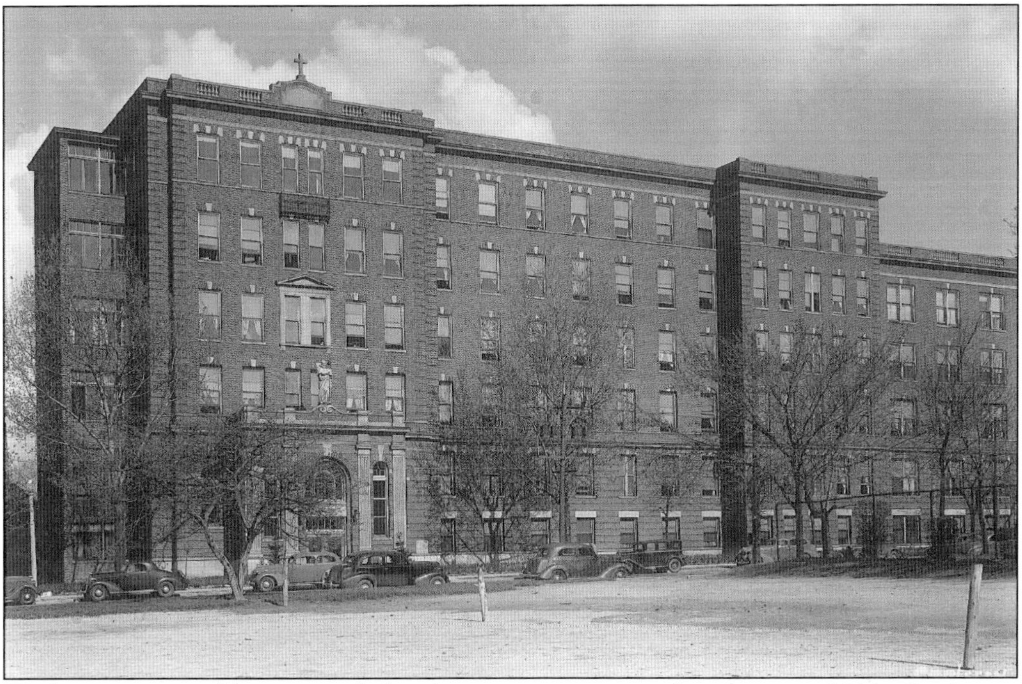

With its many additions and developments since its founding in 1911, St. James Hospital (pictured in the 1930s) has continued into the 21st century to be one of the most dynamic and enduring institutions in town.

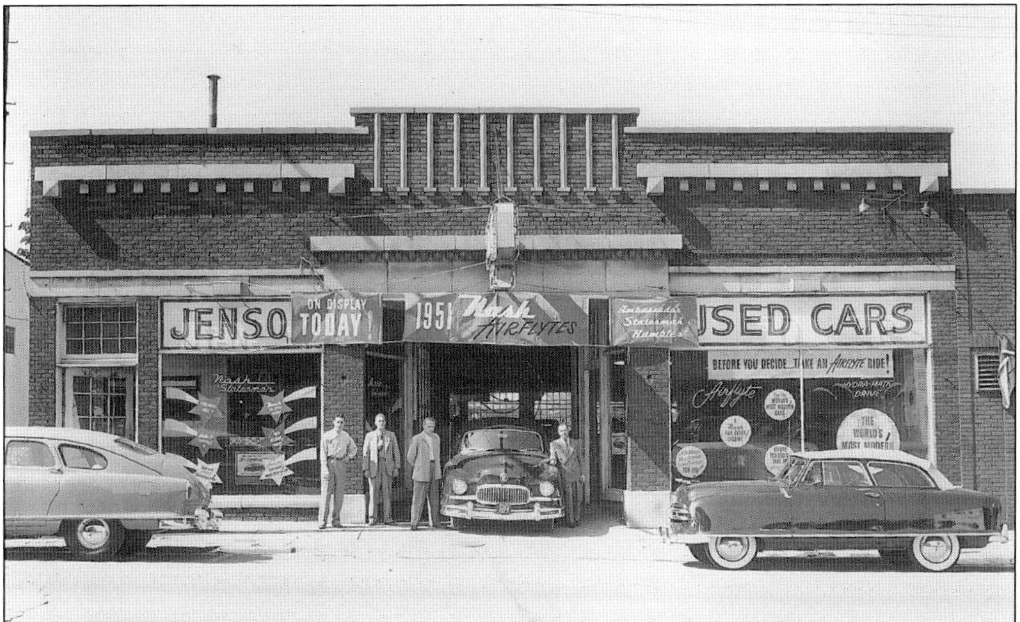

The Jenson Auto Dealership at 1644 Chicago Road dramatically announced the arrival of the 1951 Nash. "Before you decide... take an Aireflyte Ride," "The world's most modern cars," and "A Nash for every income," were the slogans of the day.

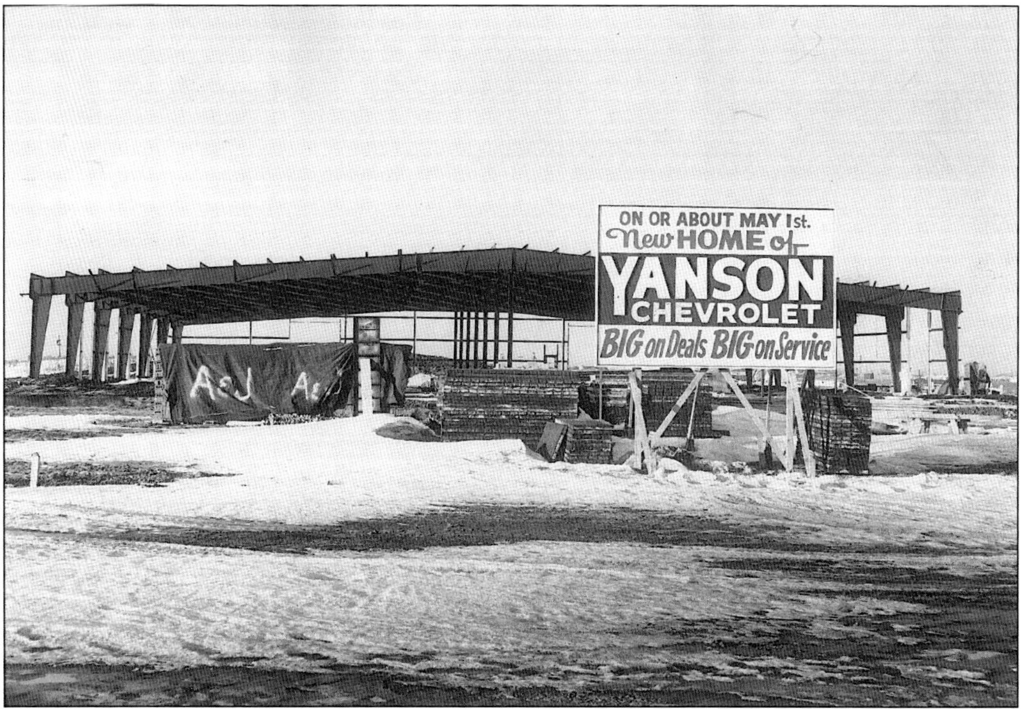

In the 1960s, the auto dealers began to move from north Halsted and the downtown area to west Lincoln Highway. Yanson Chevrolet was one of the first to do so. Forty years later, dealerships hungering for even more space moved on to regional auto malls.

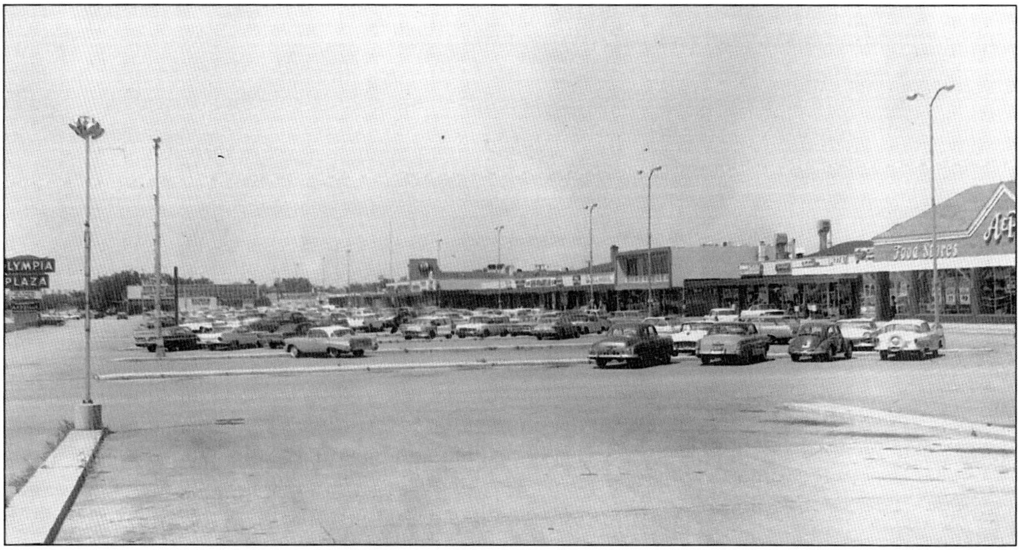

In the late 1970s, Mayor Panici proclaimed Olympia Plaza to be Chicago Heights' new downtown. This 1960s photo shows the A&P store as an anchor tenant. The development reflects the northern growth experienced in the 1950s and 1960s, when builders such as Arquilla filled up the area to the north of Bloom High School with brick bungalows, bi-levels, and tri-levels. In 1970, the population of Chicago Heights peaked at 40,000.

Six

GOVERNMENT

Our photographs representing government in Chicago Heights, though somewhat spotty, convey the same kind of pride and progressive spirit that permeated the private sector. The city enthusiastically welcomed air mail services in 1938, Vice-President Nixon in 1956, and President Reagan in 1985. The exclusively male members of the city council, police, fire, and postal workers displayed enormous pride in their work and in their city.

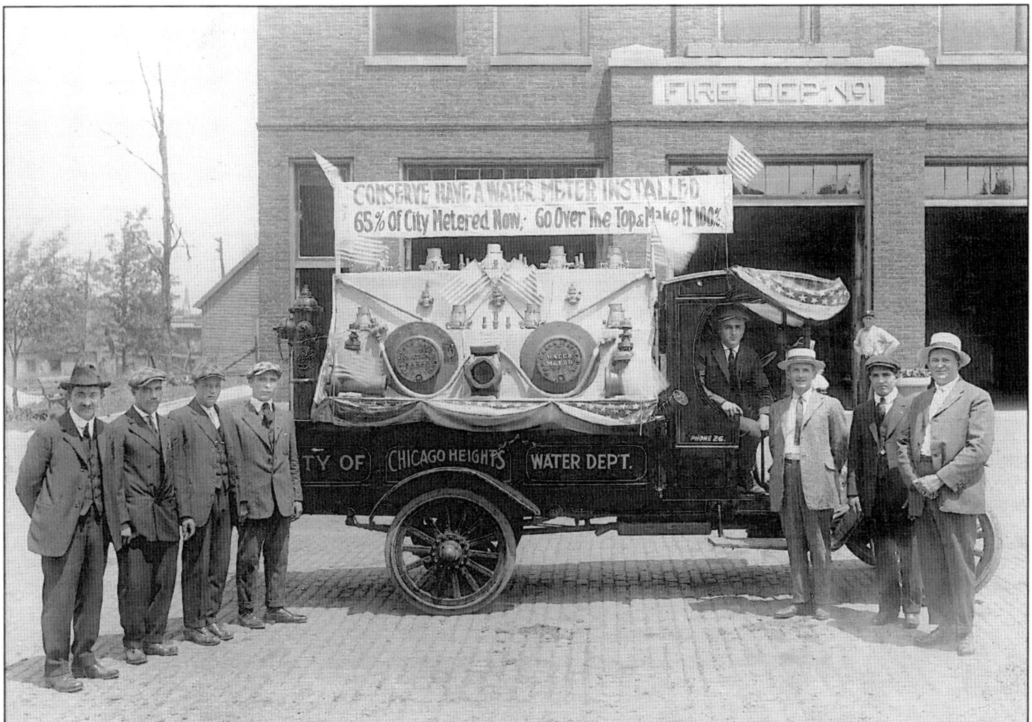

Water department employees pose in front of Station #1 on 19th Street to promote the accurate metering of Chicago Heights' water. This was an important issue for two reasons: the city's need of revenue and the city's desire to crack down on bootleggers who attempted to steal water and hide their incriminating use of large amounts of water (1920s).

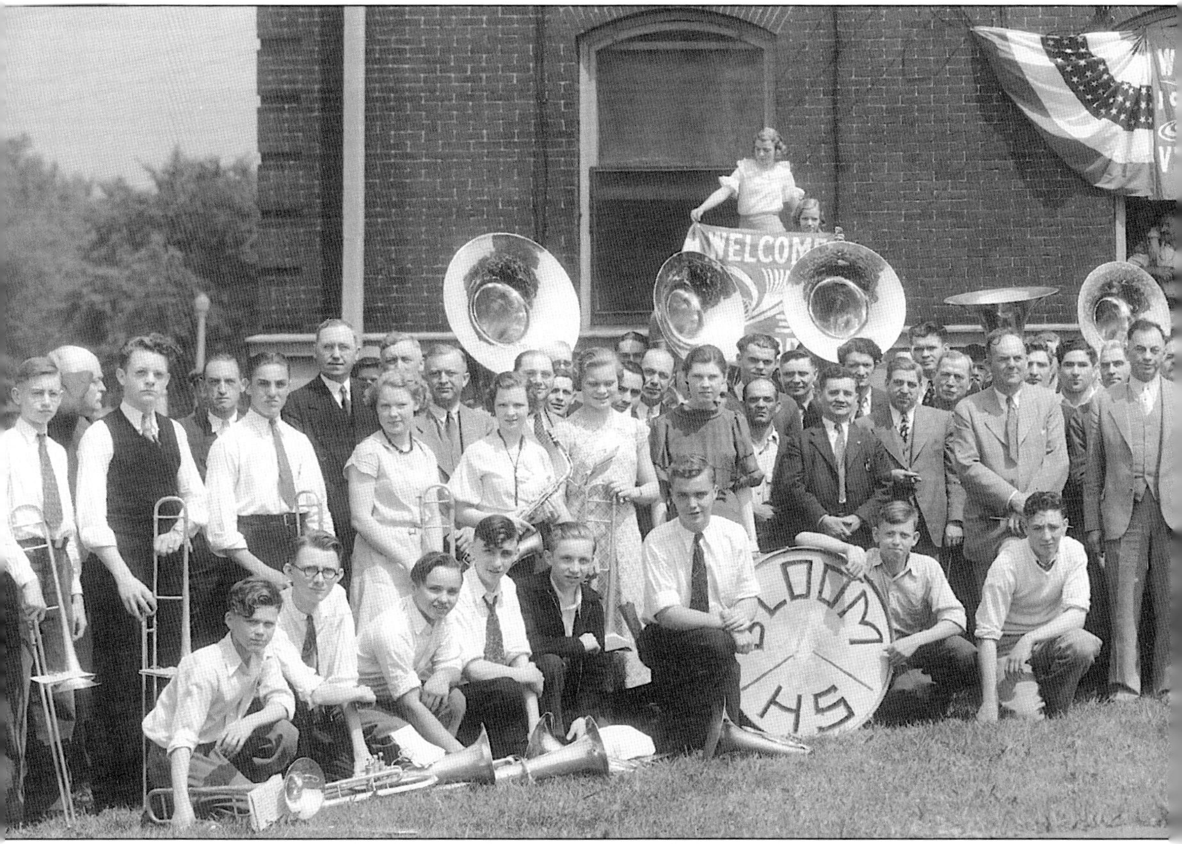

The Bloom Band and others gather on the south lawn of city hall during the Century of Progress celebration in 1933. Note the "Welcome Visitors" banners. Mayor Dan

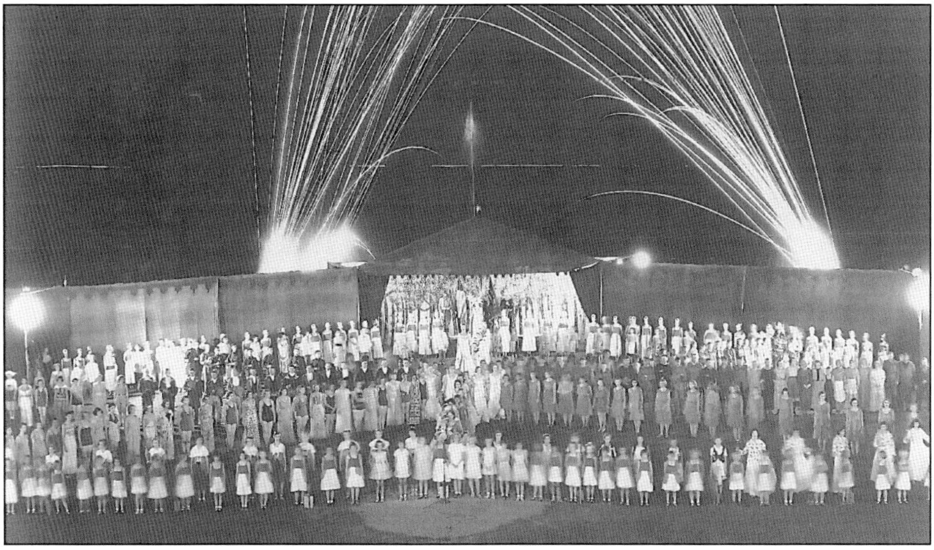

Chicago Heights celebrated its centennial in the same year that Chicago celebrated its centennial. The extravagant pageant was staged on the Bloom field and included hundreds of participants.

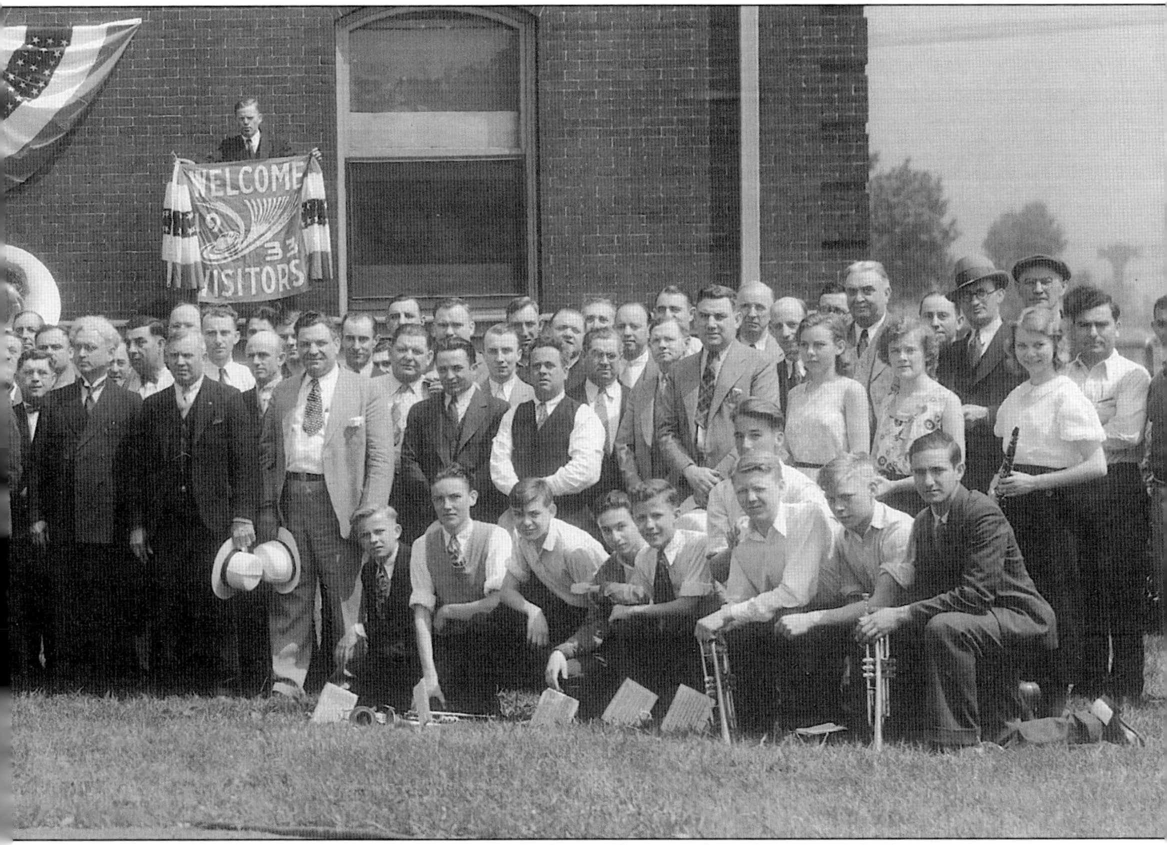

Bergin, Police Commissioner Zimny, Clerk Sadler, and Mike Costabile were among the public officials in the center of the photo.

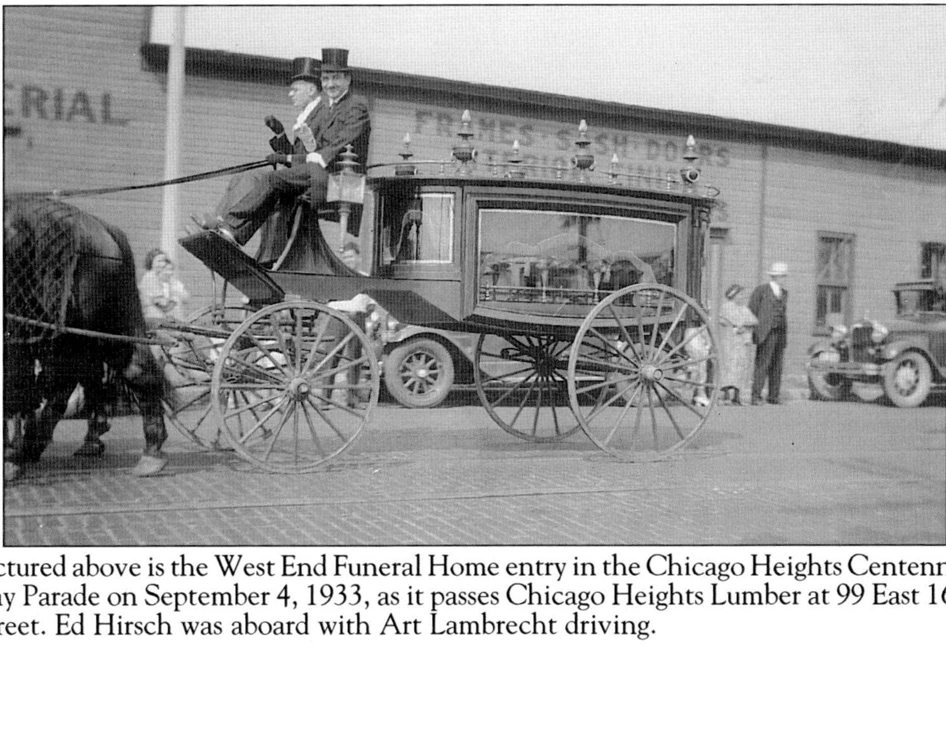

Pictured above is the West End Funeral Home entry in the Chicago Heights Centennial Day Parade on September 4, 1933, as it passes Chicago Heights Lumber at 99 East 16th Street. Ed Hirsch was aboard with Art Lambrecht driving.

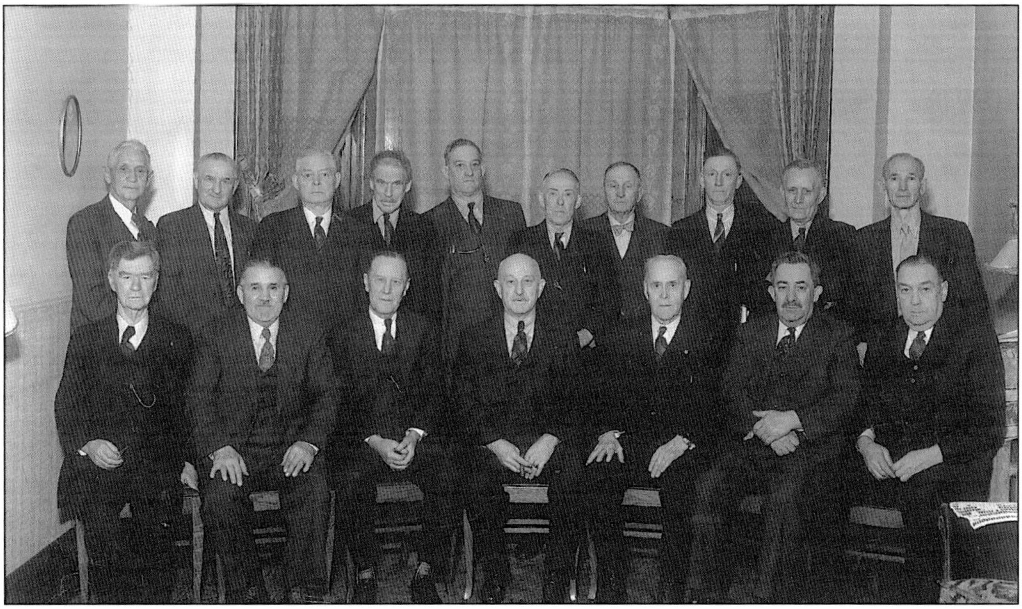

Chicago Heights Volunteer Fire Department members pose for their 46th Anniversary photo in 1939. From left to right are as follows: (front row) William Donovan, William Ritthamel, M.S. Philip, Charles Kurgis, George Fuller, Frank DeBolt, and Otto Conrad; (back row) Henry Busse, Arthur Anderson, Thomas Stone, Samuel Patterson, Oscar Williams, Harvey Manson, Elmer Somes, Skinny Wilson, Dave Peat, and Bob Forest.

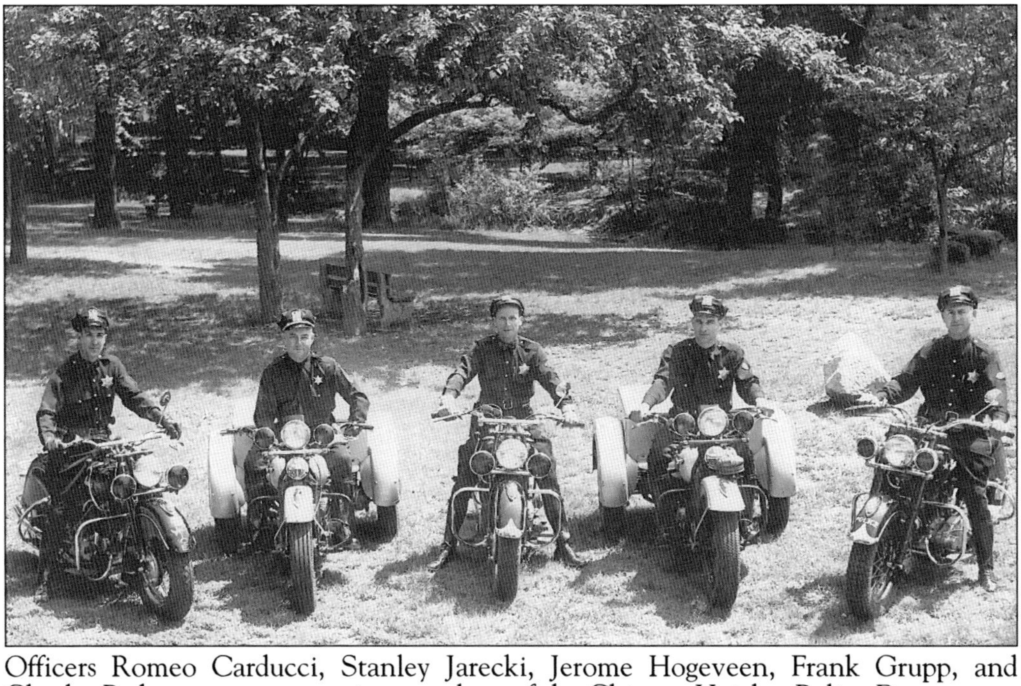

Officers Romeo Carducci, Stanley Jarecki, Jerome Hogeveen, Frank Grupp, and Charles Paduano were aggressive members of the Chicago Heights Police Department motorcycle patrol in the 1940s. The photo was taken on the banks of Thorn Creek. The department still owns one of these three-wheelers.

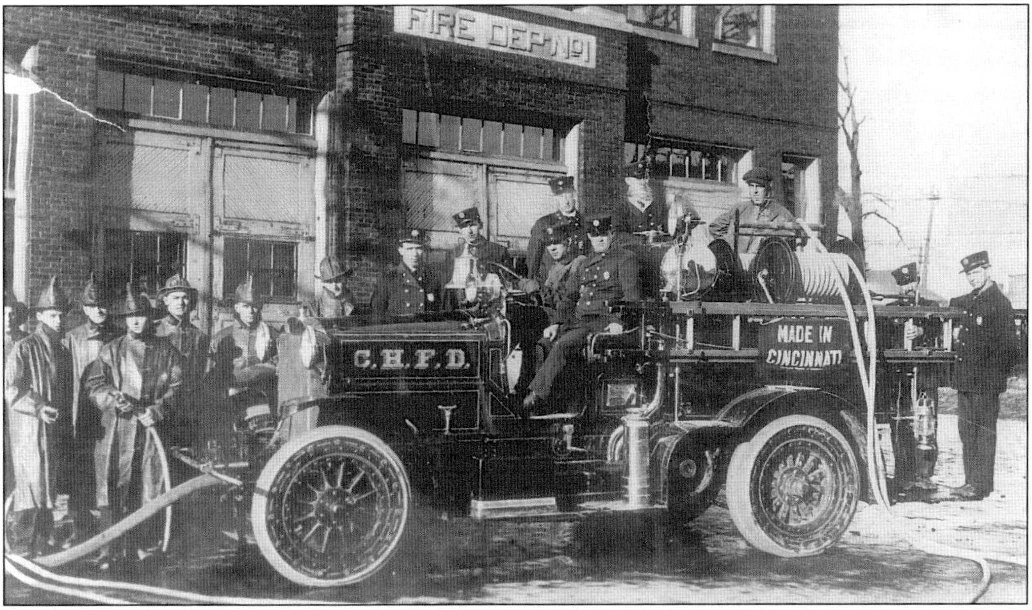

With Fire Chief Philip at the wheel, surrounded by members of the department in front of Fire Station #1 on 19th Street, the firefighters show off the city's first motorized fire truck in 1915.

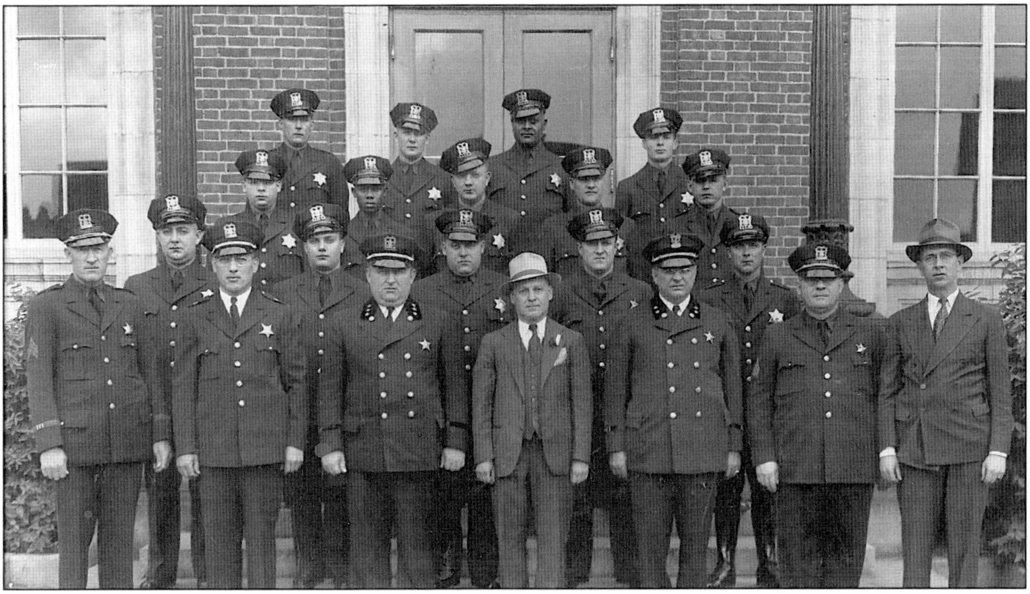

Police and Fire Commissioner John Gansen (center) poses with the police force in this official photograph taken on May 20, 1939, in front of the post office. They are, from left to right, as follows: (front row) John Lacheta, Charles Grupp, Philip Howard (chief), John Gansen, John Costabile, Frank Montesanti, and unidentified; (second row) Stanley Jarecki, Joseph Sylvester, Dominic D'Andrea, unidentified, and Elmer Quist; (third row) Max Atkin, Ben Ware, Gene Leinen, Dominic Passarelli, and unidentified; (back row) Frank Stec, William "Bloom" Kwiatkowski, Hershel "Biddy" Starks, and unidentified.

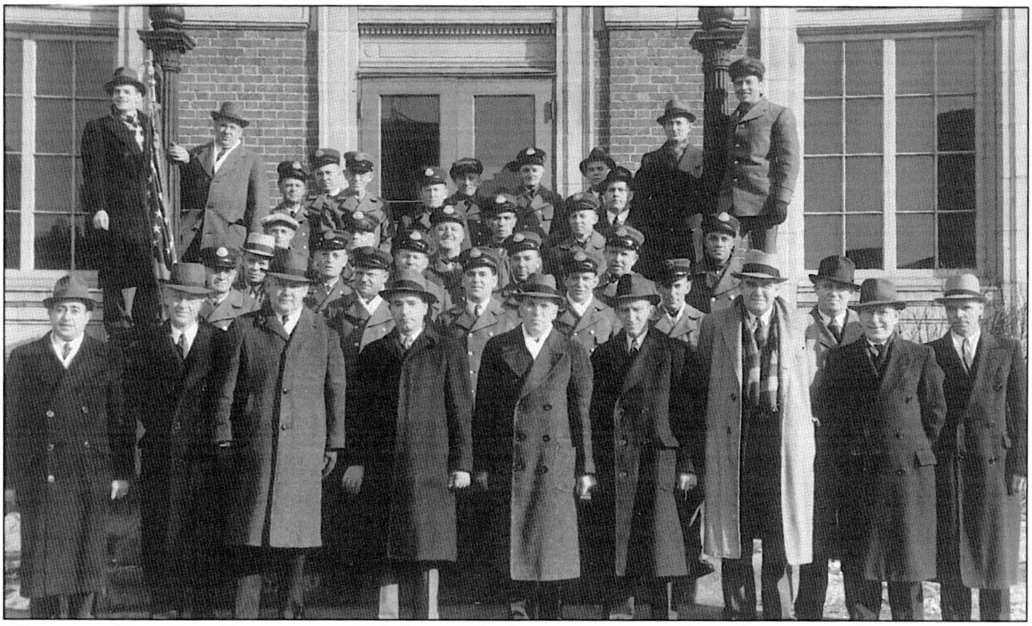

Chicago Heights Postmaster Melvin Vinlove poses with other postal workers and letter carriers in front of the post office at Halsted and Depot Court in the 1940s. The window designs and the lampposts are a small sample of the graceful architecture of the old post office.

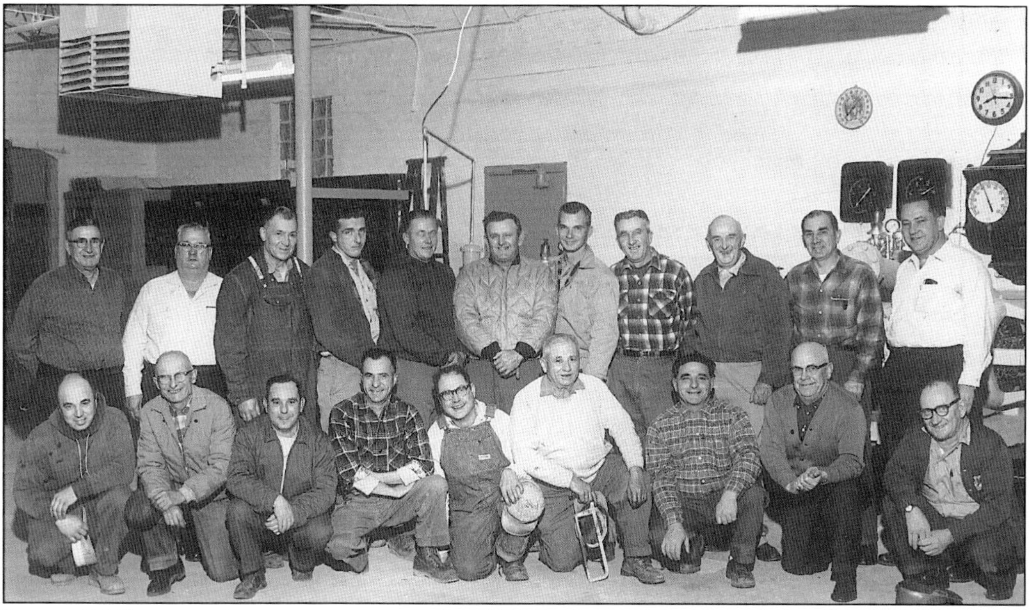

It was 8:15 on a winter morning in the 1960s when the men of the Chicago Heights Water Department gathered for this photo. In those days, the city used water pumped from 15 wells. By the 1960s, the water quality had declined precipitously and the city fathers began a campaign to bring Lake Michigan water to the residences and industries of Chicago Heights. The dream was achieved in 1976 when a 16-mile pipeline was completed, bringing water from Hammond to Chicago Heights.

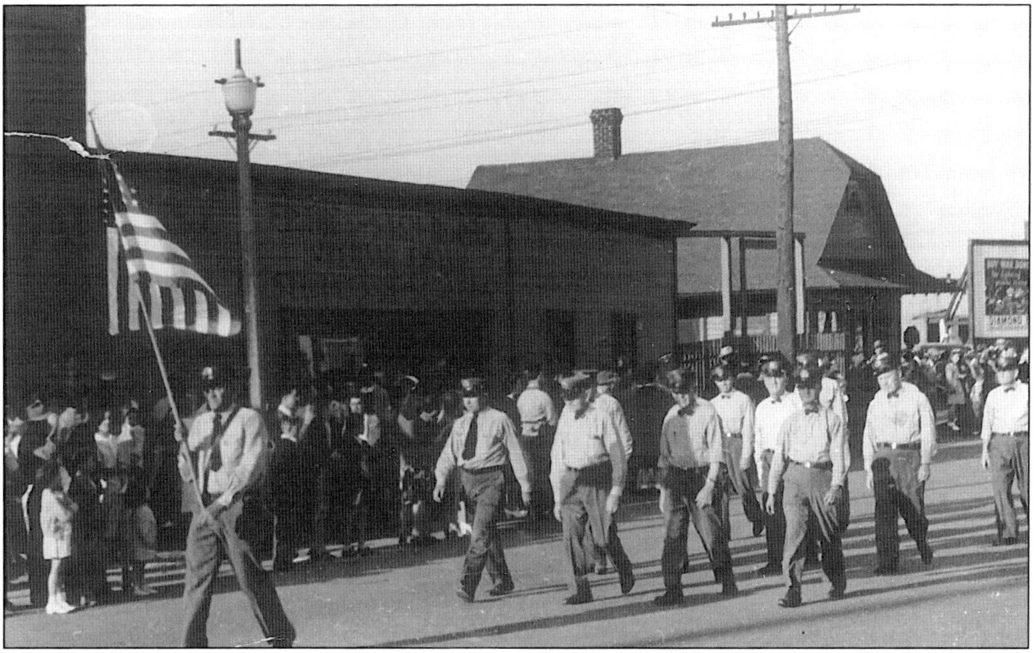

Postal employees parade on 16th Street near East End past the lumberyard in 1949. John Bell, the city's first African-American mail carrier, is the flag bearer.

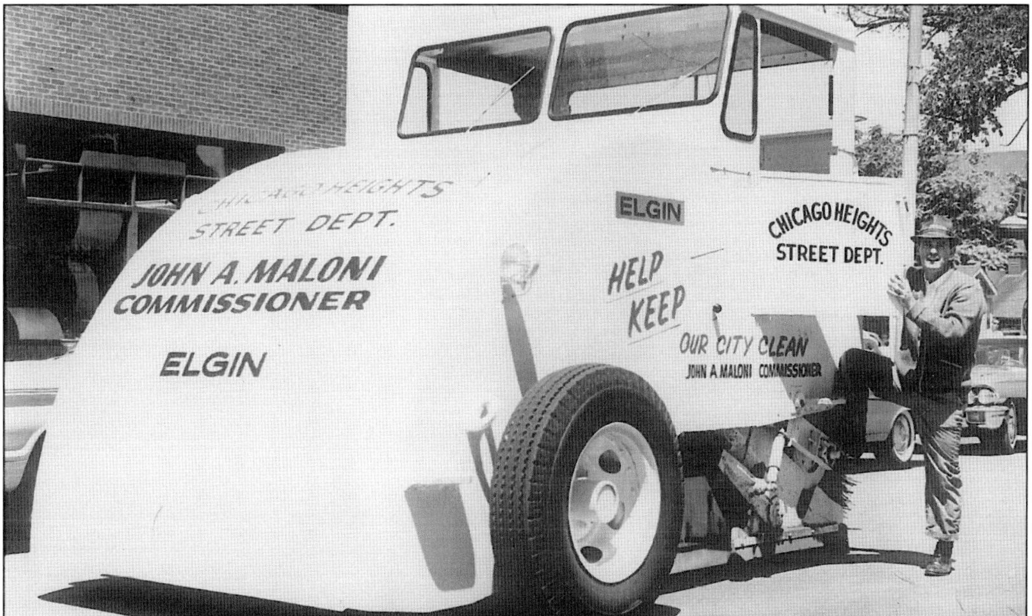

A Chicago Heights Street Department employee boards his street sweeping machine in the early 1960s on Otto Boulevard in front of the Star Building. The vehicle, purchased for $13,000 in 1963, left no doubt of whom to credit for clean streets.

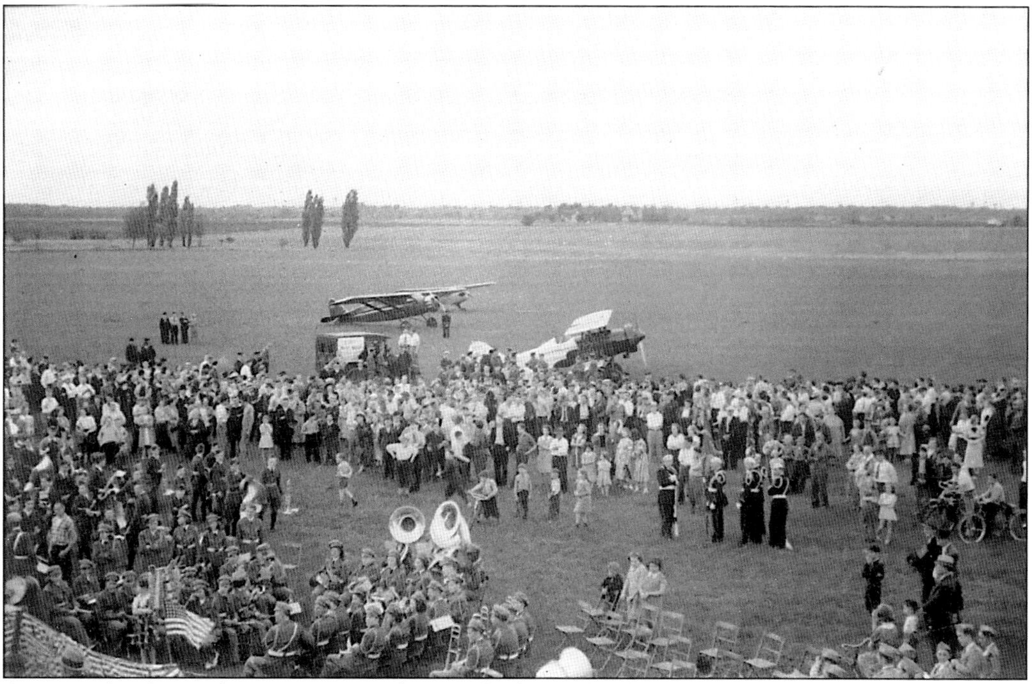

A crowd of nearly 1,000 people, including the high school band and kids on bicycles, gathered to witness the first air-mail pickup May 19, 1938, at the Chicago Heights airport, located at Ashland Avenue and Joe Orr Road (now Marian Catholic High School).

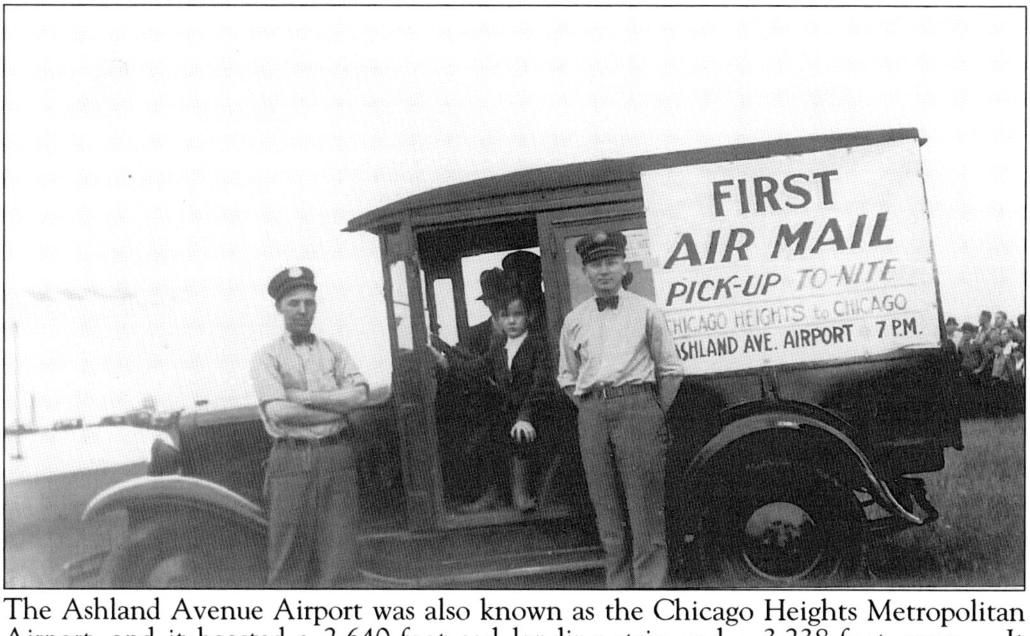

The Ashland Avenue Airport was also known as the Chicago Heights Metropolitan Airport, and it boasted a 2,640-foot sod landing strip and a 3,238-foot runway. It operated only during daylight hours. The airport closed in 1947 when the operators lost their lease.

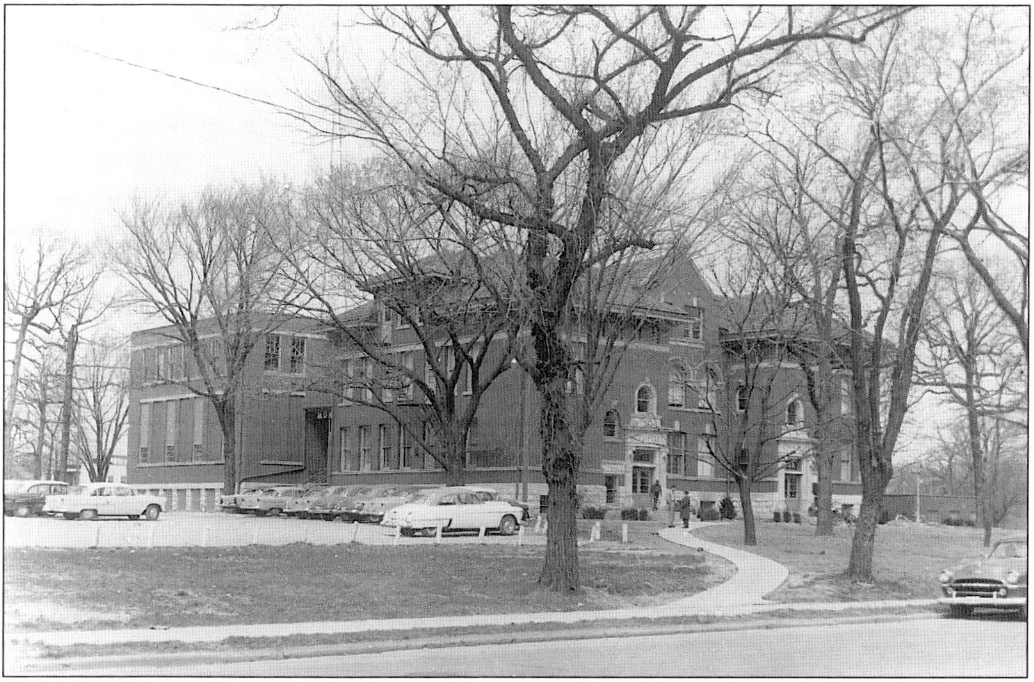

The old Bloom High School building, constructed in 1901, served as the Chicago Heights City Hall building from 1953 until 1975. The structure also housed a courtroom, police and fire stations, a roller rink, and "The Morgue"—a gothic-named youth center.

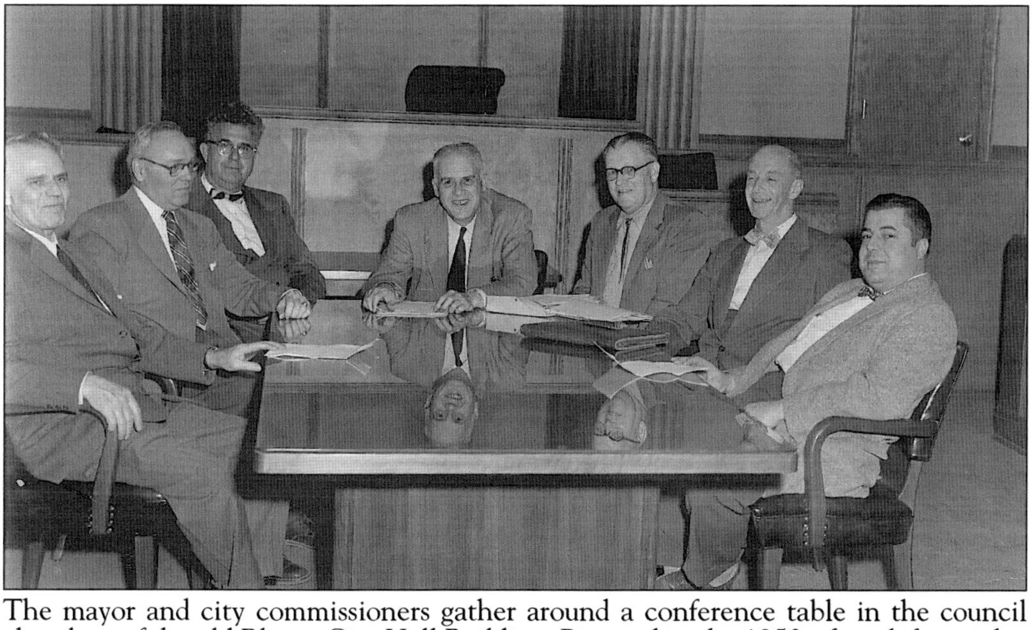

The mayor and city commissioners gather around a conference table in the council chambers of the old Bloom City Hall Building. Pictured in the 1950s, from left to right: George Brooke, William Schramm, Ernest Lawler (corporation counsel), Mayor Carl McGehee, Paul Soderman (clerk), Andy Foley, and Louis Marks.

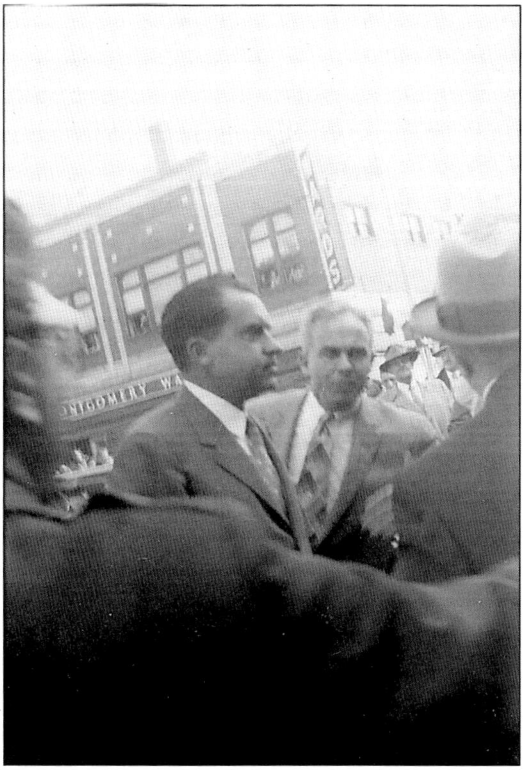

Vice President Nixon visited Chicago Heights on October 5, 1956. He is shown here shaking hands on Illinois Street in front of the old Montgomery Ward's store that stood at the northeast corner of Halsted and Illinois Streets.

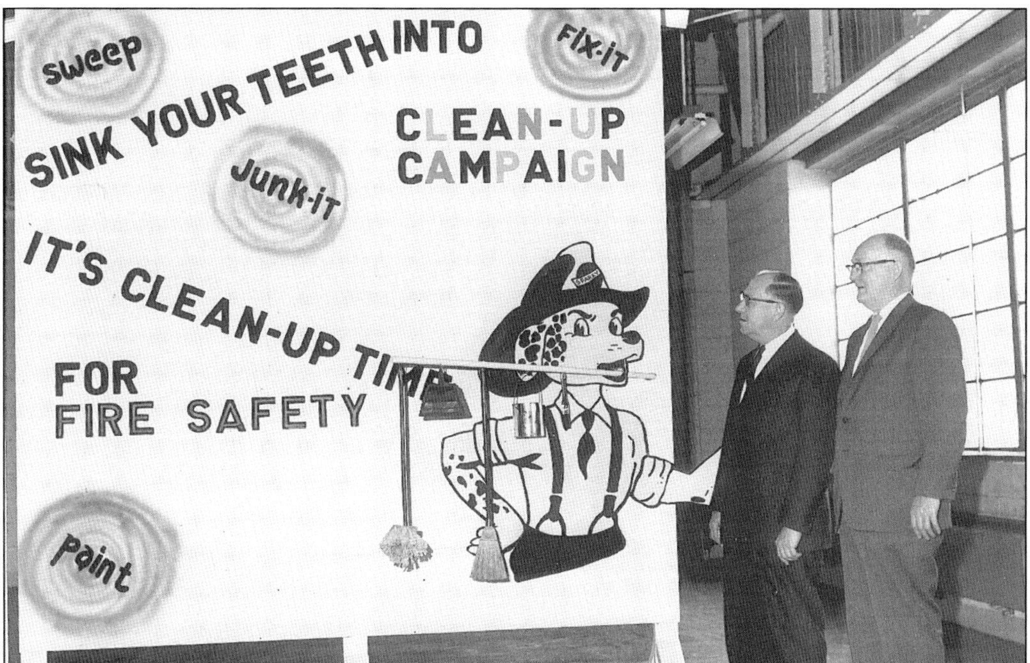

The Committee for Chicago Heights, as always, spent a good deal of time urging residents to clean up for safety as shown in this 1963 photo.

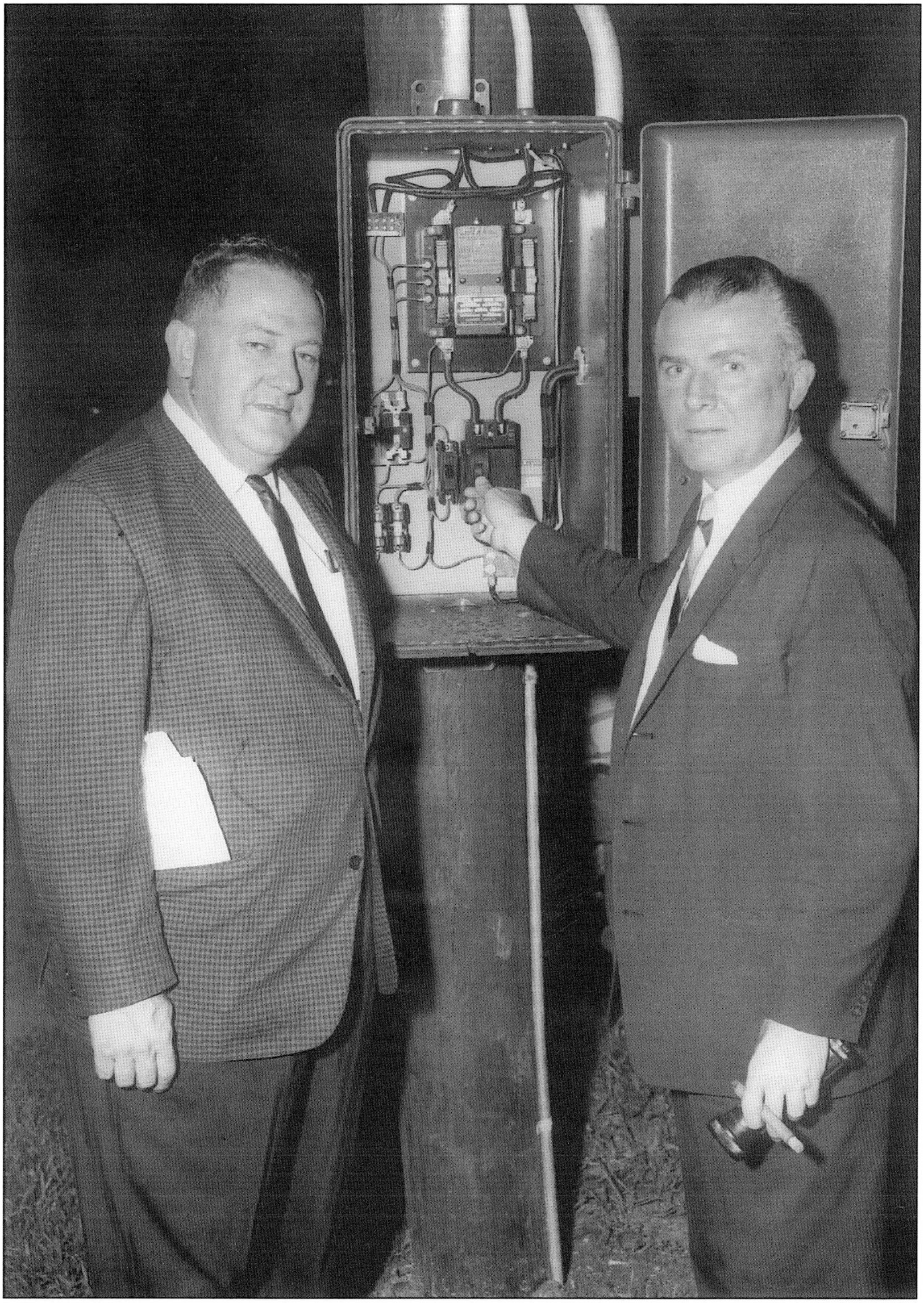

With the flick of a switch, Mayor Maurino Richton illuminates a section of high intensity street lights on Halsted Street from 14th Street to Joe Orr Road. Commissioner Robert DeBolt is on the left of this picture taken on July 22, 1963.

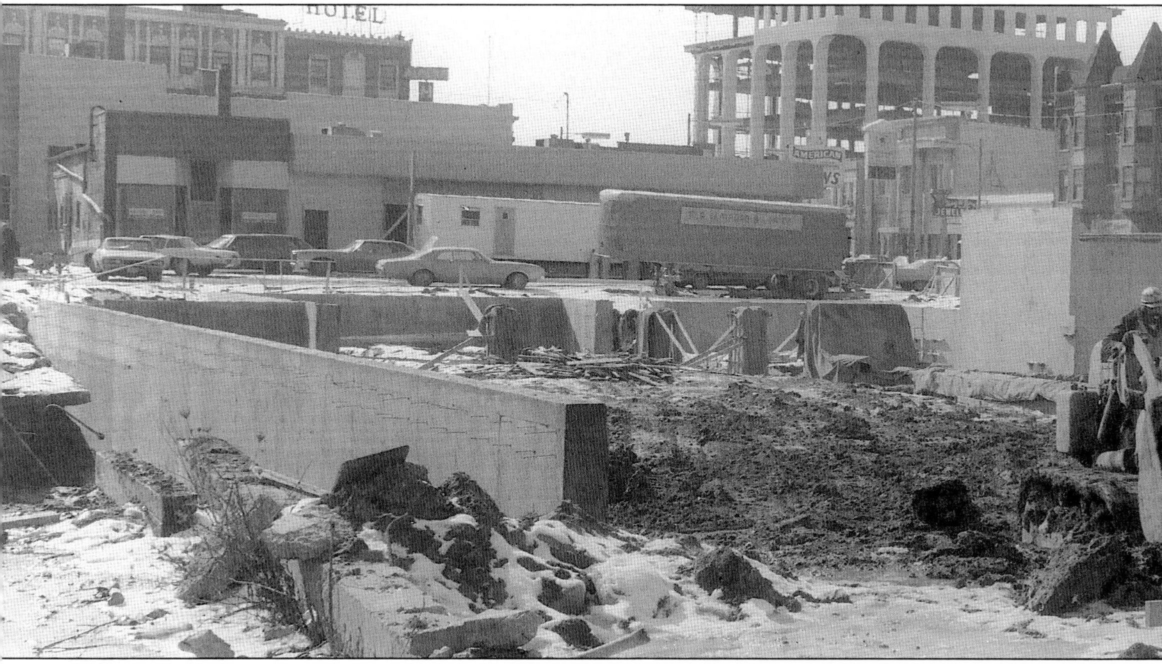

This 1970 view looks southwest from the construction site of the current Safety and Justice Building toward the new First National Bank Office highrise. Before the

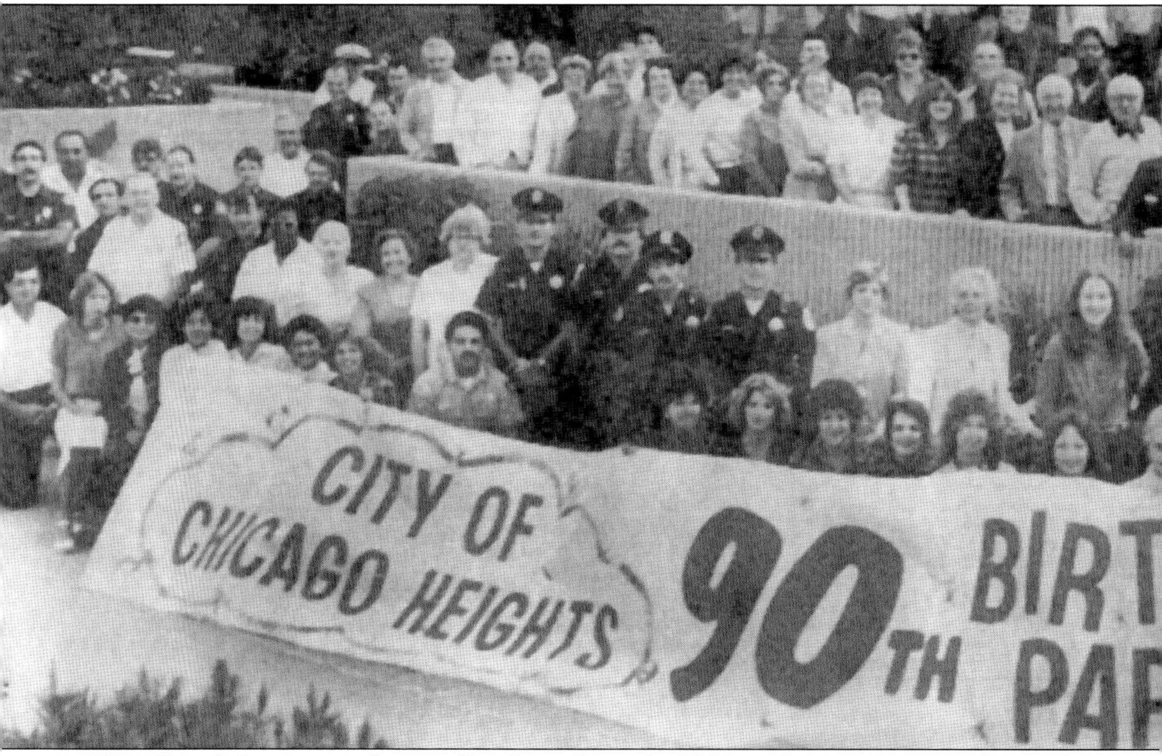

This "family" portrait of city officials and nearly 200 employees was staged in order to promote the 90th birthday celebration in September 1982. Although settlement in the

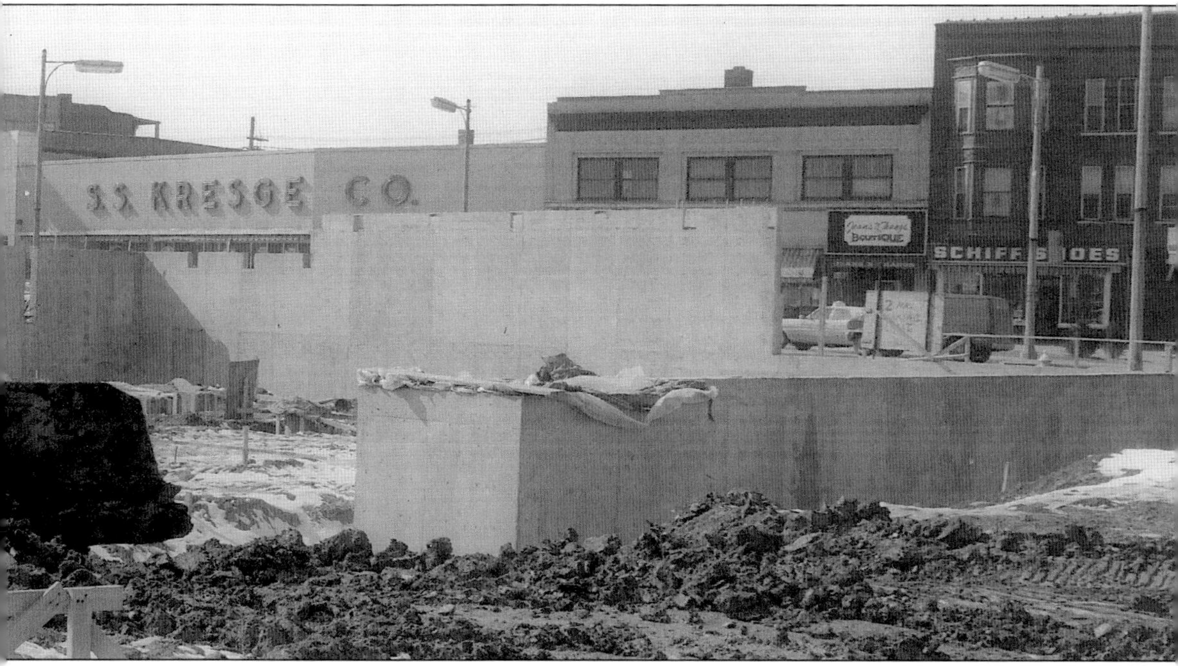

abandonment of the downtown redevelopment, photos like this one seemed to promise continued vitality for the heart of the city.

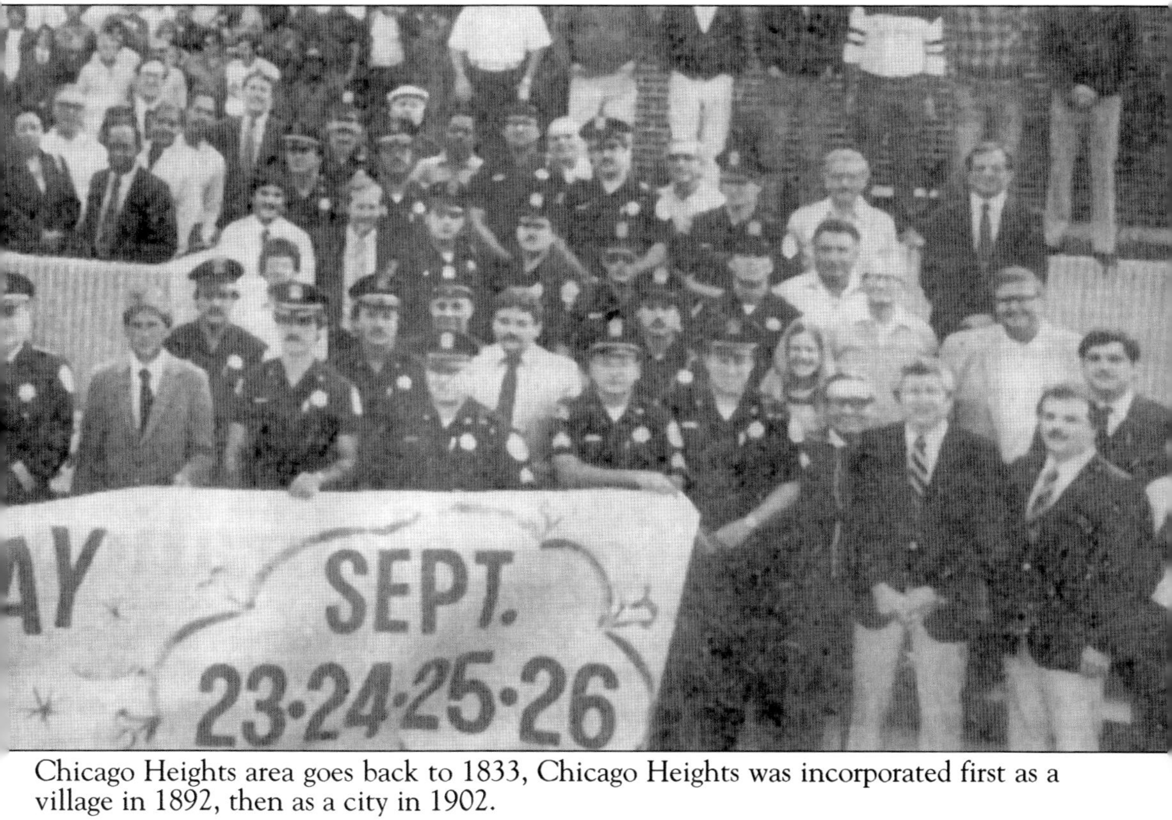

Chicago Heights area goes back to 1833, Chicago Heights was incorporated first as a village in 1892, then as a city in 1902.

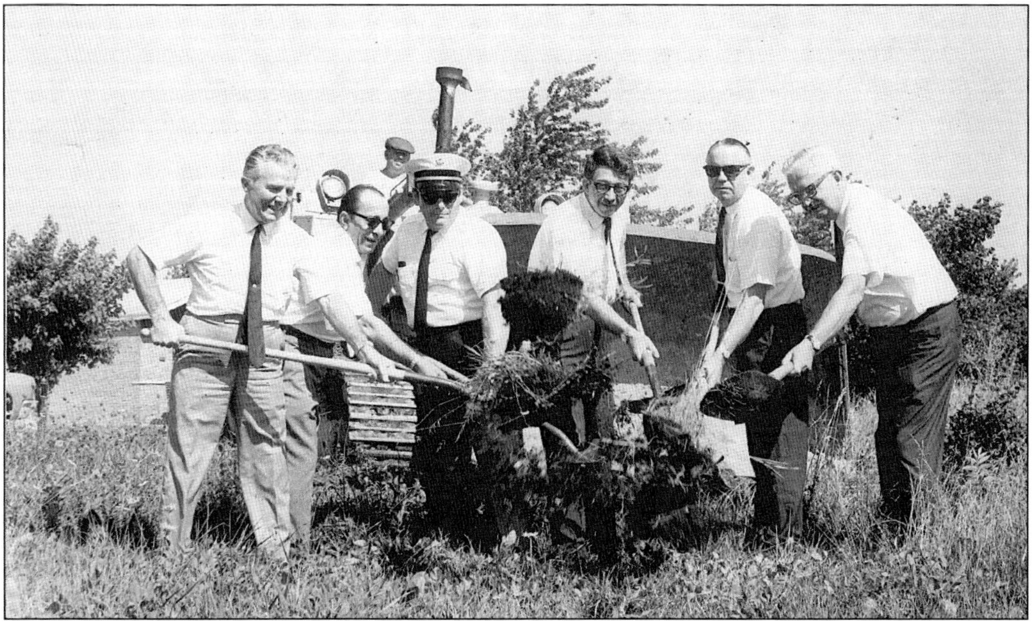

Municipal officials broke ground for Fire Station #3 on Joe Orr Road on August 19, 1968. Wielding shovels, from left to right, are Mayor Maurino Richton; Commissioner John Maloni; Fire Marshal Emmanuel Fried; Ben Pitcher, vice president of the Chicago Heights Chamber of Commerce; Charles Gies, its president; and William Thorsness, executive director of the Manufacturers Association of Chicago Heights.

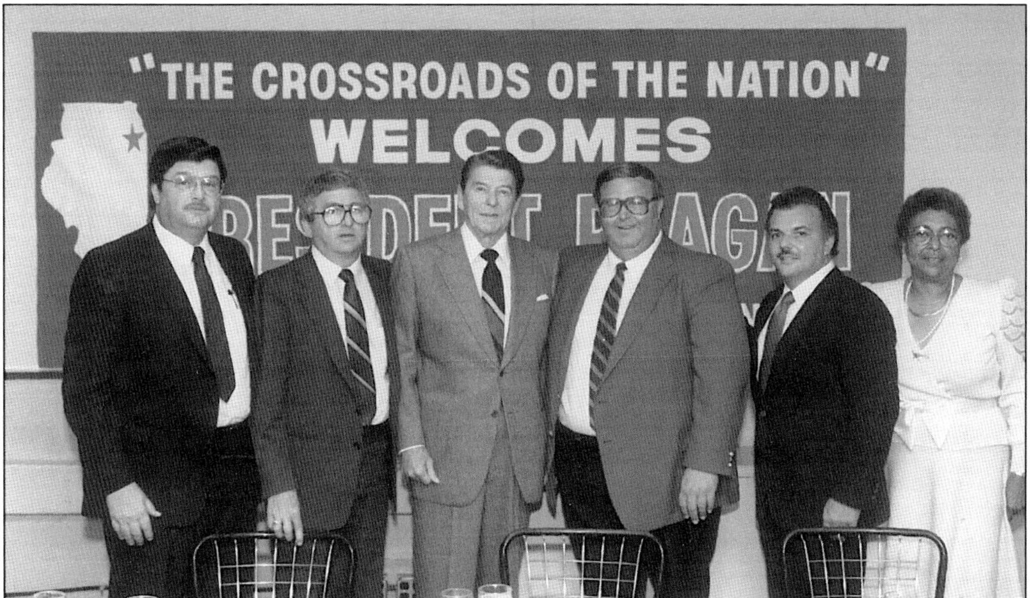

President Ronald Reagan visited Chicago Heights on June 28, 1985, where he met with the mayor and the city council in the Bloom cafeteria. Pictured, from left to right, are Eugene Sadus, Mayor Panici, President Reagan, John Gliottoni, Nick LoBue, and Louise Marshall.

Seven

CHURCHES

Churches, along with the groups and activities they sponsor, are an important element of the history of Chicago Heights. Churches in our town have often reflected the ethnic diversity and neighborhood characteristics of the people, going back to the First Presbyterian Church founded in 1843. Photos in this section reflect the continuity of that congregation, the role of Lutheran, Methodist, and African-American churches, and the growing importance of ethnic Catholic parishes.

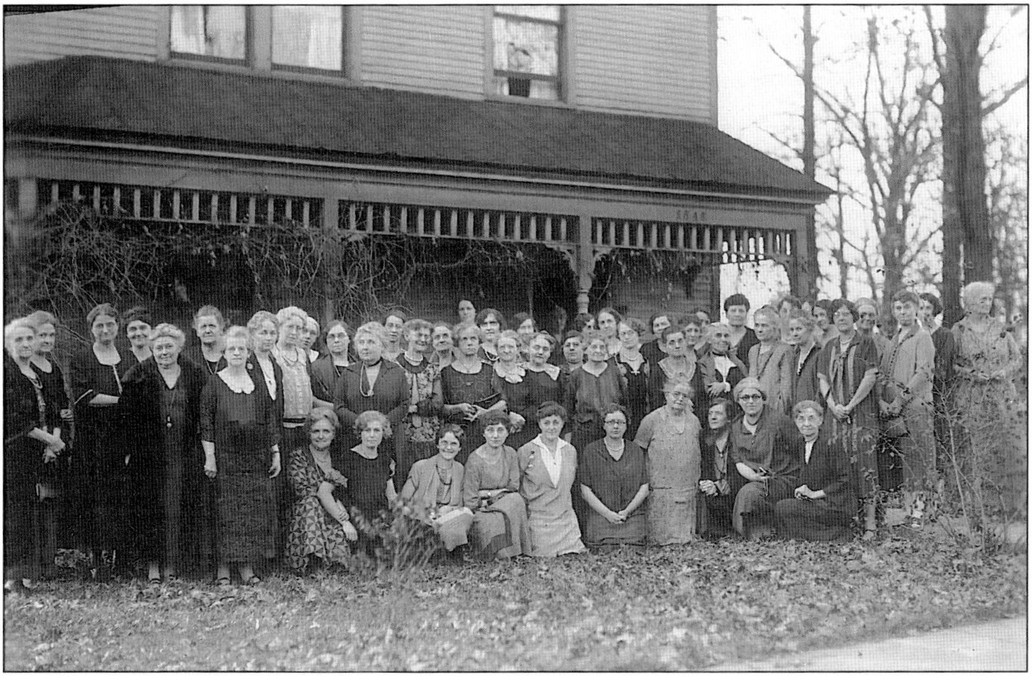

Ladies of the First Presbyterian Church pose in front of 1546 Euclid. This congregation was especially noted for founding the first church in what was then Thorn Grove in 1843. Among those pictured are Mrs. Bischoff, Mrs. G. McEldowney, Mrs. R. Palmquist, Mrs. J. Caskey, Mrs. C.H. Wallace, Etta Bowles, Miss Winter, Mrs. W.E. Williams Sr., Mrs. Mount, Mrs. Frank Caskey, Mrs. Kelley, Mrs. Vance, Marge Frank, Rose McEldowney, Mrs. Sheehean, Mrs. Helfrich, Miss Anna McEldowney, and Mrs. Estes, c. 1925.

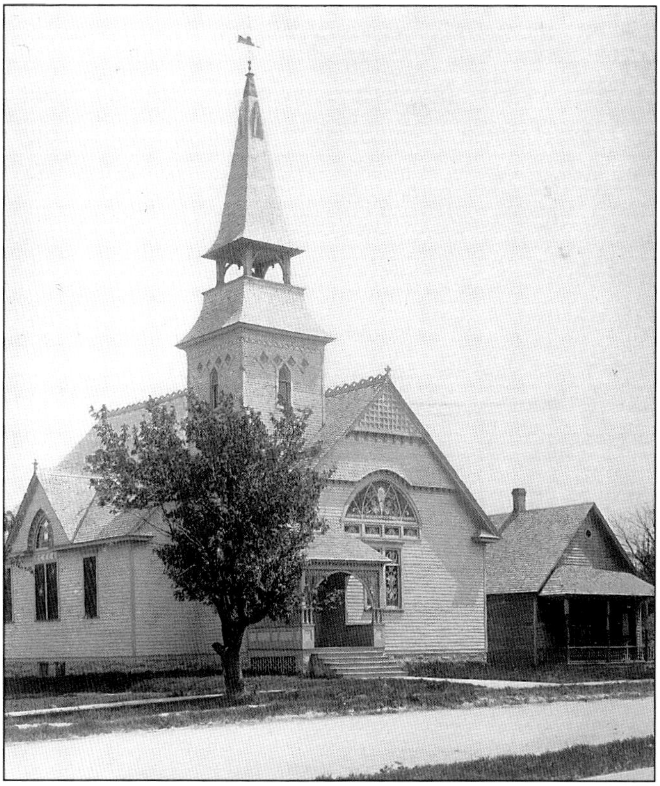

This frame building, home of the First Methodist Episcopal Church, stood at the southeast corner of Oak and 16th Street. Dedicated in 1894, it was replaced by the current structure in 1920. The church and its congregation played a major role in the social and spiritual life of the city for many decades. In 1995, the First Methodist Church dissolved and the building was sold to the Miracle Temple.

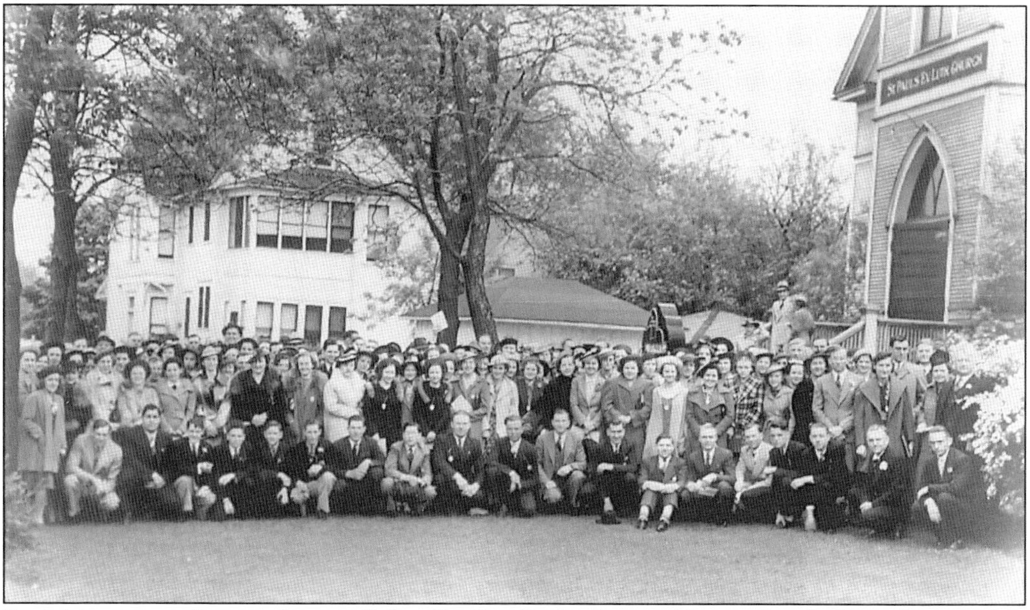

Parishioners gather in front of the St. Paul's Lutheran Evangelical Church on 14th Street. The building was located just to the east of the original St. James Hospital building. Kneeling on the far right, second from the end, is Pastor Brauer.

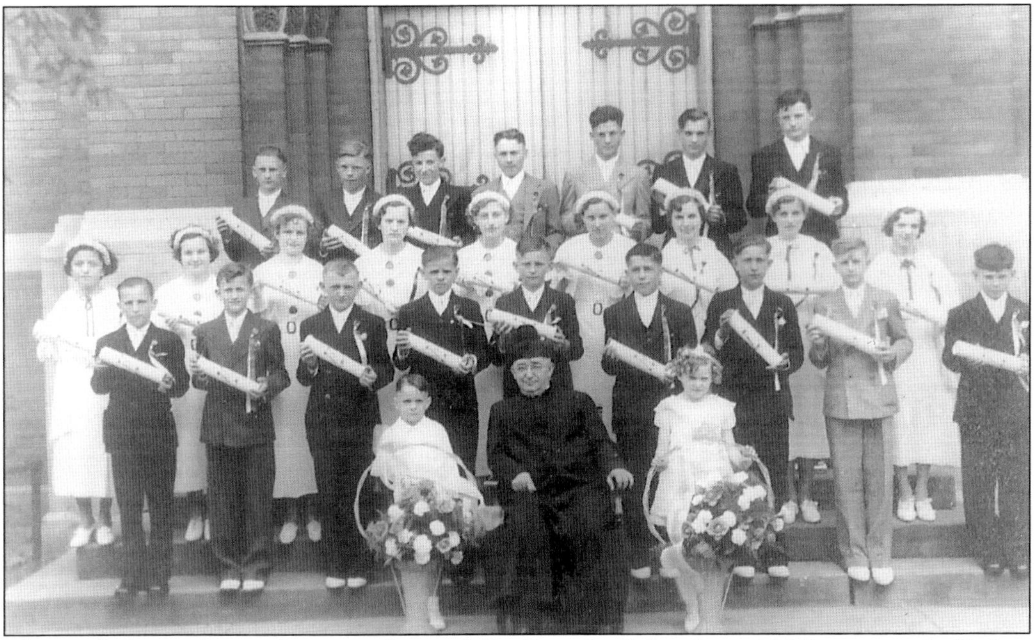

The eighth grade graduation class of St. Joseph School in 1935 surrounds Father Doberstein. Genevieve Wlos is the girl to the far right.

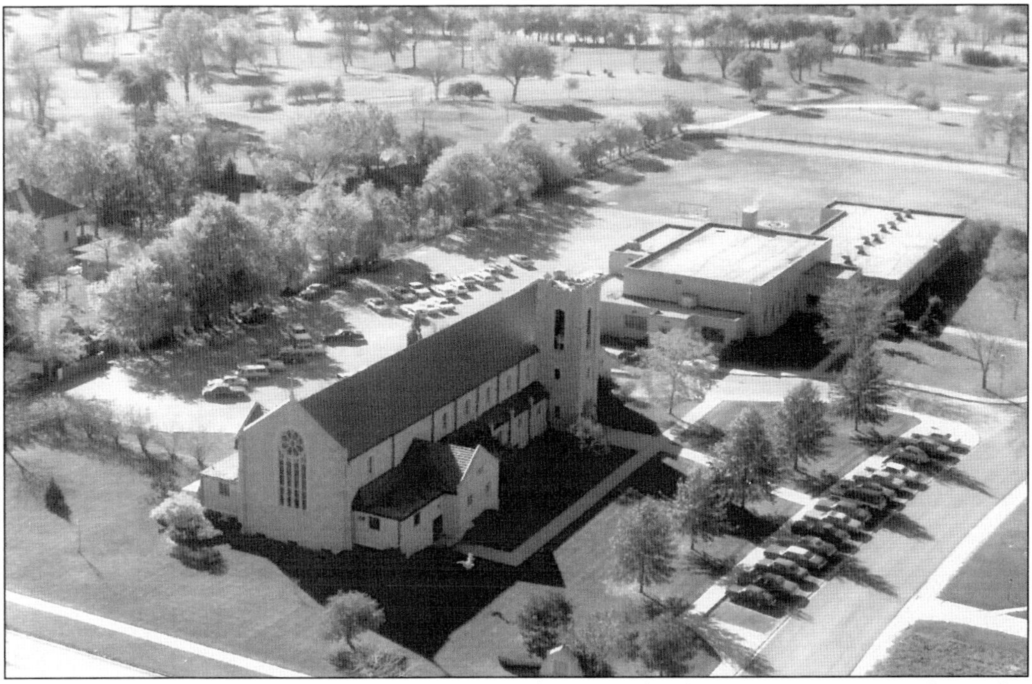

The Lutheran community in Chicago Heights goes back to 1882. Moving from the original St. Paul's Lutheran on the south side of 14th Street to the physical plant pictured here in 1951, the Lutheran community continues to play a major role in the city through both its church and its school.

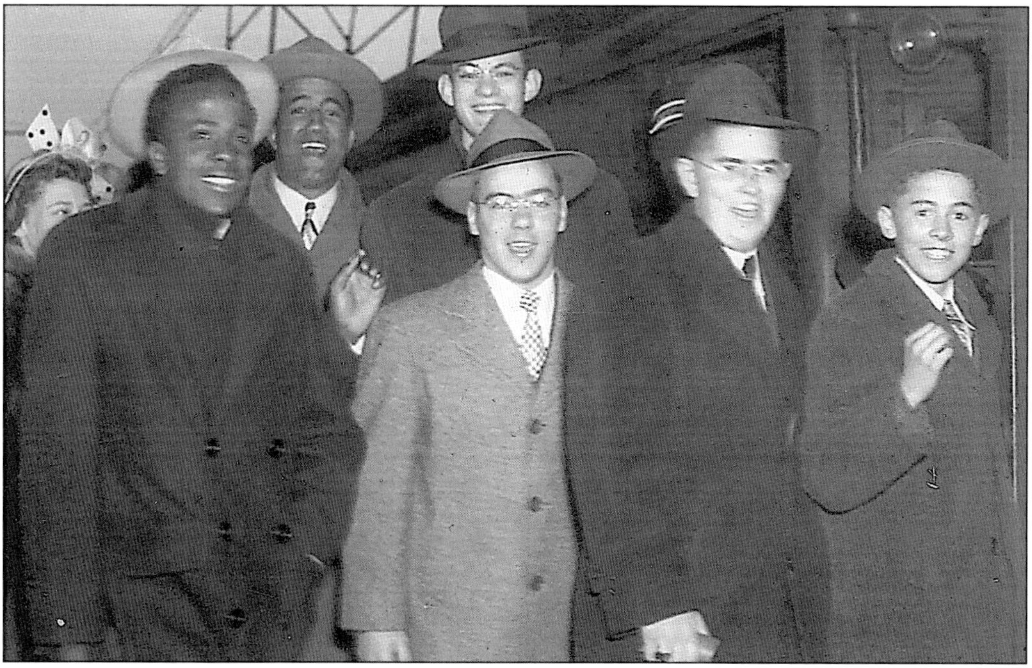

Marcelle C. Webb (third from left) and nearly 200 members of the Christian Youth Council were among the crowd as Chicago Heights young people boarded a special chartered train at the 211th Street Illinois Central station for a trip to Easter sunrise services at Soldier Field, April 1946. The event took on extra meaning because it was the first peace time Easter celebration since 1941.

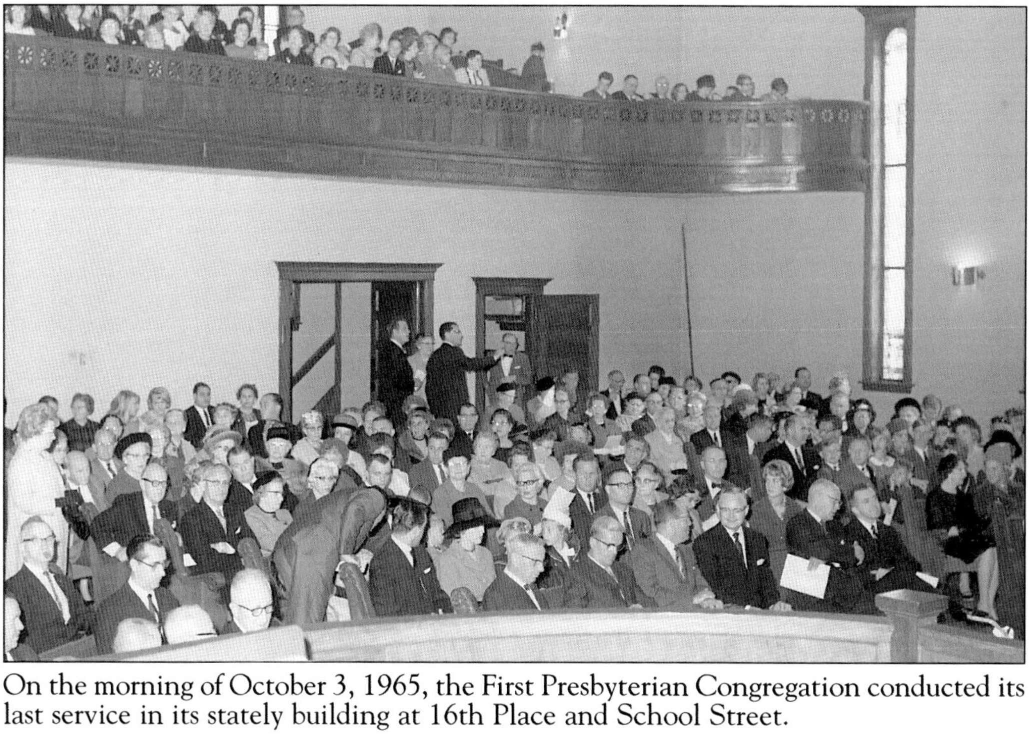

On the morning of October 3, 1965, the First Presbyterian Congregation conducted its last service in its stately building at 16th Place and School Street.

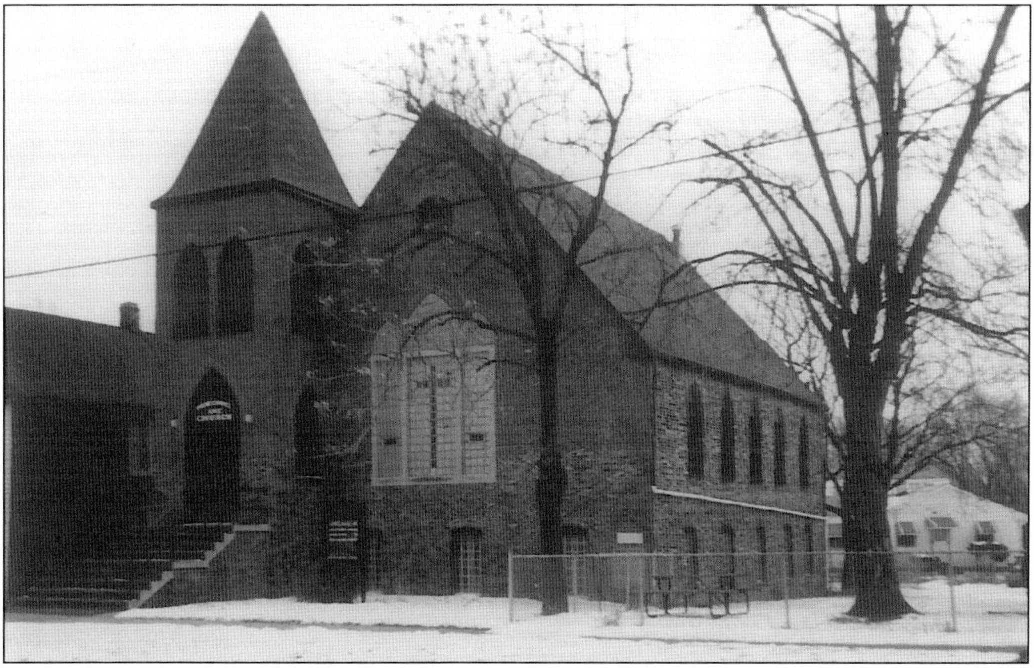

Payne Chapel African Methodist Episcopal Church began as a mission in 1907 at 1440 Park Avenue with 18 members in attendance. After a series of moves, the congregation located permanently to this building at 1511 Center Avenue, right across from Lincoln School. Payne Chapel is the oldest African-American church in Chicago Heights and has been designated by the Historic Preservation Committee as a local landmark.

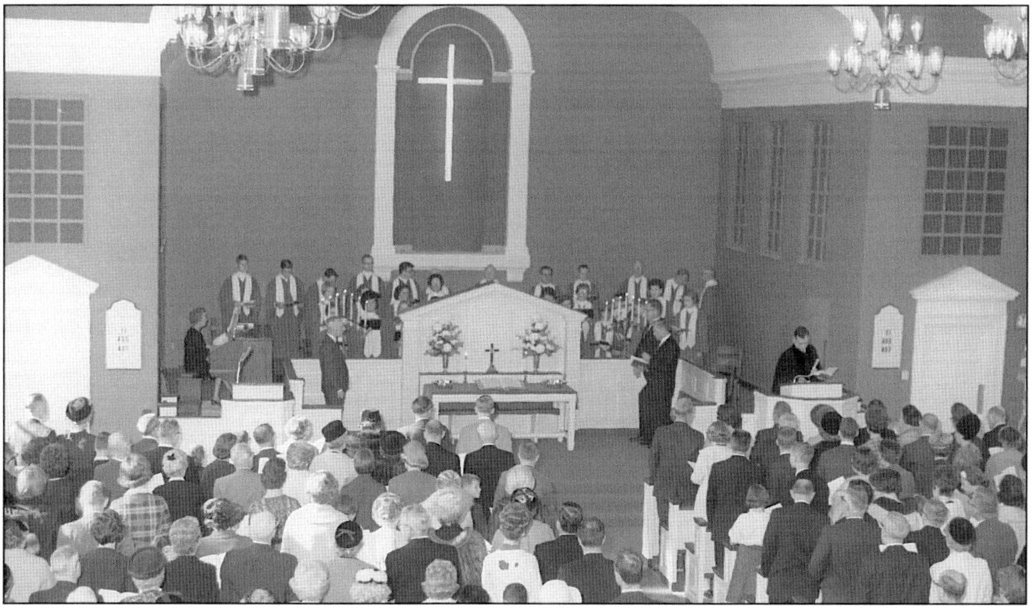

At 3:30 P.M. on October 3, 1965, the First Presbyterian Congregation held its first service in the current church building at 10th and Thomas. The original church was built in 1843 at 21st and Chicago Road, the current site of the First Presbyterian Cemetery.

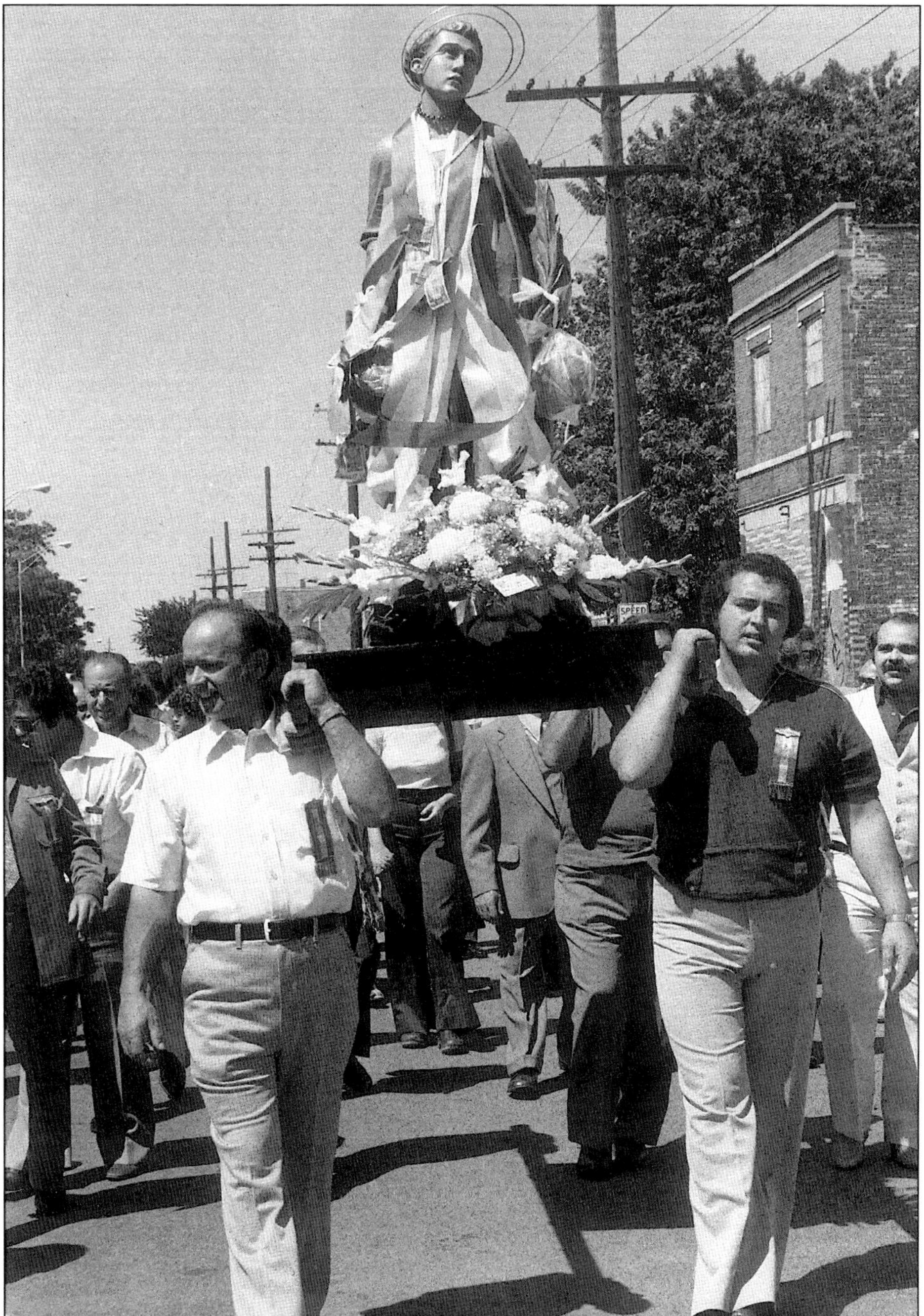

Livo Planera and Mario Cipolla carry the statue of San Lorenzo on August 11, 1979, in the annual procession originated by the Amaseno Society in 1974. A good number of Italians in Chicago Heights have origins in the town of Amaseno (40 miles south of Rome) whose patron saint is San Lorenzo. The August street festival, combined with the feast of San Rocco in recent years at the lodge headquarters at 24th and Union, has been a highlight of summer activities in Chicago Heights.

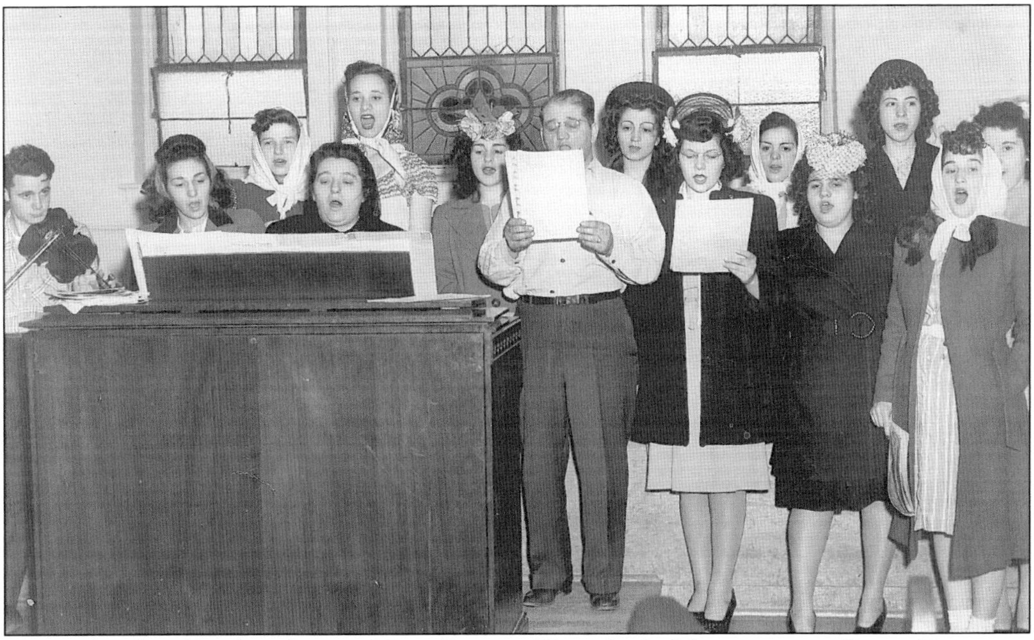

Here, the St. Cecilia choir of San Rocco Church, led by organist Grace Bamonti, perform in the choir loft in 1947. Left to right are as follows: Vincent Ranieri, Yolanda Apponi, Sylvia Bamonti, Mary Bruni, Grace Bamonti, Carmella Malito, Joe Biasella, Helen Ranieri, Vera Macchioni, Katherine Poeletta, Philomena Stella, Mary Longo, Jane Pratico, and Josephine DiMaggio.

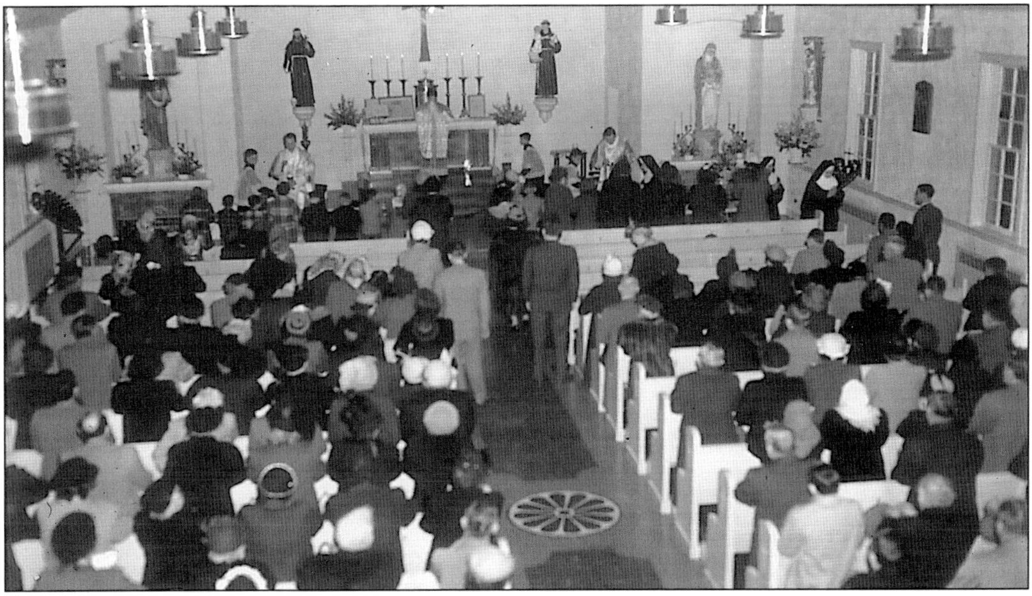

St. Ann's Church, at Chicago Road and Main Street, is pictured at Communion time in the 1950s. After the Second Vatican Council, Catholic altars were repositioned to face the congregation while communion rails were eliminated. This congregation, which included many German Americans, was devastated when the Church was ordered closed in the early 1990s.

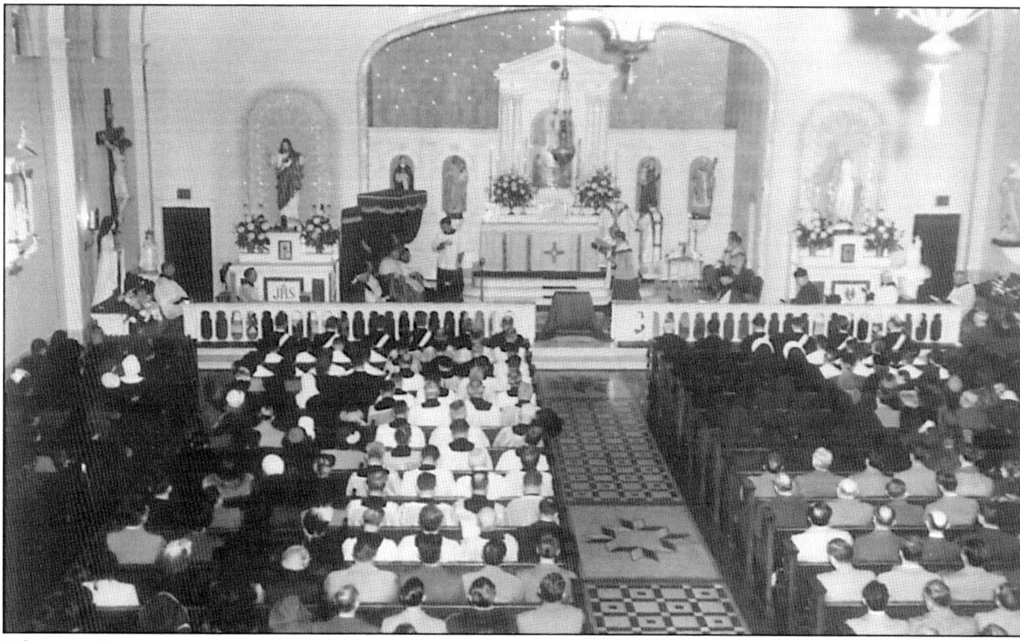

The 50th Anniversary Mass at St. Agnes, conducted by Monsignor Croarkin, took place on November 18, 1948.

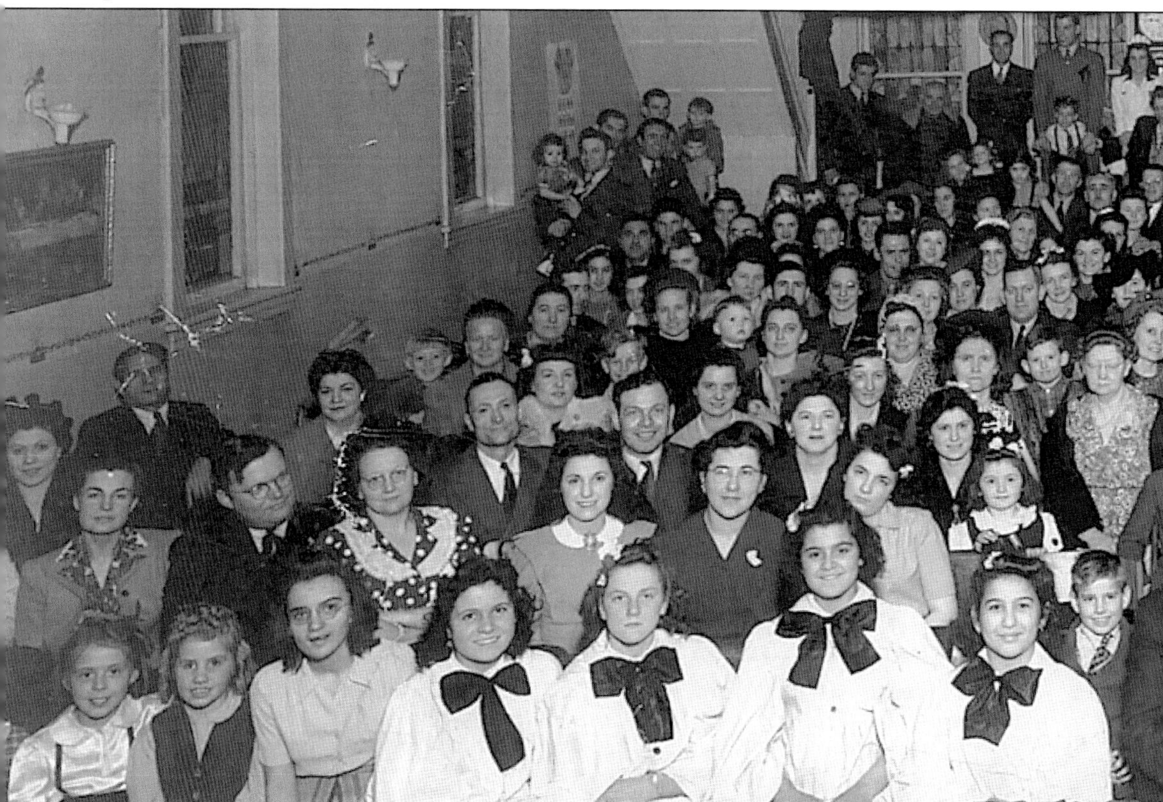

Pictured above is a full house at the Church of Our Savior at 24th and Wallace in the

St. Joseph parish was formed on September 11, 1905, by 40 Polish immigrant families. This imposing edifice was dedicated on October 15, 1914. Often described as the most beautiful church building in the city, St. Joseph's was one of the three Chicago Heights Catholic churches ordered closed by the Archdiocese in 1990. The building is currently operated by the Christian Vision Center.

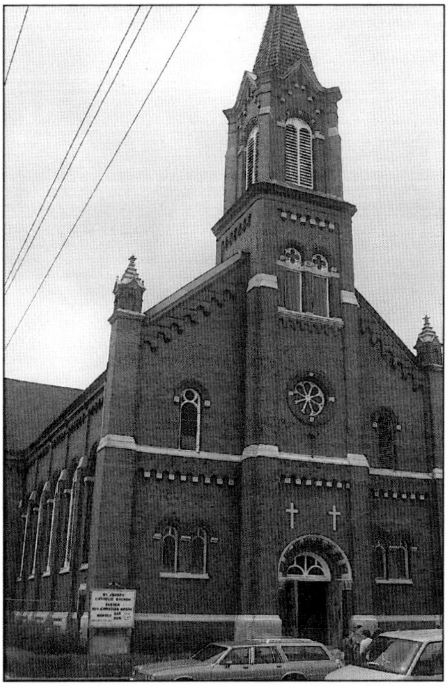

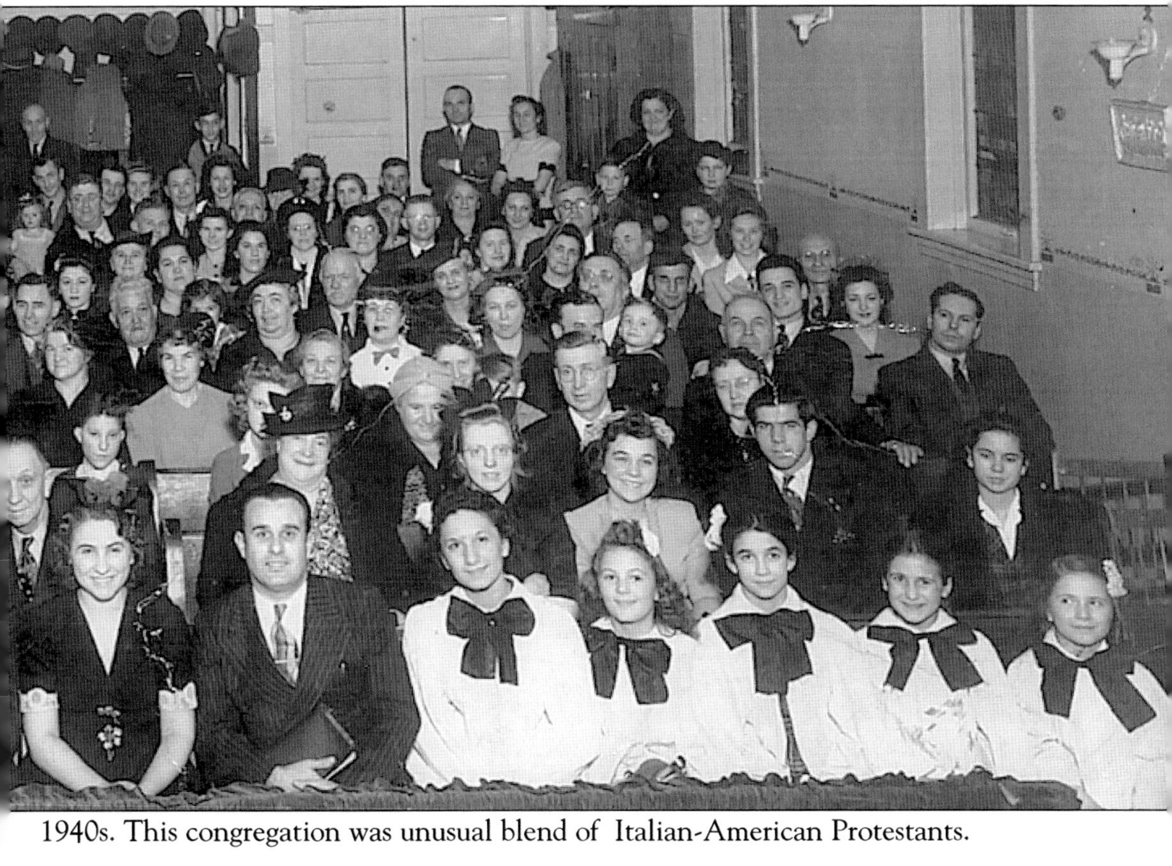

1940s. This congregation was unusual blend of Italian-American Protestants.

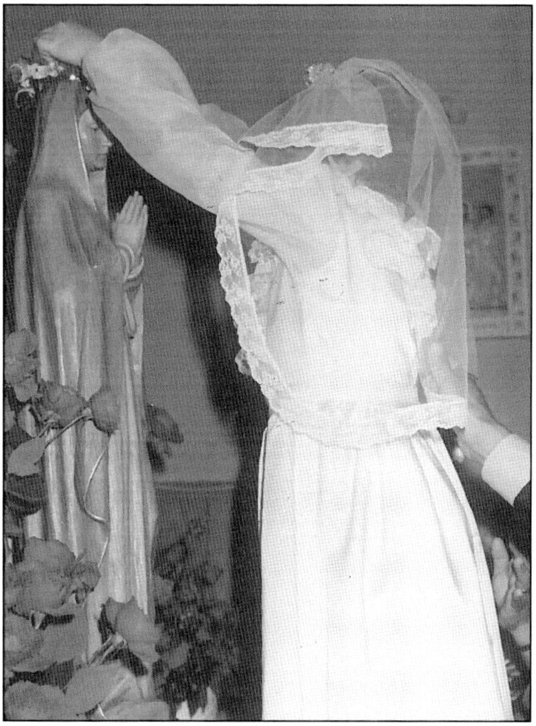

Karla Ruiz places the crown on Our Lady of Guadalupe at St. Casimir Church in 1979. The Church was founded in 1912 on East 14th Street as a Lithuanian Catholic parish and became heavily Mexican American in the 1960s until it closed in the 1970s. After its closing, the Mexican American parishioners transferred to St. Paul's Catholic Church on the Hill.

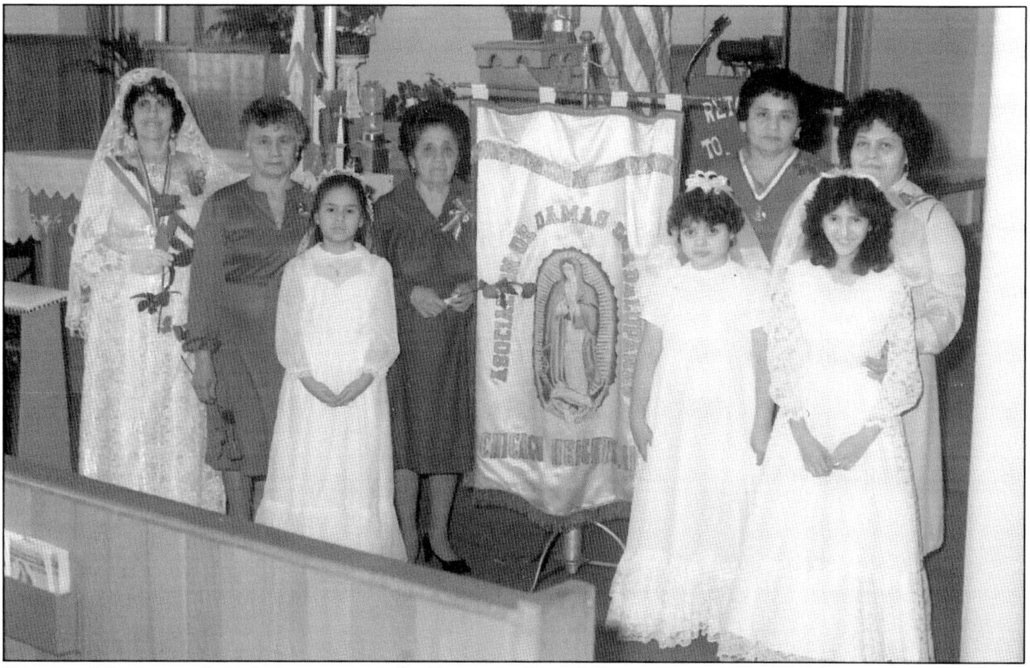

Pictured here is the Associazion de Damas Guadalupanas on December 12, 1970—El dia de la Virgin at St. Casimir. This celebration and the re-enactment of the Way of the Cross on Good Friday are two of the many cultural traditions that Mexican Americans have brought to Chicago Heights.

Eight

SOCIAL GROUPS

Voluntary associations have enriched the cultural and social fabric of Chicago Heights. Sports like baseball and bowling, as well as ethnic, musical, dramatic, charitable, recreational, service, fraternal, and civic organizations have complimented the world of business, working to create a lively and progressive sense of community. These organizations gave Chicago Heights a unique identity in a time before the dominance of mass media and pop culture.

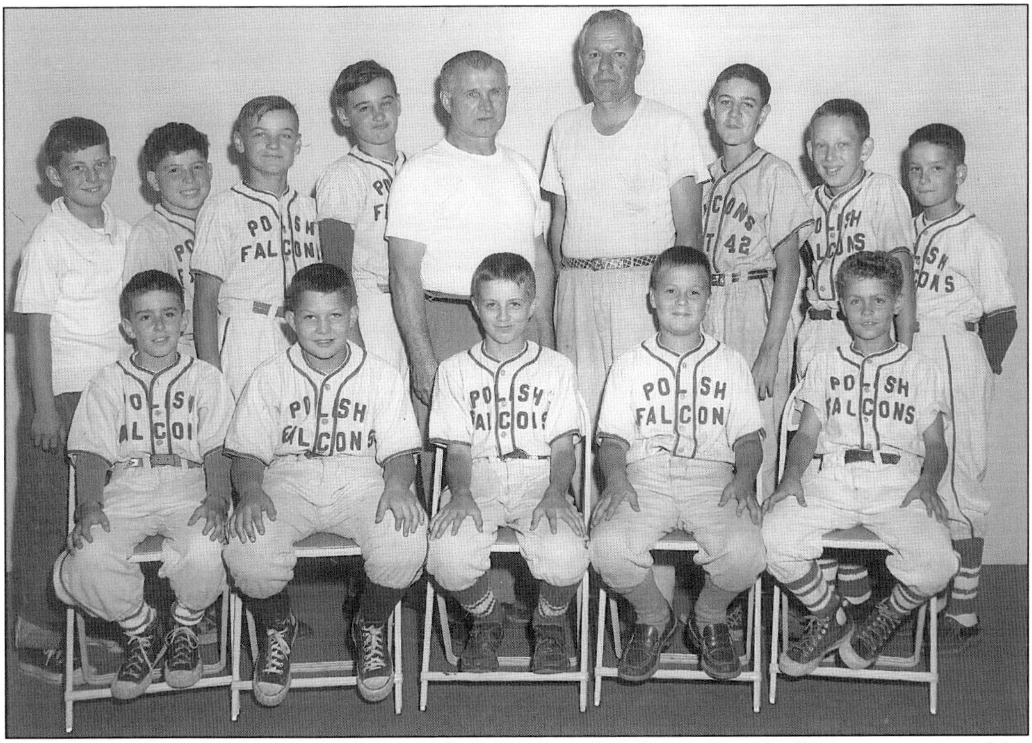

Pictured is the 1954 edition of the Polish Falcons Small Fry Baseball Team managed by John Wooten and Louis Capps. Small Fry, or Little League, baseball was introduced in Chicago Heights in the late 1940s with the building of the Small Fry baseball field on the banks of Thorn Creek near Chicago Road in the Cook County Forest Preserve.

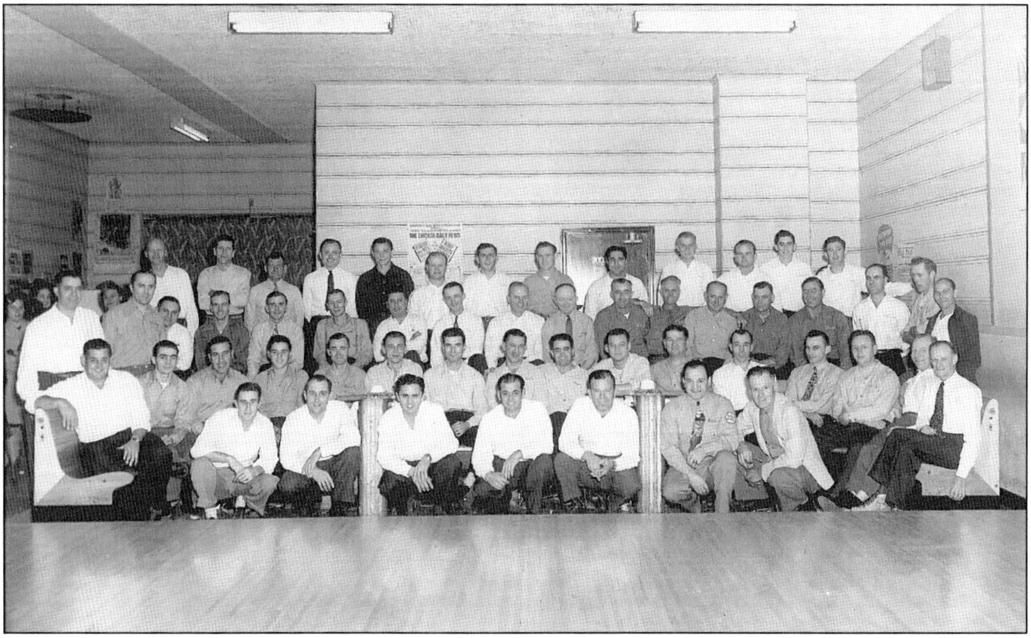

The Junior Bowling League poses in 1942 at the Bowl Aire located at 1529 Halsted. The Bowl Aire was one of three downtown bowling venues that included the 10-Pin across the street and the 20th Century Lanes on 19th and Chicago Road.

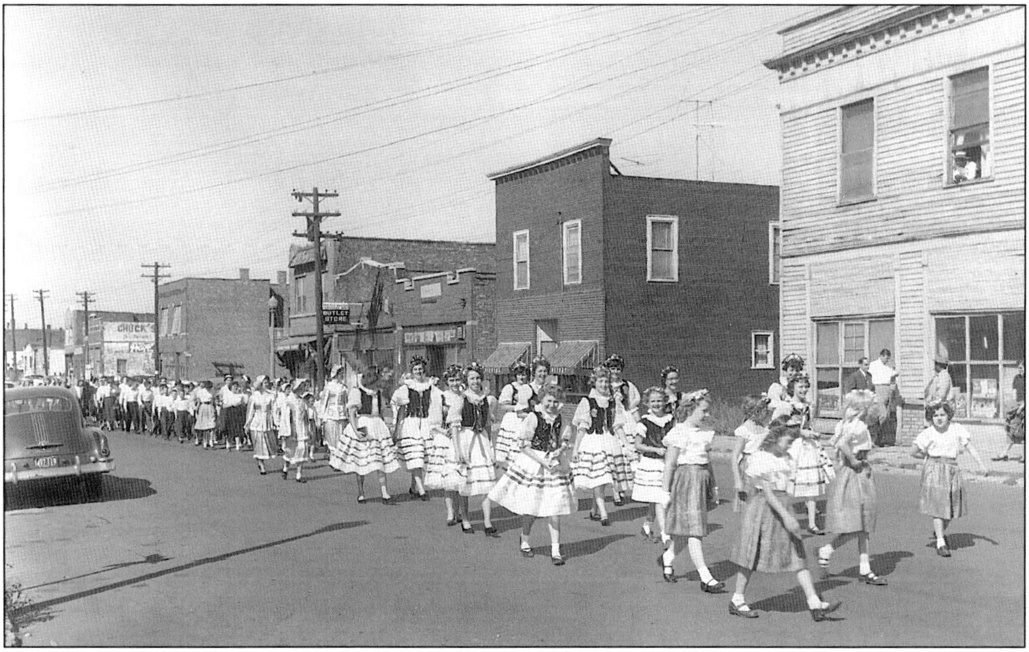

Young people of the Polish Falcons parade east on 16th Street clad in Polish costumes, c. 1950. The Falcons Hall was a popular place for weddings. The Falcons recently celebrated their 95th anniversary. Note the commercial nature of 16th Street including Chuck's Service Station, Pierandozzi's Market, an outlet store, Pete Simone's Candy store, Silberg's Furniture, and Skinny Miller's Poultry store.

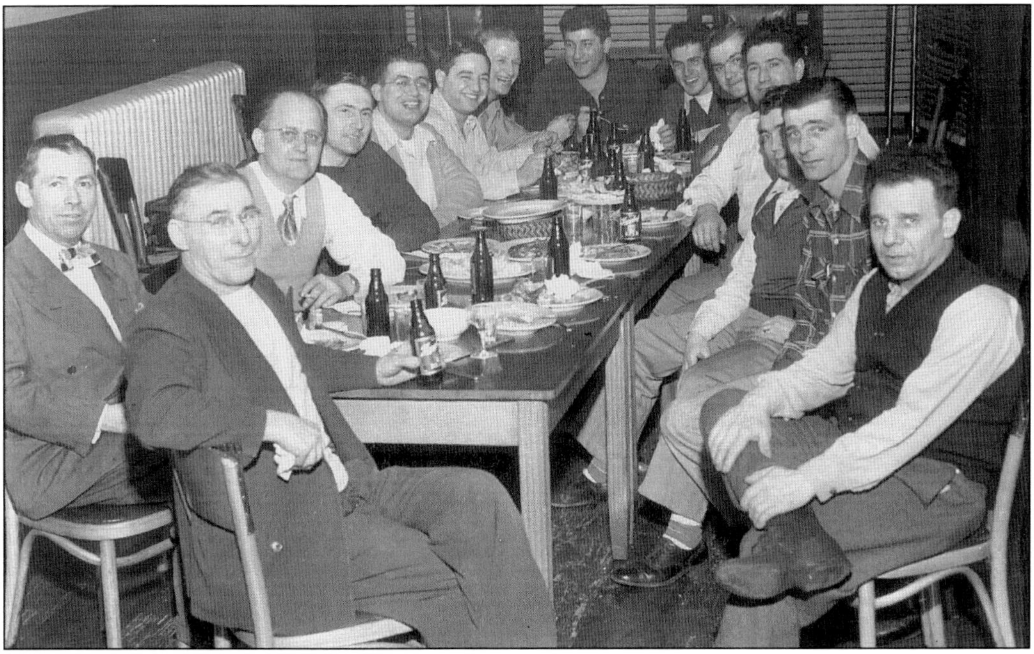

The ABEX bowling league members gather for refreshments in this c. 1945 photo. Guido Falaschetti is seated at the far right.

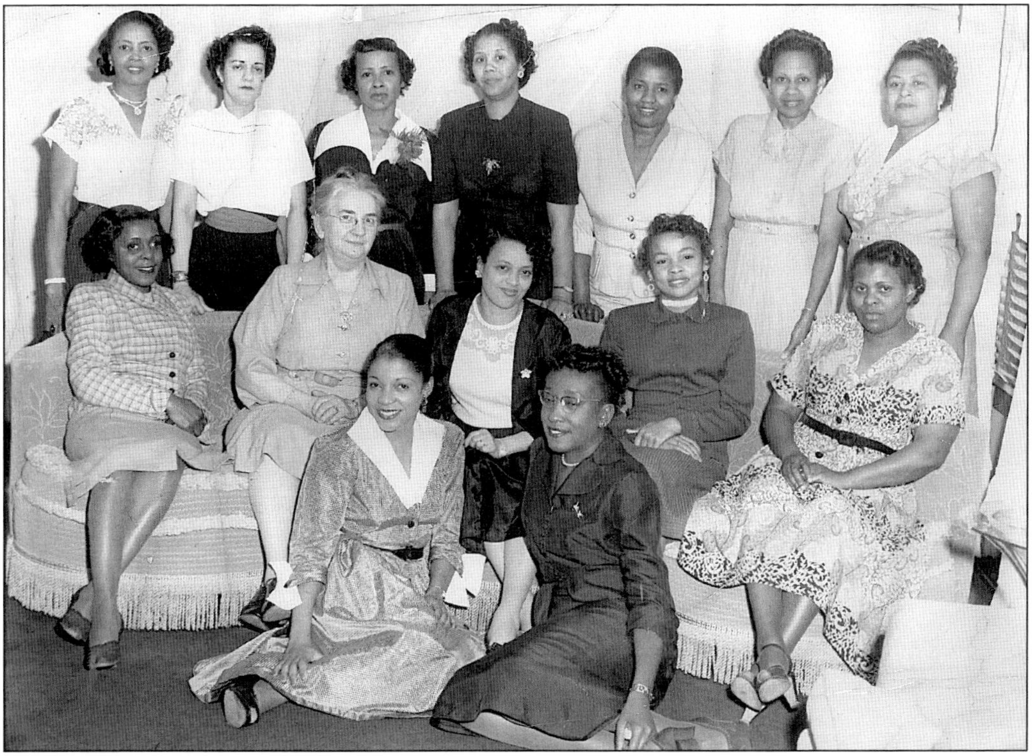

Pictured is a first-aid class taught at the Jones Community Center in 1945. Standing in the center is Cora Covington—restaurateur, social activist, and community leader.

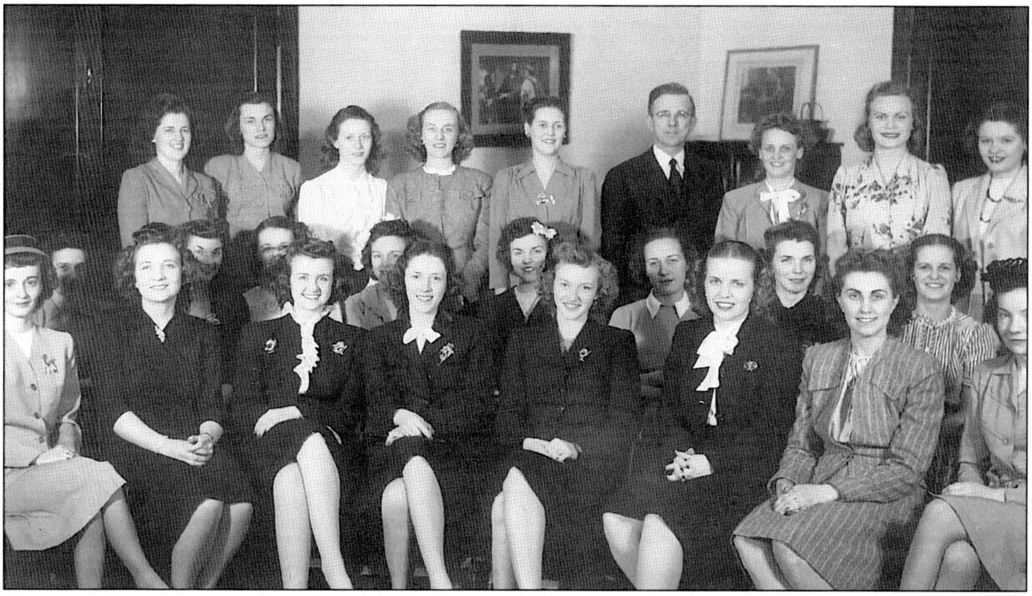

Among those pictured in this 1943 photo of the First Presbyterian Church War Wives and Sweethearts Club are, from left to right, as follows: (front row) Janis Mickelson Hines, Rosemary Sheehan Morgan, Frances Guy Vogel, Marjorie Bergstrand, Virginia Hansen Steeley, and Edith Flexman; (second row) Margaret Cheminsky Goodman; (third row) Eileen Reithel Hohenstein, Norma Elstedt, Maureen Kiestra Hjemnick, Rev. Clarence Showalter, Clara Kiestra Feehery, and Charlotte Franck Hienze.

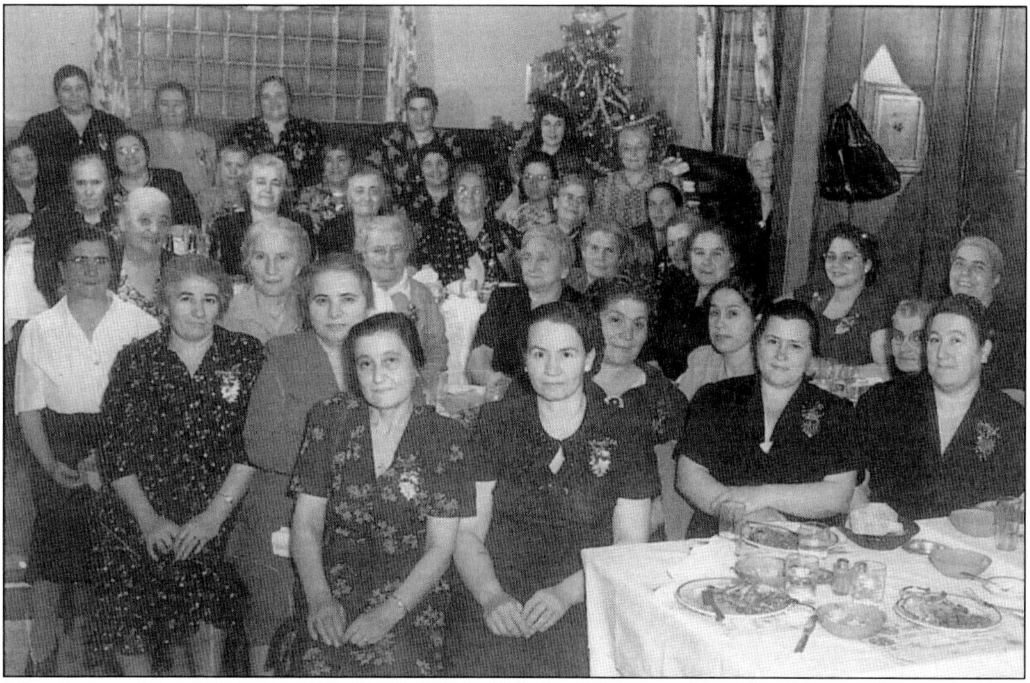

Members of the Christian Mother's Club (Madre Cristiane) of San Rocco Church pose for a photo following their Christmas banquet at the old Savoia's Restaurant in the 1940s. The Christian Mothers served as a kind of PTA for the Mount Carmel School.

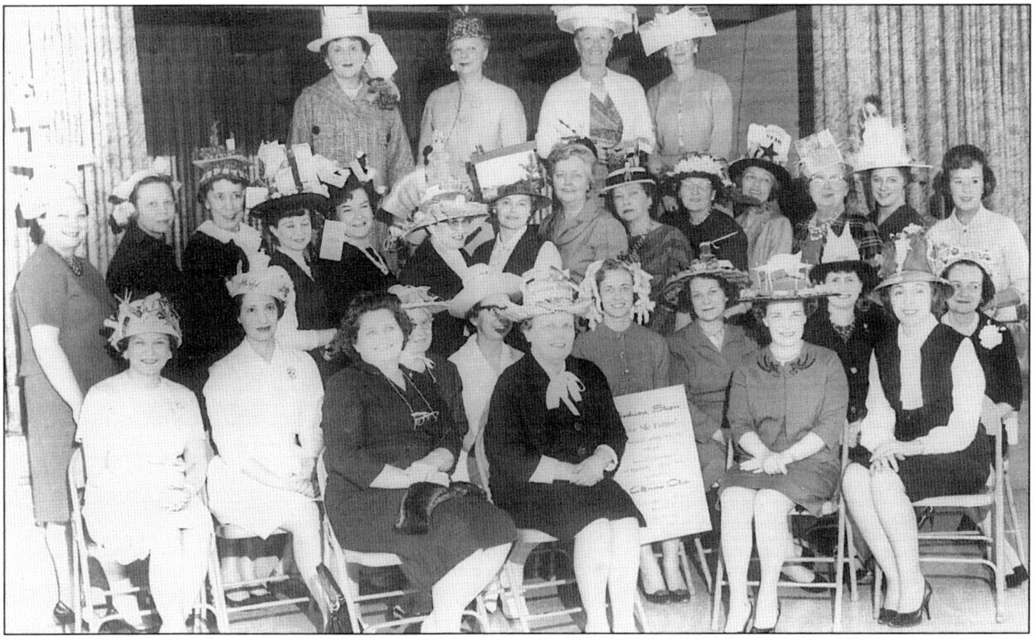

The Altrusa Club of Chicago Heights was organized in 1956. It soon became the club of the leading professional and businesswomen of the city. Here the members pose with extravagant head gear and a poster to promote the group's fashion show. Among those pictured are as follows: Sophie Modzelewski, Ruth Wilkening, Hazel Hirsch, Kay Fuller, Lenore Saller, Evelyn Bultema, Marie Cottrell, Helen Sergeant, Marge Gansbergen, and Alyce Murphy.

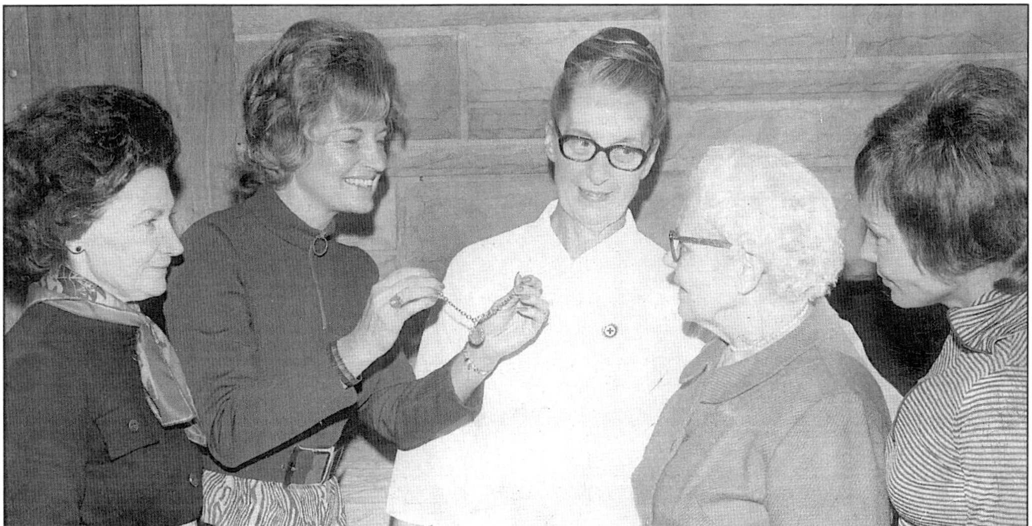

Community volunteers and volunteer nurses from 1935 to 1978 operated the Infant Welfare League and its Well Baby Clinic. Most notable among those who supported the League was nurse Gunhild "Gunnie" McAllister. For over 17 years, McAllister volunteered her free days to treat children at the Well Baby Clinic. From left to right are as follows: Kotch Luecke, Pat Trainor (president), Gunhild McAllister, Dr. Margot Arak, and Dr. Green.

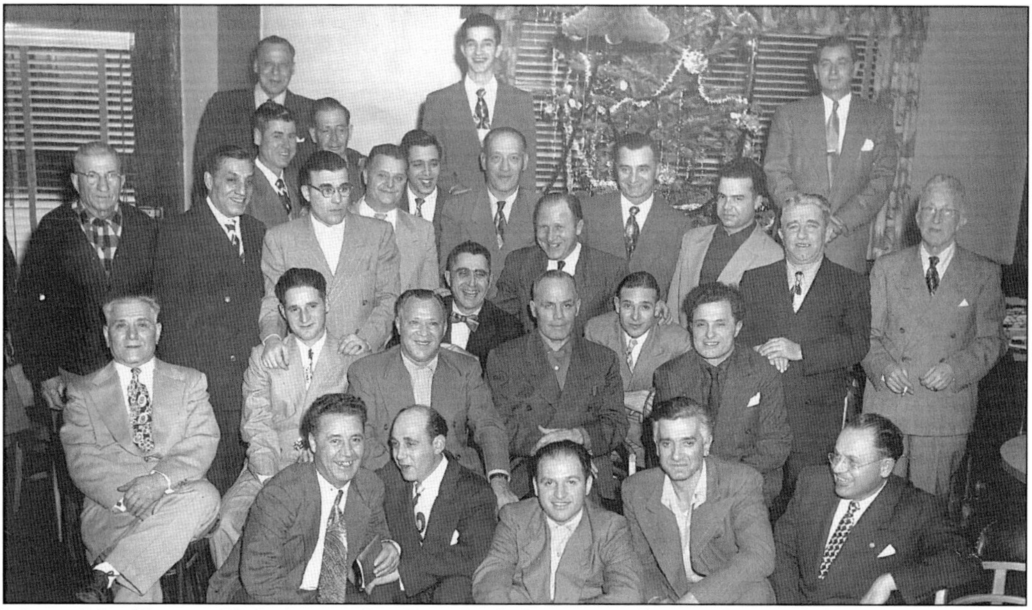

Men of the Dante Club, located at East 24th Street, gather in front of the Christmas tree at their headquarters in the late 1940s. An organization of second generation Italian Americans, the Dante Club promoted the sale of bonds during World War II. From left to right are as follows: (front row) Charles Rufo, Anthony Giannetti, Max DiGiulio, Orlando Passarelli, and Anthony D'Andrea; (second row) Frank Tintari, Joe Novelli, Lee Monacelli, A. Grossi, Jack Perry, Sam Mele, and Bill D'Amico; (third row) Chuck DePeso, A Mascitti, Americo Lagone, Tony Tiberi, Charles Grupp, Mario Bruno, Joe Grilli, Phil Macozzi, and Joe DeBaberi; (back row) Mr. Rotondi, Salty Rydewicz, Pete Monacelli, Jerry Higgins, Mike Bruno, and Raldo Rotoloni.

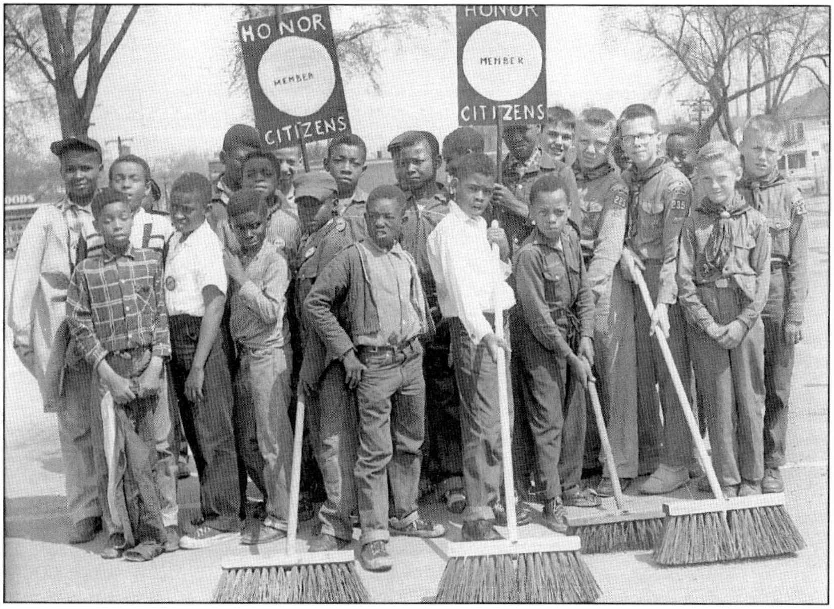

Members of Boy Scout Troop 235 and the Honor Citizens of Chicago Heights spruce up the Washington School grounds in 1958.

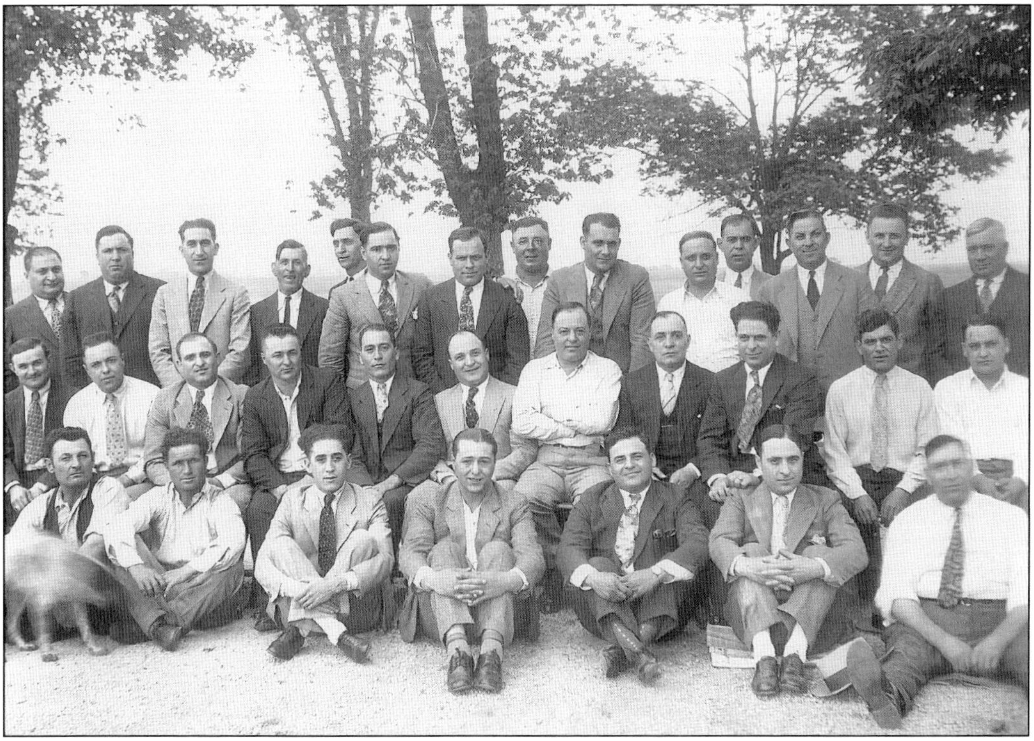

Friends gathered for a Sunday dinner at Nick Neroni's (top row center, no tie) located at 22nd and State Streets, c. 1938.

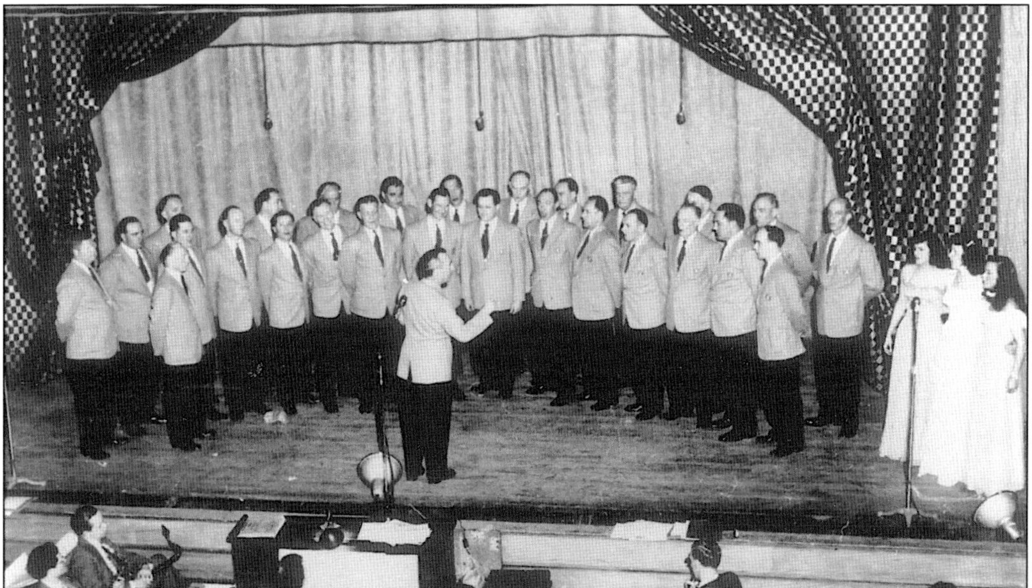

Group singing was common in Chicago Heights up to the 1970s. In addition to the Kiwanis Chorus pictured here in the late 1950s, school glee clubs, service organizations, and churches had choral groups which fostered a sense of community and group awareness.

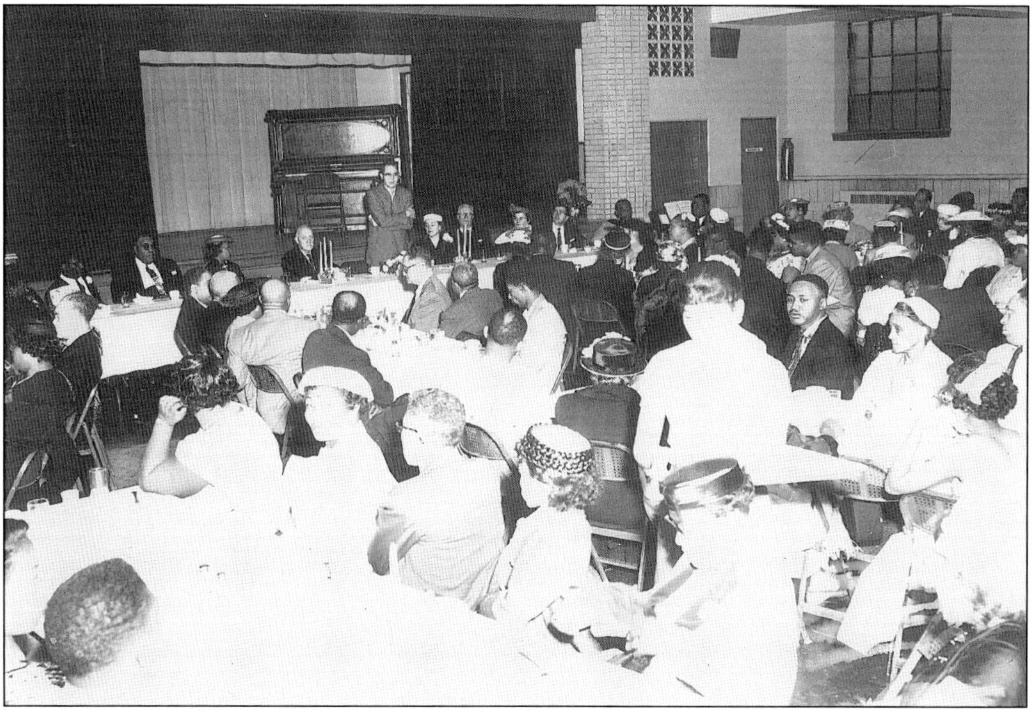

Dr. Emerson Lights speaks at a Goodwill Charity Club meeting at the Jones Center. Lights was a former member of the Chicago Heights Health Department and the Plan Commission before becoming a commissioner with the Cook County Housing Authority. He died in 1977.

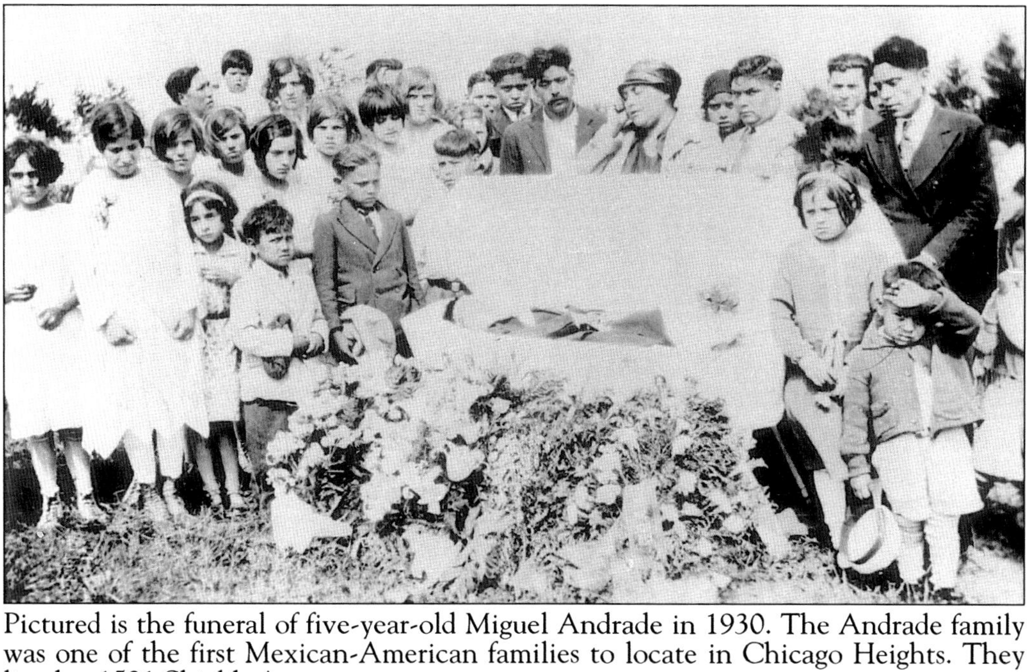

Pictured is the funeral of five-year-old Miguel Andrade in 1930. The Andrade family was one of the first Mexican-American families to locate in Chicago Heights. They lived at 1531 Shields Avenue.

In 1966, Shirley Kennedy (left) was crowned Miss Chicago Heights by the Chicago Table Employers Scholarship club. Runners-up included Macie Beck (center) and Katherine Williams.

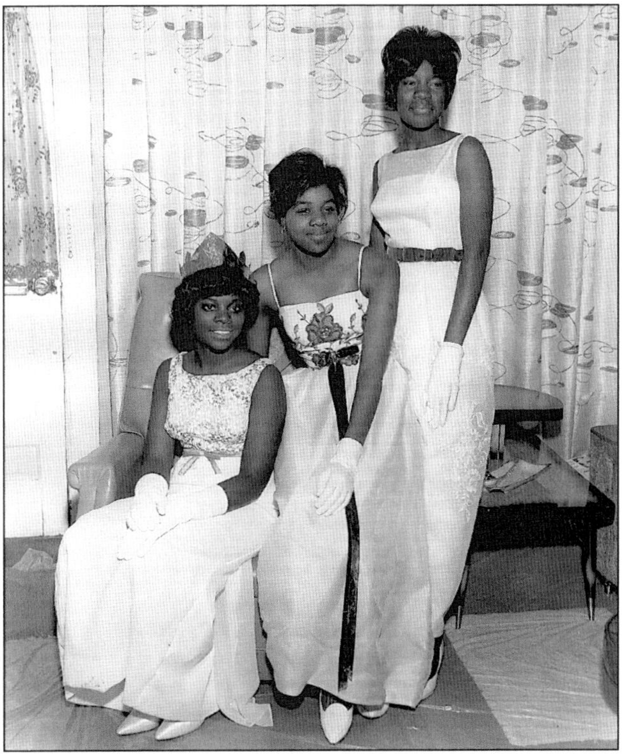

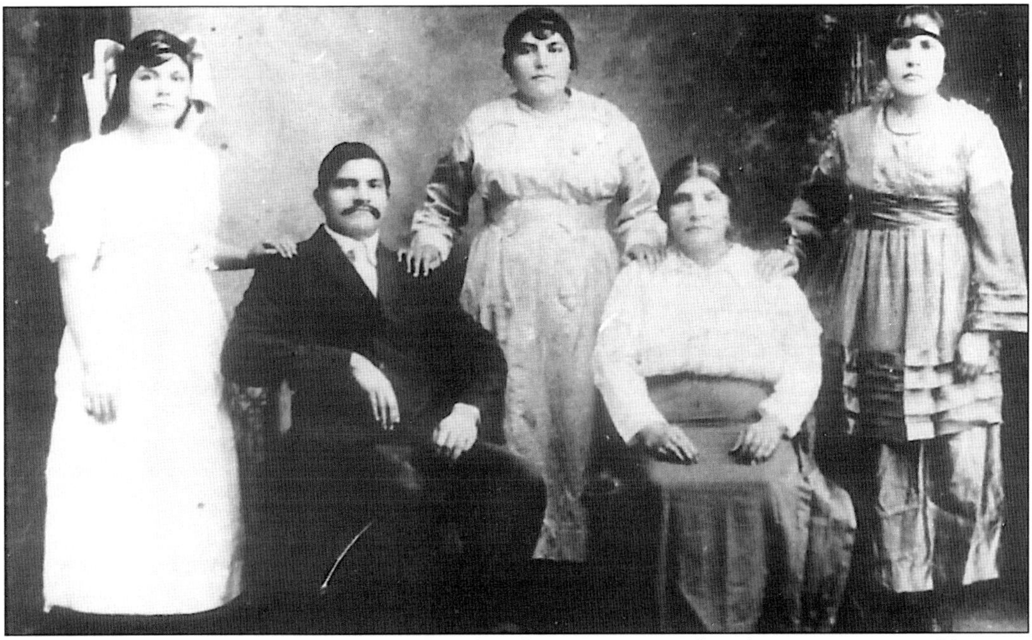

The Fonseca family is reputed to be the first Mexican family to arrive in Chicago Heights in 1916.

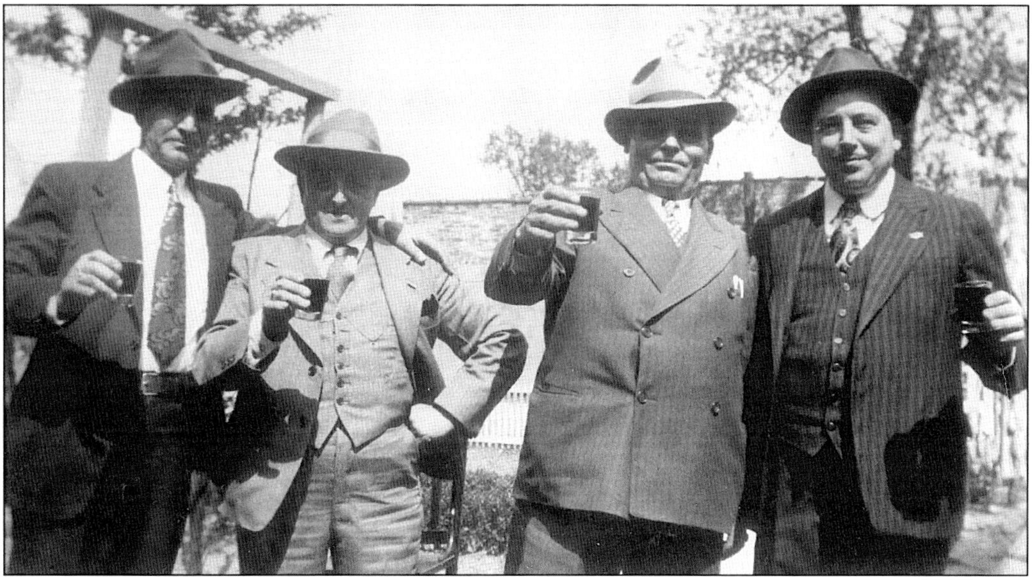

Salute! Louis Longo, Agostino Ciambrone, Sam Sesto, and Angelo Ciambrone gather in the backyard on 17th Street to enjoy a glass of wine on a festive 1940s Sunday afternoon.

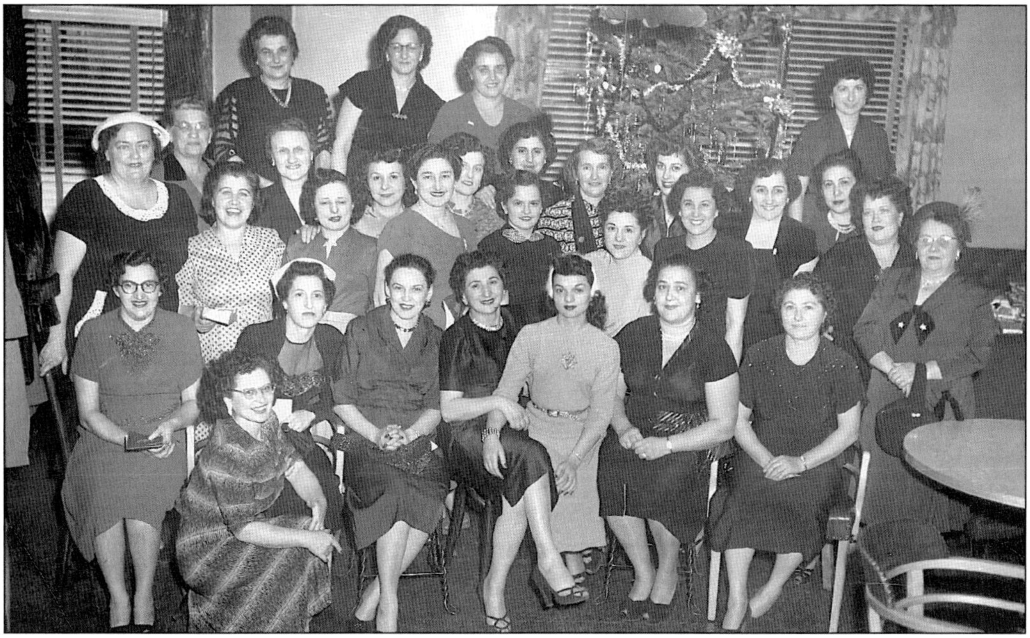

The women of the Dante Club posed at the headquarters on 24th Street for this Christmas photo in 1951. From left to right are as follows: (front row) D. Monacelli, Florence Dandrea, Augusta Rufo, Julia Monacelli, Gussie Pasarelli, Lydia Paris, Lena Rotoloni, and Sue Grilli; (second row) Angeline Cipolla, Rose Rotondi, Theresa Giannetti, Clara Tiberi, Fil Mele, Mary Lagone, Benedetta Farina, Jean Girardi, and Minnie Perry; (third row) Bernardine Grossi, Marie Grupp, Hilda D'Amico, Lena Mascitti, Margaret Higgs, Ann Novelli, Celeste DiGiulio, Vicki Bruno, and Terri Bruno; (back row) Emma DePeso, Julia Rydlurcz, Emma Tintari, and Gloria Grilli.

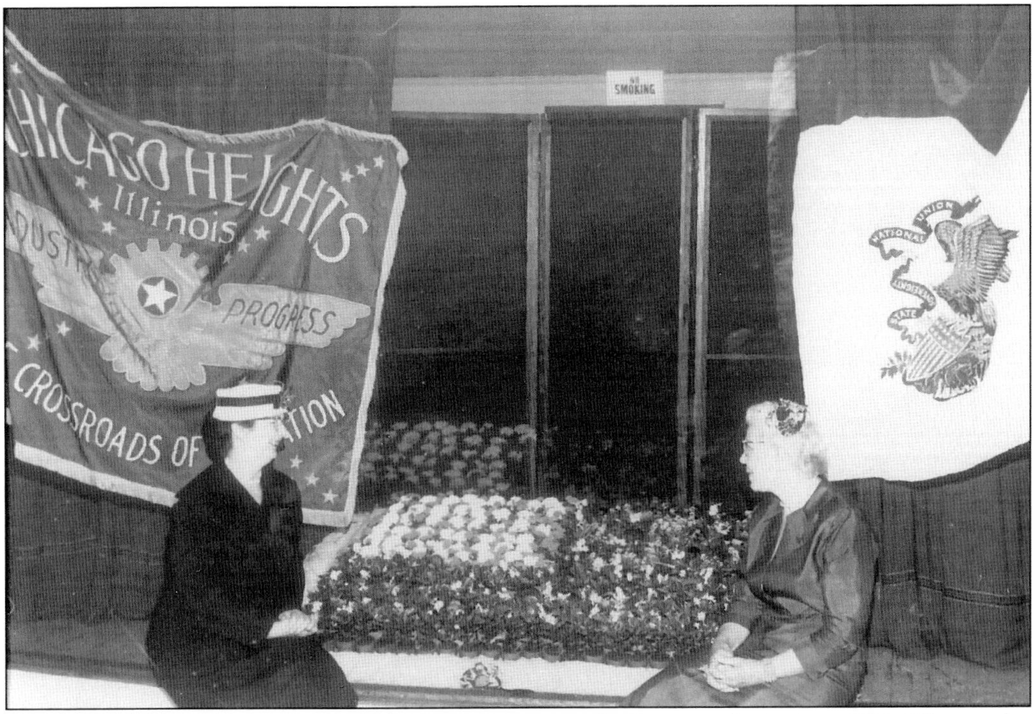

Beautification promoters at Culturama pose with flowers depicting Old Glory, the Chicago Heights flag embossed with the message "Industry and Progress, Crossroads of the Nation," and the Illinois state flag.

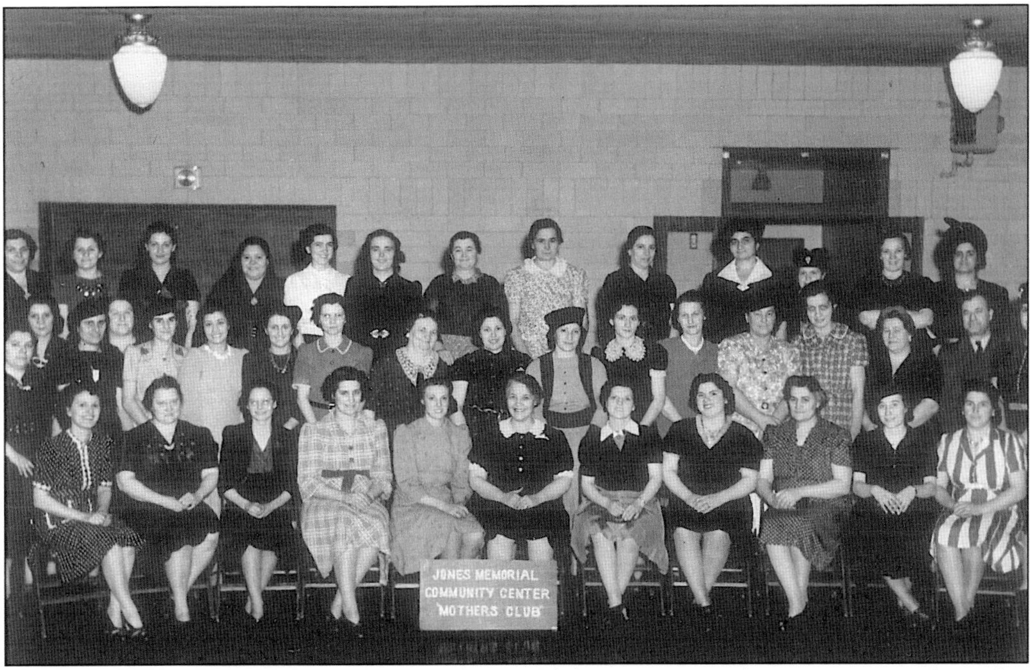

In the 1940s, the Jones Center Mother's Club was a social organization that also enhanced the homemaking and parenting skills of its members.

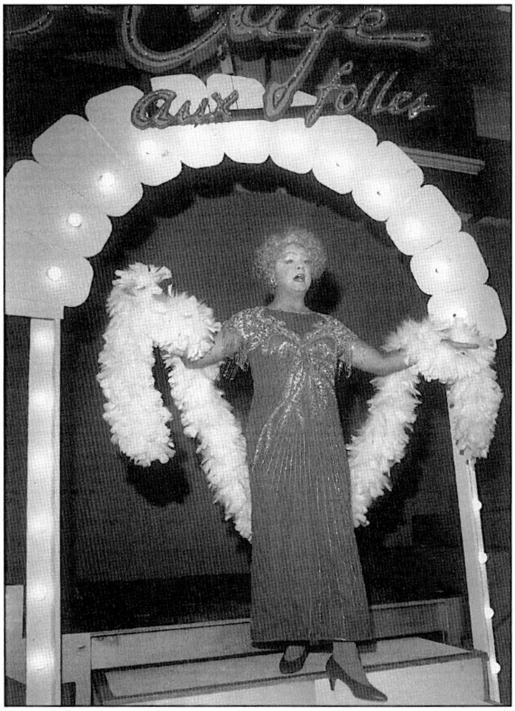

Rick Rapp portrayed the flamboyant Zaza in the Chicago Heights Drama Group's 1995 production of *La Cage aux Folles*, continuing the grand tradition of community theater that began in the early 1930s. As the 21st Century dawned, the Drama Group was still going strong.

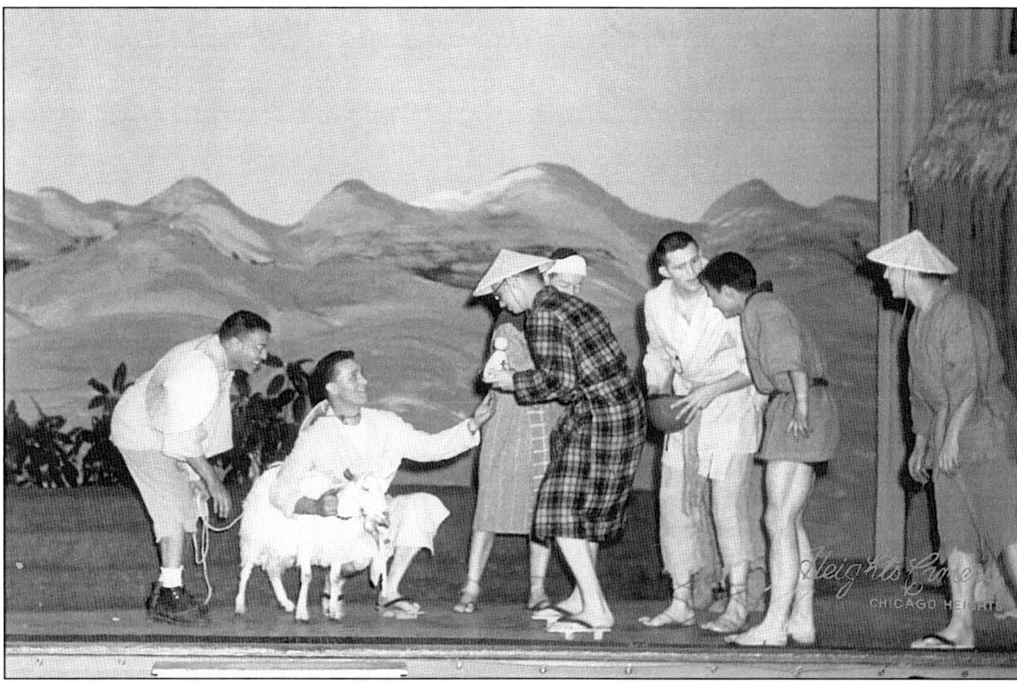

"Lute Song"—the Bloom senior class play in 1955—was presented at Washington School auditorium in an era before the construction of the Bloom auditorium. School programs combined with Drama Group productions created quite a lively entertainment scene.

Armando Giampaolo, a lifelong resident of Chicago Heights, accompanies yet another musical event in our city. In the 1990s, he became a civic institution appearing with the Miracle Temple Choir, the San Lorenzo Celebration, and the CrossRoadsFest.

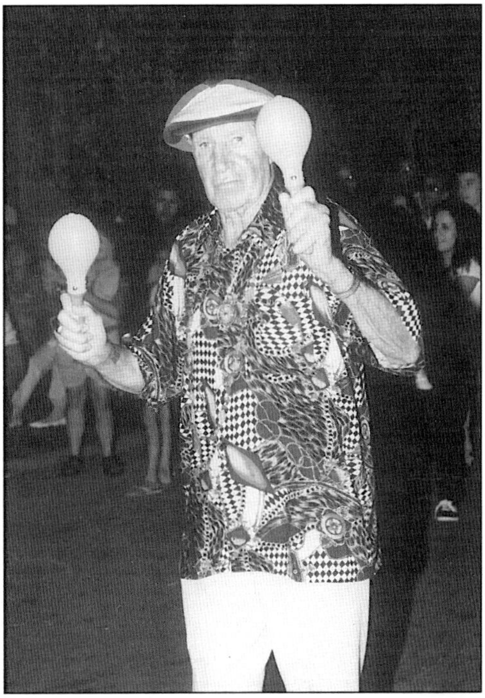

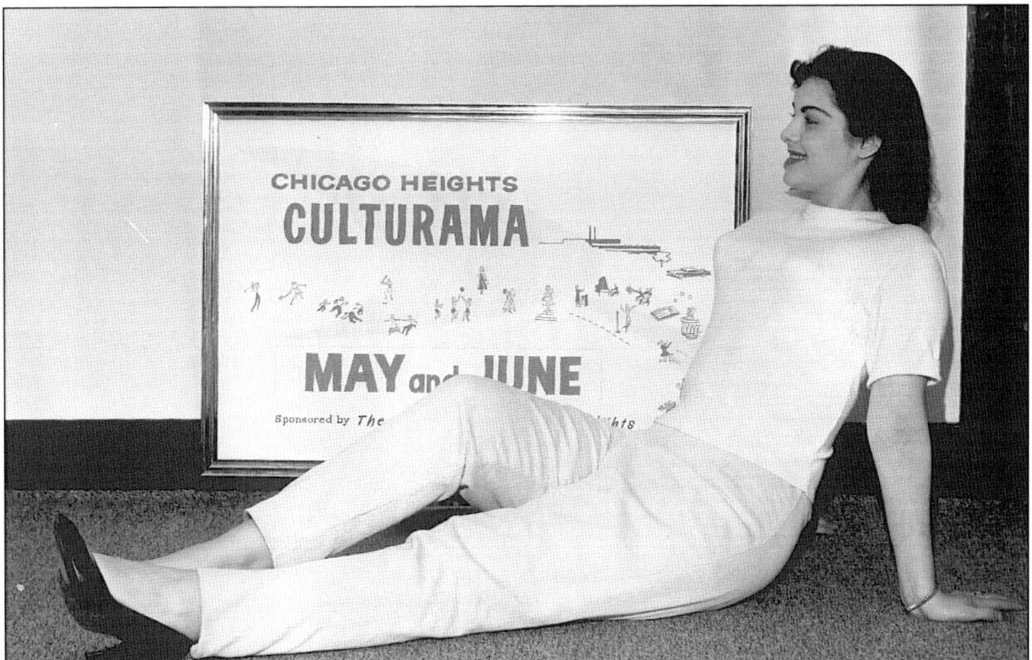

In 1958, Culturama commemorated the 125th anniversary of the settlement of the Chicago Heights area. It was designed by the Committee for Chicago Heights to reawaken the community to its own rich heritage and cultural life. Many celebrities, including Vincent Price, Jan Peerce and Herb Shriner, were featured entertainers during the two-month celebration.

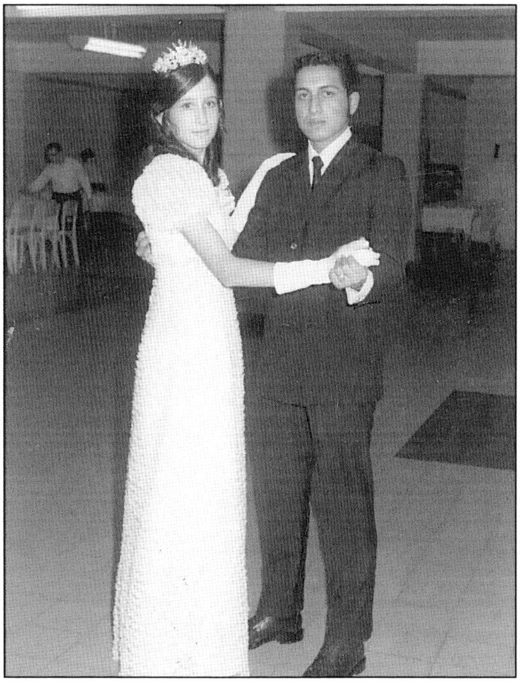

Sonja Ruiz and her cousin Jose Ruiz (age 17) dance together at Sonja's Quinceanera October 15, 1969, in the reception hall at St. Casimir Church. The Mexican tradition of the Quinceanera is a "coming out" occasion for 15-year-old girls and is marked with formal parties and social events that rival a wedding.

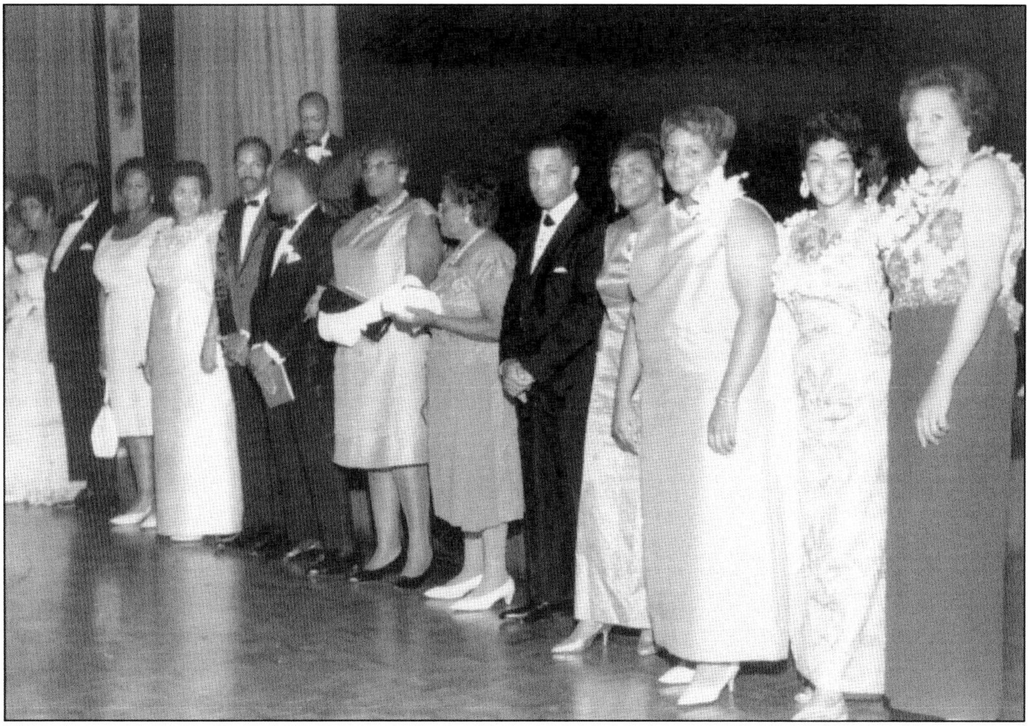

The Chicago Heights Scholarship Foundation Committee included Marvin Gavin and Joseph Hawkins among its members.

Nine

SCHOOLS

For many of us, our most vivid memories of Chicago Heights are linked to our school days. The friendships we made in grade school, the manner in which the community followed the fortunes of Bloom sports teams, and the memories that we connect with the school buildings themselves, pervade our recollections of times past. The image of the Bloom building, class pictures, the Junior High band, and the memory of those stern, dedicated, caring teachers come to mind.

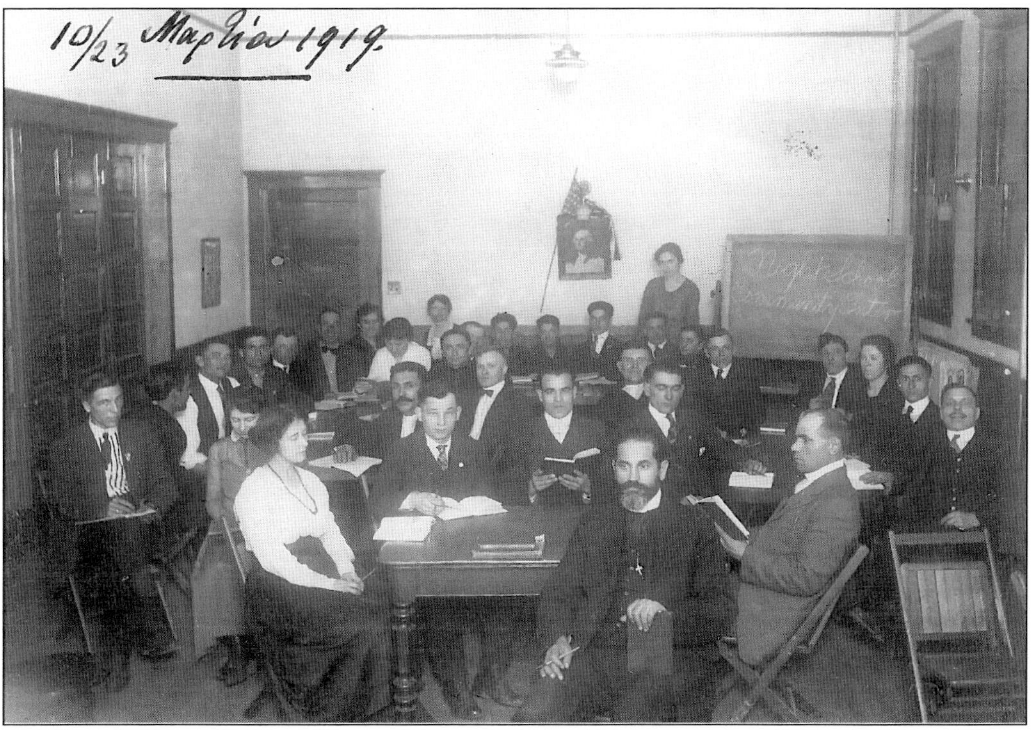

This Jones Community Center night school English class had a wide variety of European immigrants as students. They are pictured here on October 23, 1919. A settlement house modeled on Jane Addams' Hull House, the Jones Center has served newcomers and needy in Chicago Heights since 1915.

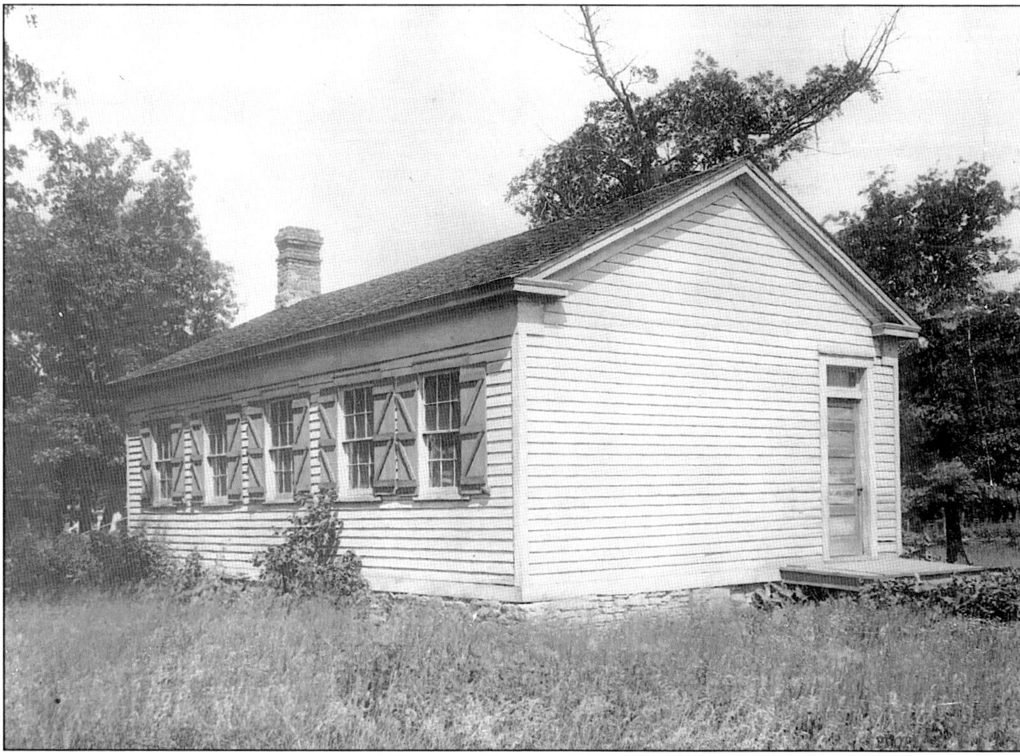

The North School stood at the southwest corner of 14th and Chicago Road from the 1880s to 1920. After the high school was built nearby, this building was used as the Town Hall of Bloom Township until it was torn down to make way for tennis courts after World War I.

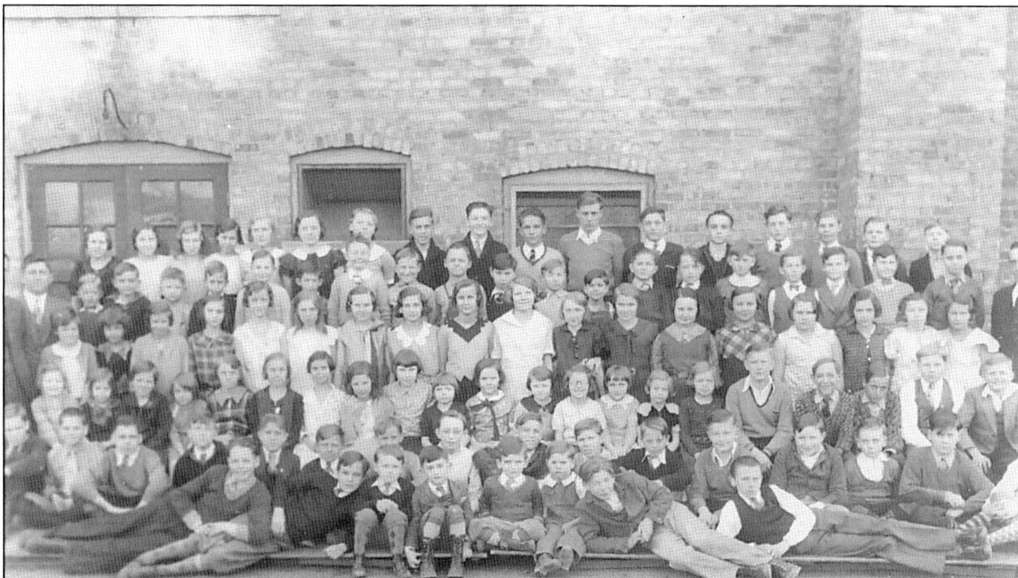

St. Paul Lutheran School teachers and students are pictured above, *c.* 1935.

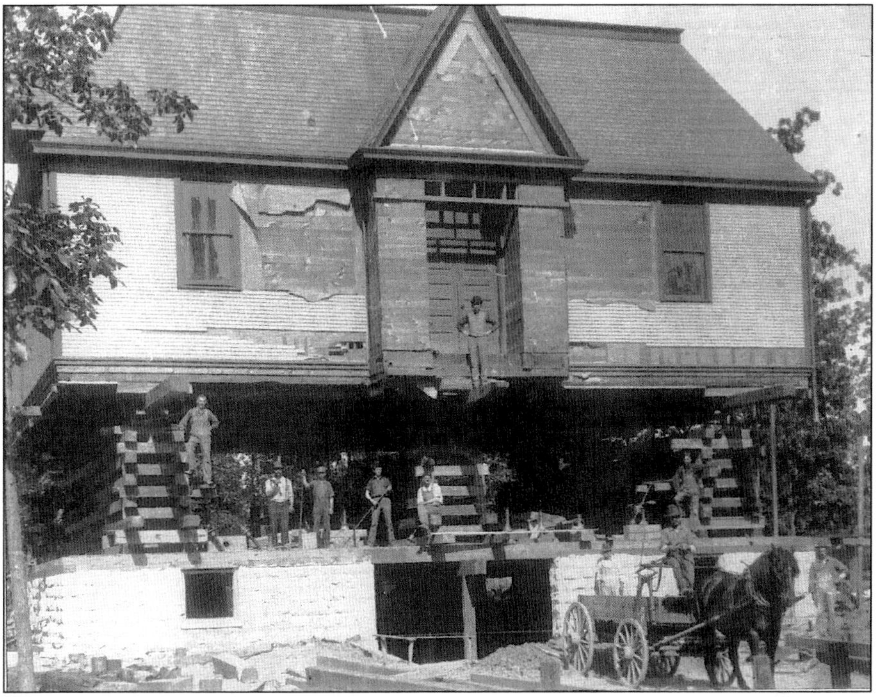

One of the earliest school structures in Chicago Heights was jacked up by house-mover E.E. Somes so a first floor could be added.

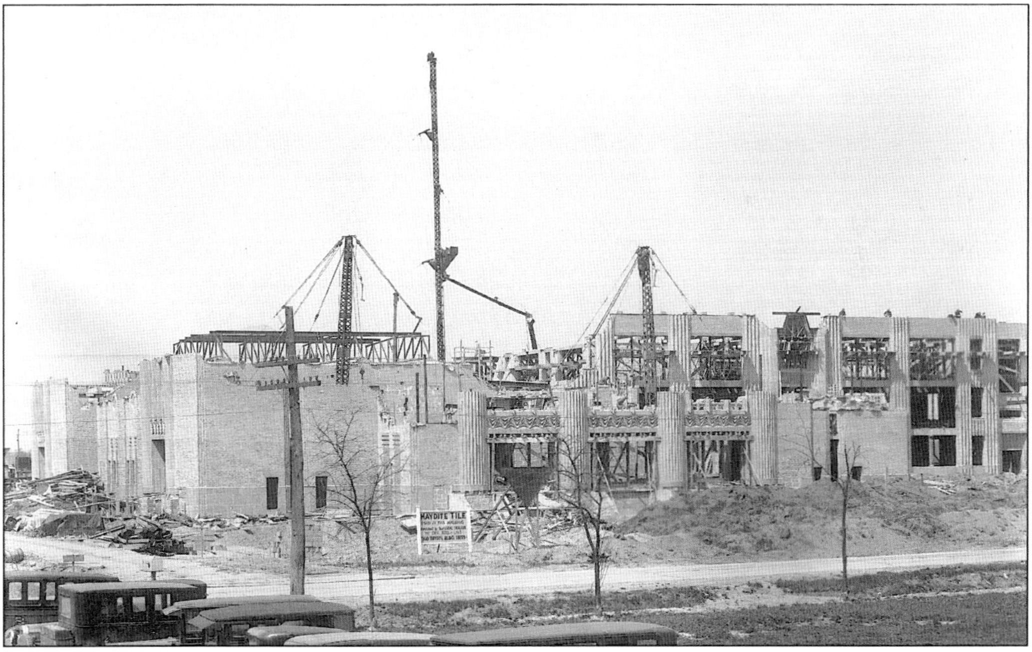

Under construction in April 1931, the east section of the original Bloom building begins to show the classic Art Deco motif of its architecture. Bloom High School is the only Chicago Heights building on the National Register of Historic Places, and has been described as the best example of Art Deco architecture in the state.

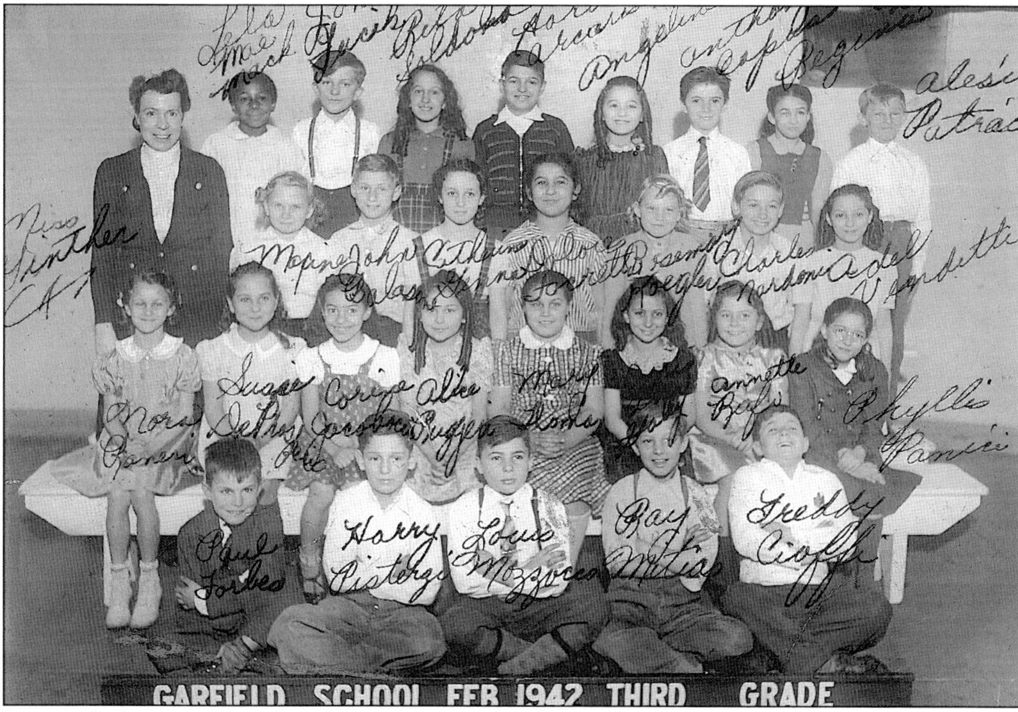

Pictured above is Miss Ginther's third grade class at Garfield School. The donor of this 1942 photo has conveniently identified each of the youngsters; they are now about 67 years old.

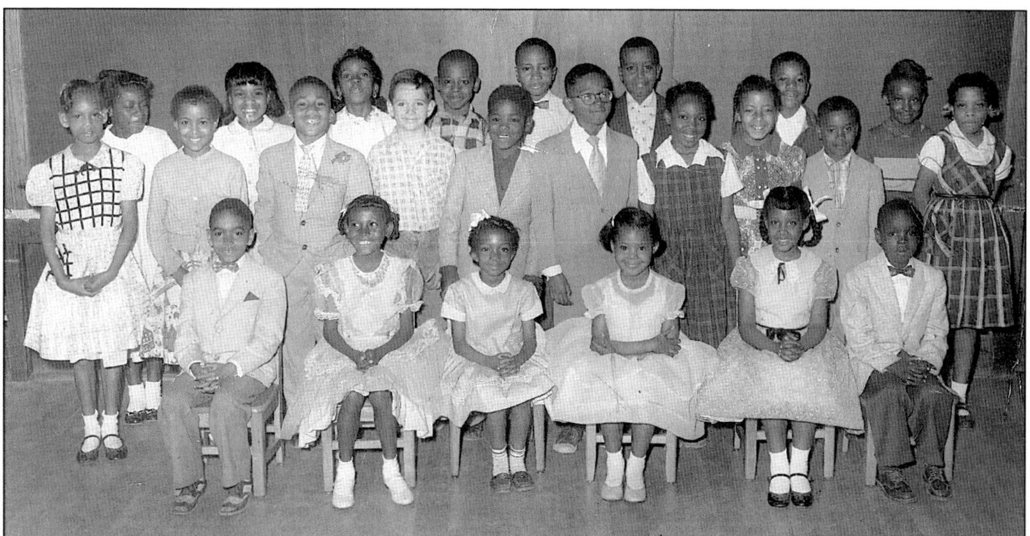

Katherine Gavin Wilkerson got most of her students to smile on picture day for the third grade class at Lincoln School in 1956. One of the bright young ladies in this class is Rhodena Covington McIntosh.

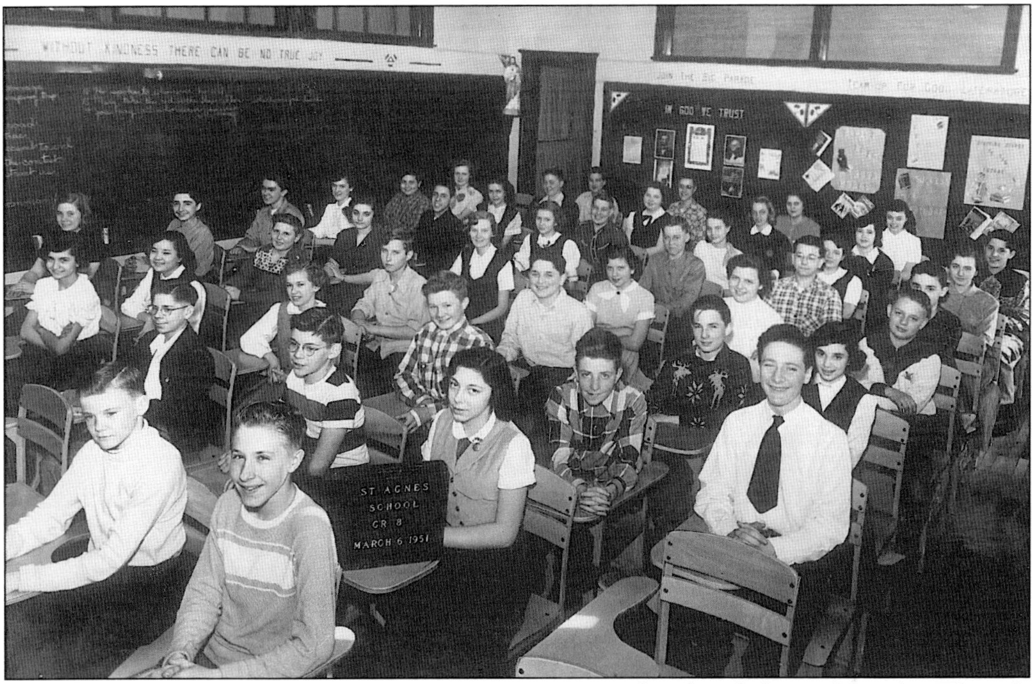

Pictured is a typical classroom scene at St. Agnes school eighth grade 1951. Though the students were not yet sporting uniforms, they were nicely dressed.

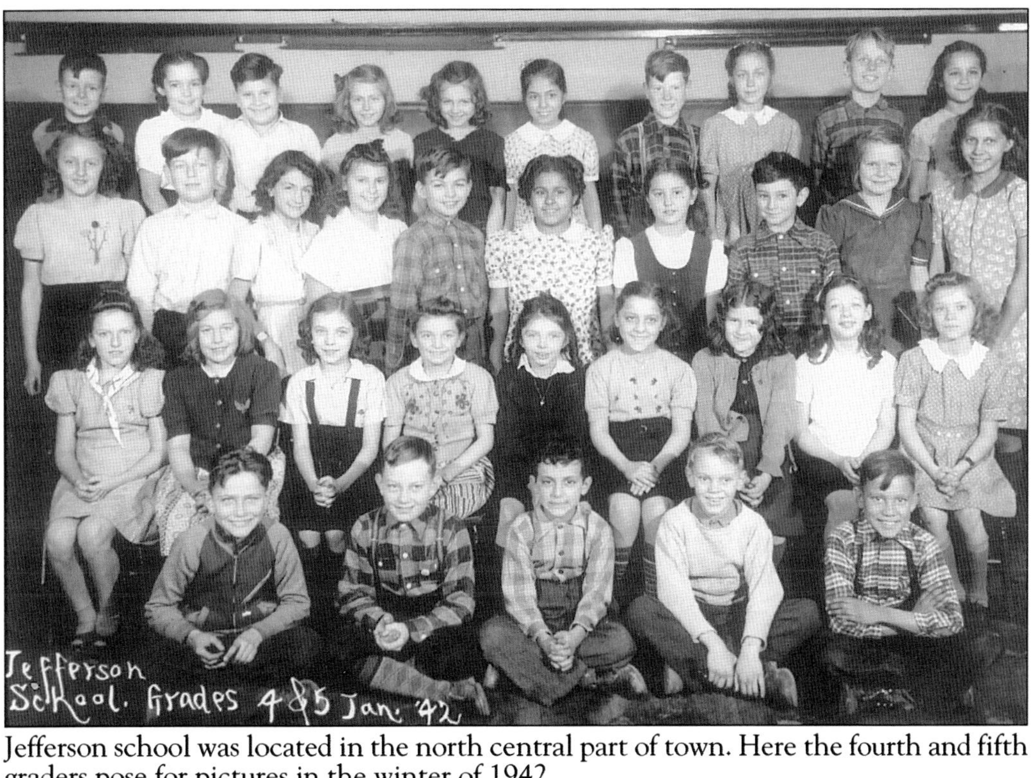

Jefferson school was located in the north central part of town. Here the fourth and fifth graders pose for pictures in the winter of 1942.

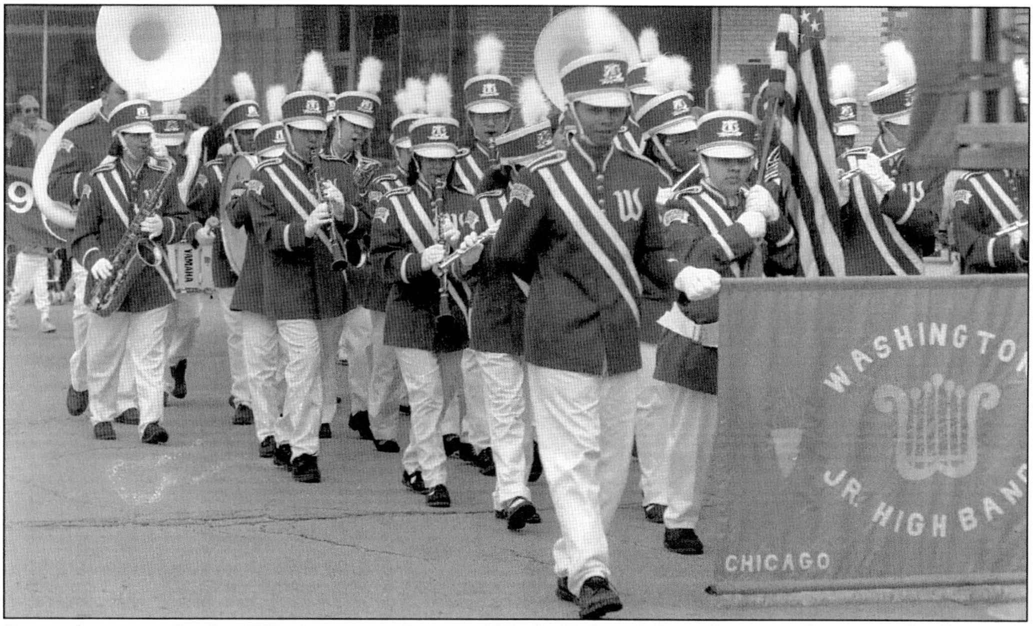

Smartly attired, the Washington Junior High School Band is on the march through Olympia Plaza in the 1960s. In those days, local parades were much more frequent and more elaborate than they are today.

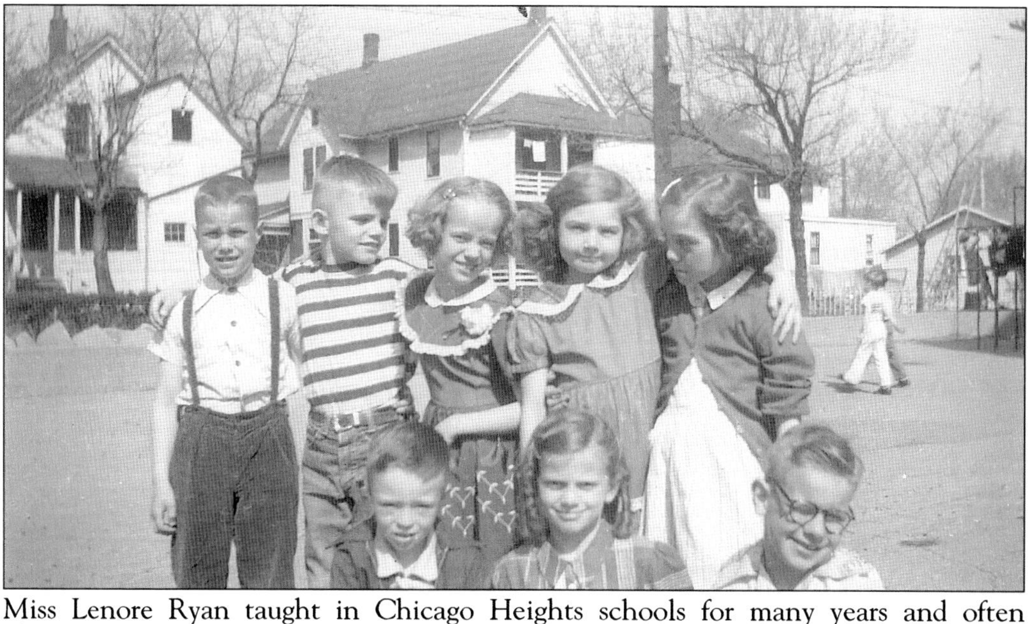

Miss Lenore Ryan taught in Chicago Heights schools for many years and often photographed her students. This group photo was taken in the early 1950s on the Washington School playground.

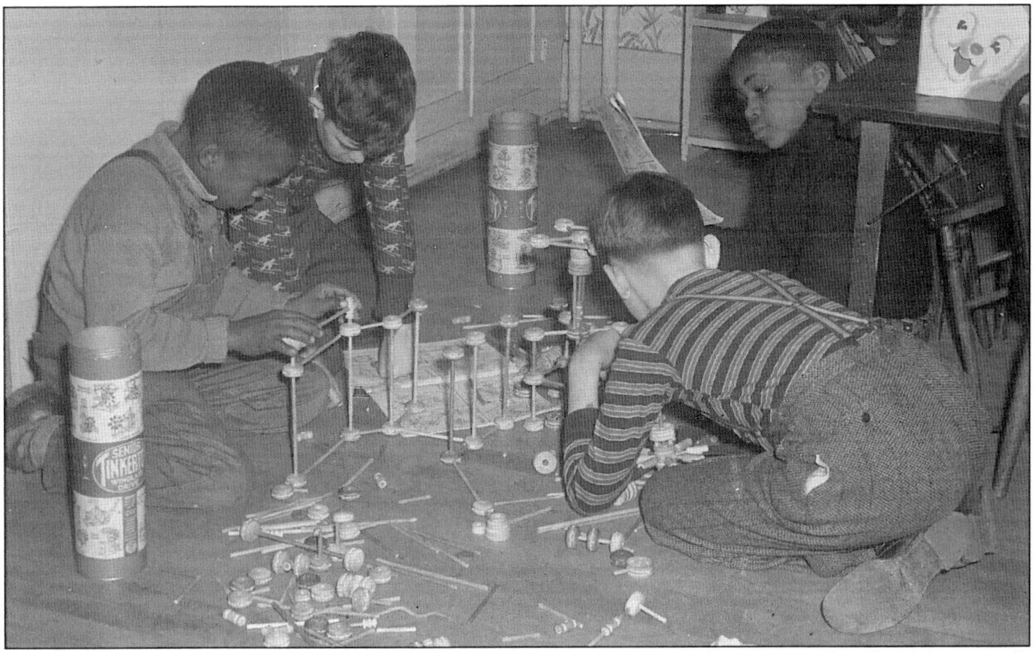

Youngsters at Lincoln School during the 1950s are pictured engrossed in building with Tinker Toys.

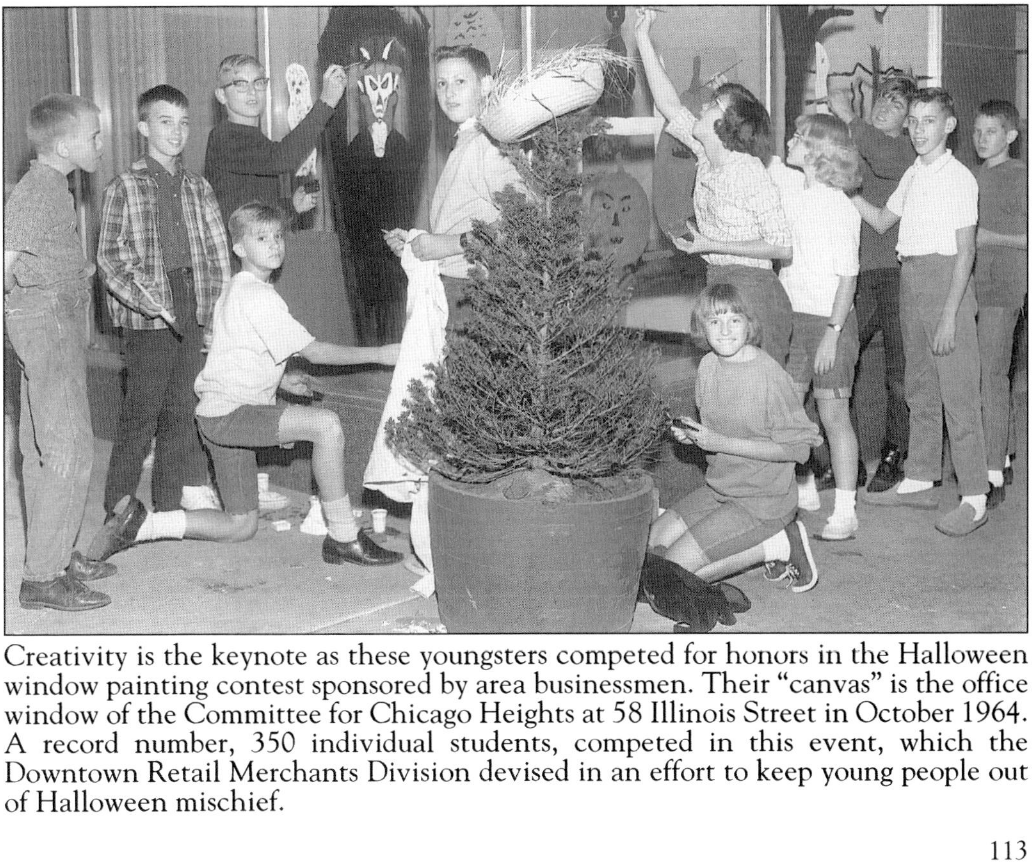

Creativity is the keynote as these youngsters competed for honors in the Halloween window painting contest sponsored by area businessmen. Their "canvas" is the office window of the Committee for Chicago Heights at 58 Illinois Street in October 1964. A record number, 350 individual students, competed in this event, which the Downtown Retail Merchants Division devised in an effort to keep young people out of Halloween mischief.

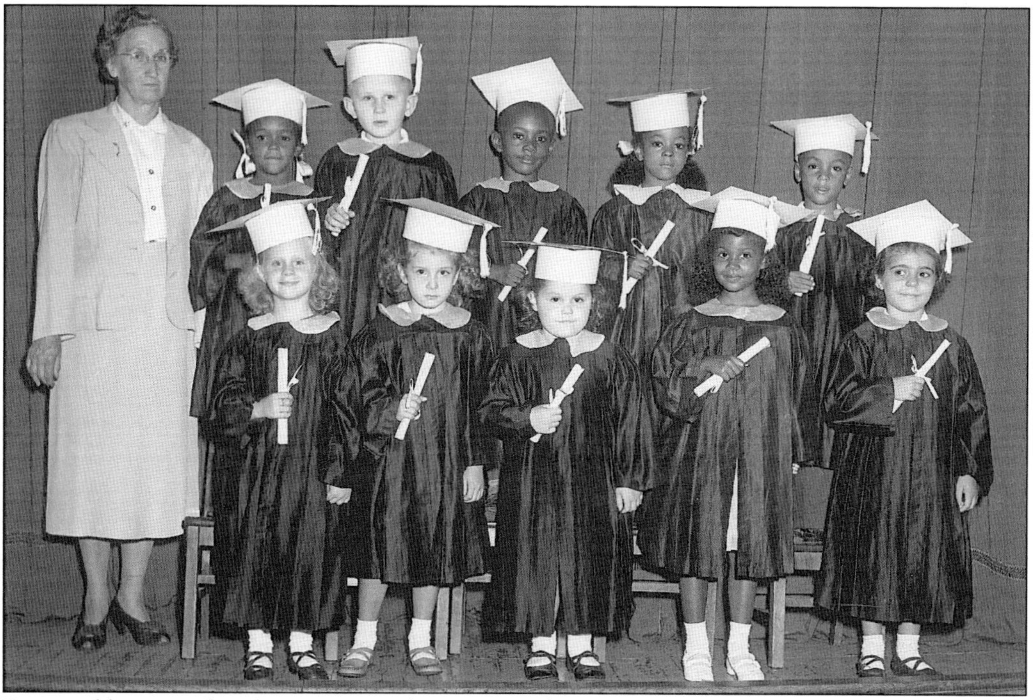

Pictured here is a kindergarten graduation on the stage at the Jones Community Center in the 1950s.

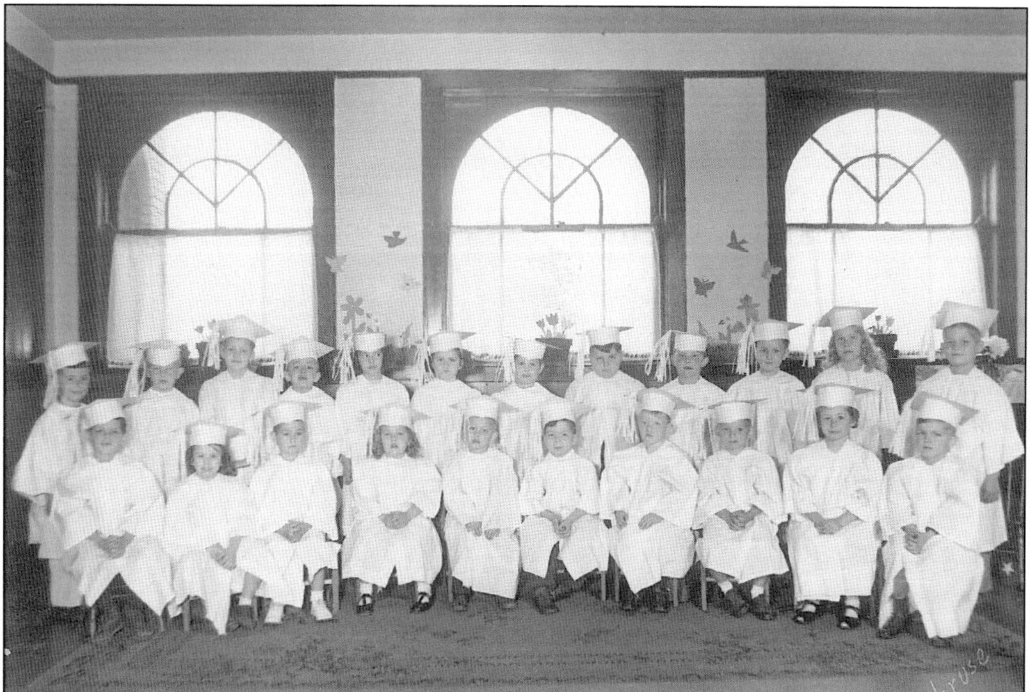

Kindergarten graduation at Ashland "Smith" Park on Ashland Avenue is pictured above in this c. 1945 photo.

Ten

NEIGHBORHOODS

Neighborhood places—homes, stores, streets, parks, and backyards—are the stages on which we play out our lives. This section looks at a variety of places in our town. The grand Victorian homes, modest cottages, neighborhood stores, and meeting places tell a story of change and diversity. From the Hill to the Euclid Area to Country Club Road, these images evoke a sense of energy and elegance.

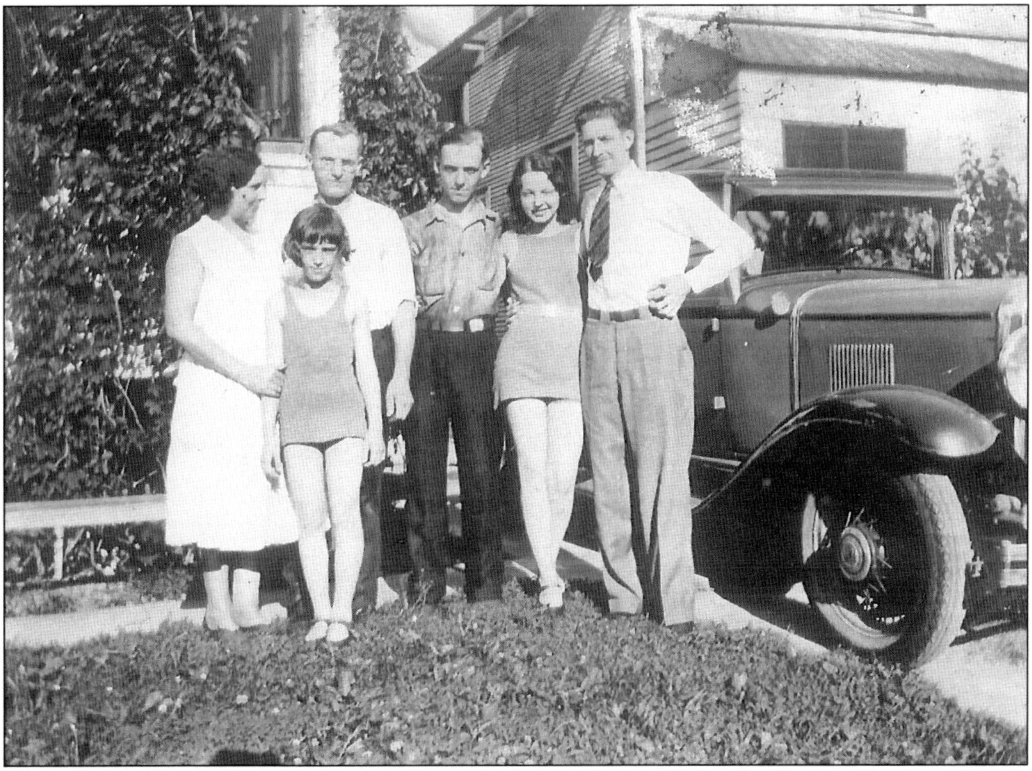

The photo above shows a summertime get-together of Myrtle, Irma, George, Gene, Peg, and Harry Robey on Emerald Avenue in June 1931.

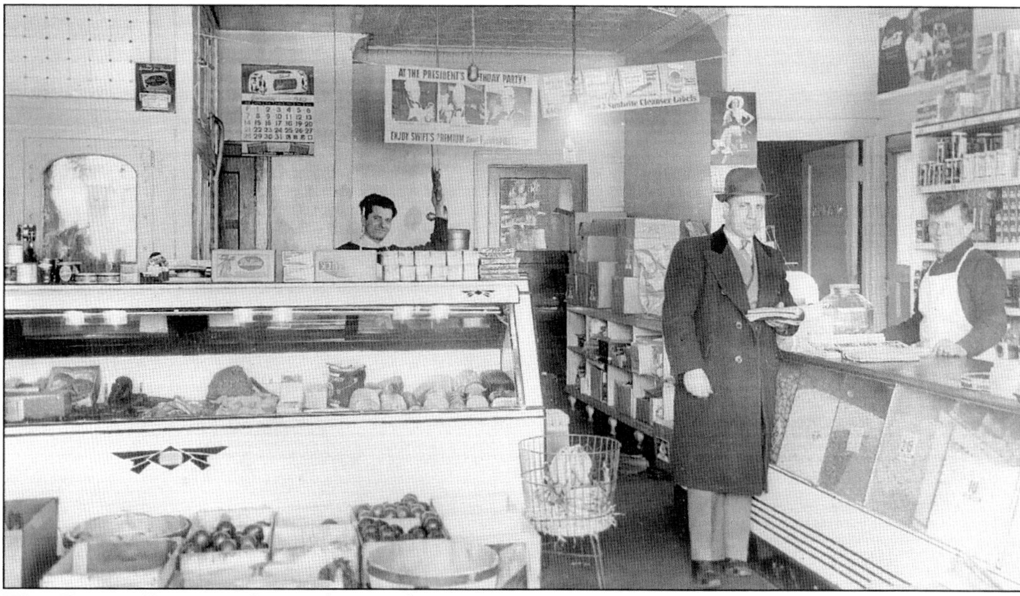

The Bruni Grocery Store, located at Cottage Grove and Lincoln Highway, was not technically in Chicago Heights. This January 1940 photo shows Emedio Bruni waiting on Frank Angone with Louis Bruni behind the deli counter. Note the advertising icons of the day like Wonder Bread, Coca Cola, and Salada Tea. Many East Side residents walked to victory gardens which they maintained in East Chicago Heights. In 1950, East Chicago Heights had a population of 1,548.

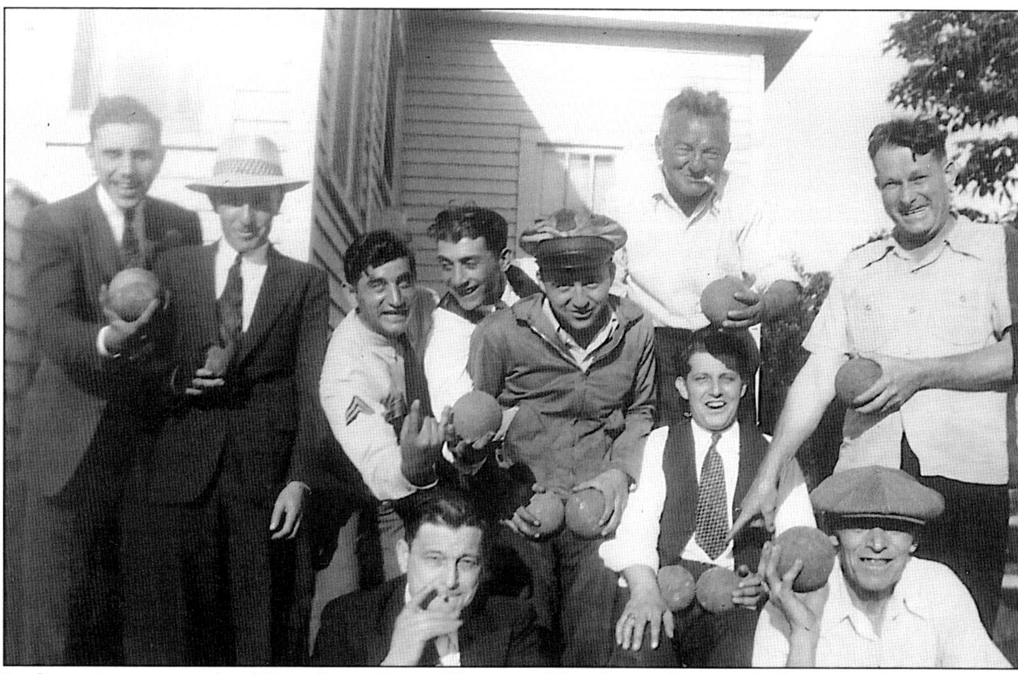

Italian American buddies from East Chicago Heights relax and clown with a game of bocce in the 1940s. Among those pictured are Vince Scarligilia, Ernie Malizia, Jim Malizia, and Quindo DeAngelis.

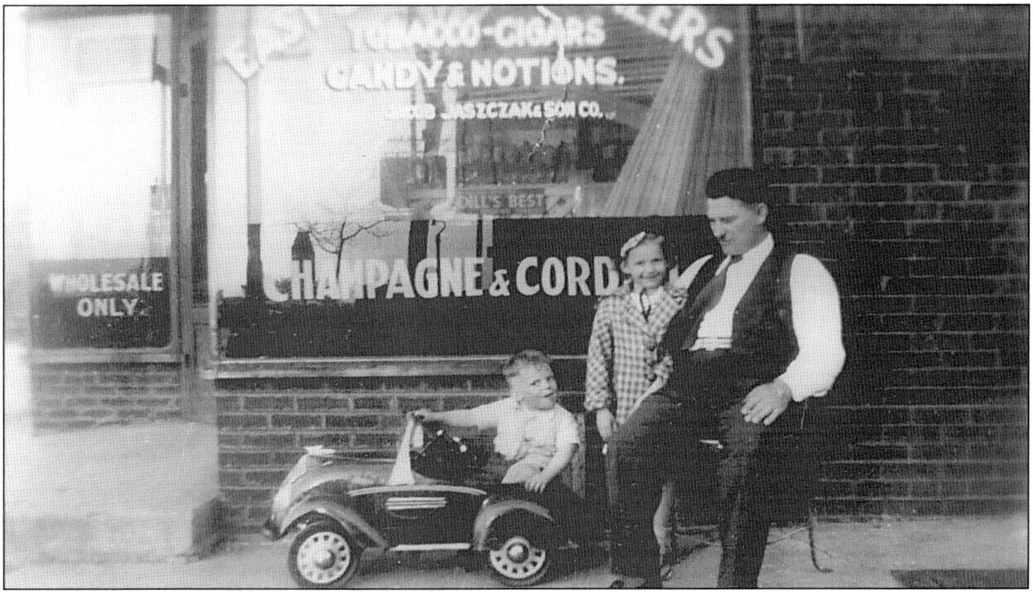

Ray, Florence, and Jacob Jaszczak relax in front of the Eastside Wholesaler at 14th and Green Streets. The Eastside Wholesale Company, one of the many Polish-American businesses, has survived into the 21st Century.

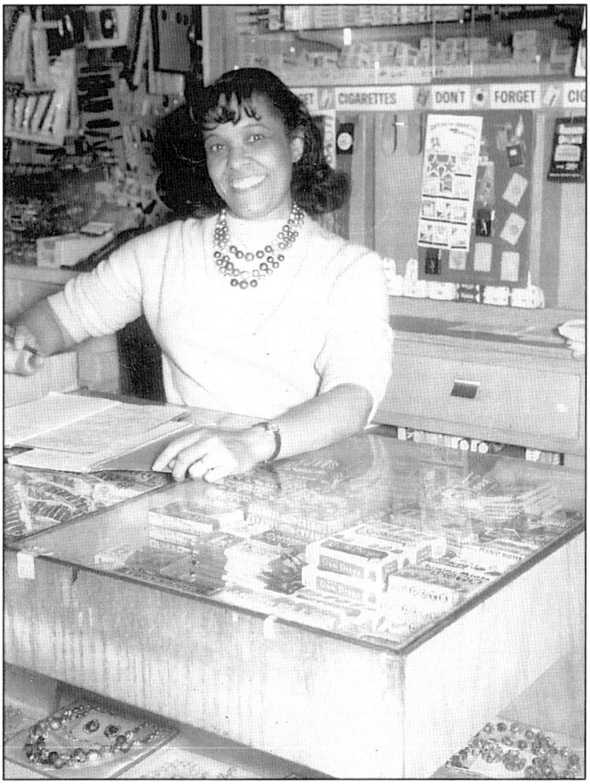

Malvolua Tapp minds her 1950s candy store on the East Side.

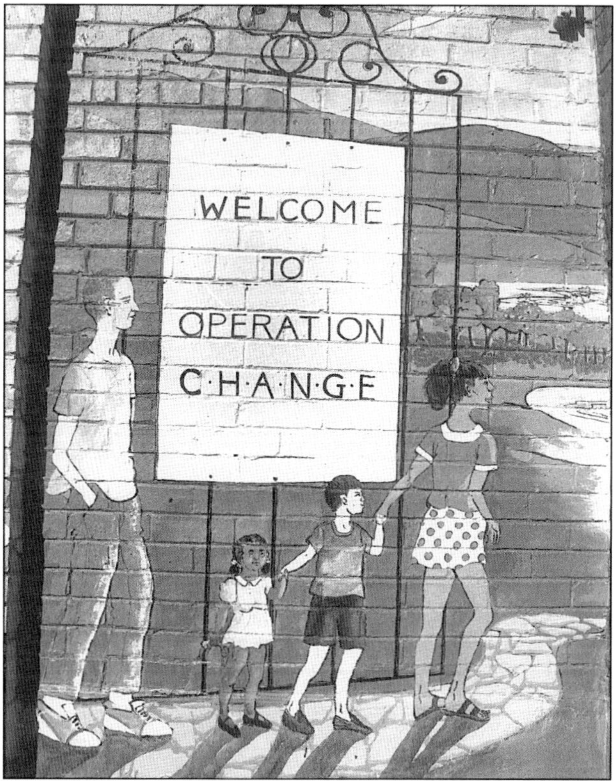

In the early 1990s, Operation Change conducted anti-gang and anti-drug programs among the city's youth, using such projects as this mural on the ComEd wall on 22nd Street near East End. The message of peace and brotherhood spreads 10-feet high along the 150-foot length of a brick wall.

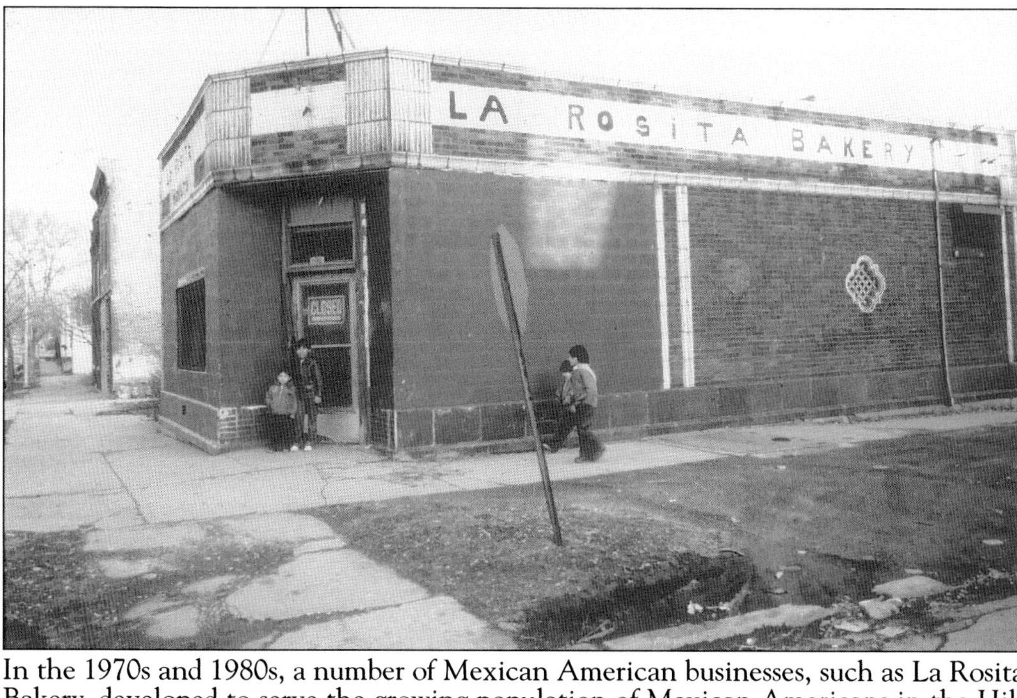

In the 1970s and 1980s, a number of Mexican American businesses, such as La Rosita Bakery, developed to serve the growing population of Mexican Americans in the Hill area and elsewhere in the city. The structure had formerly been Biasella's Drugstore.

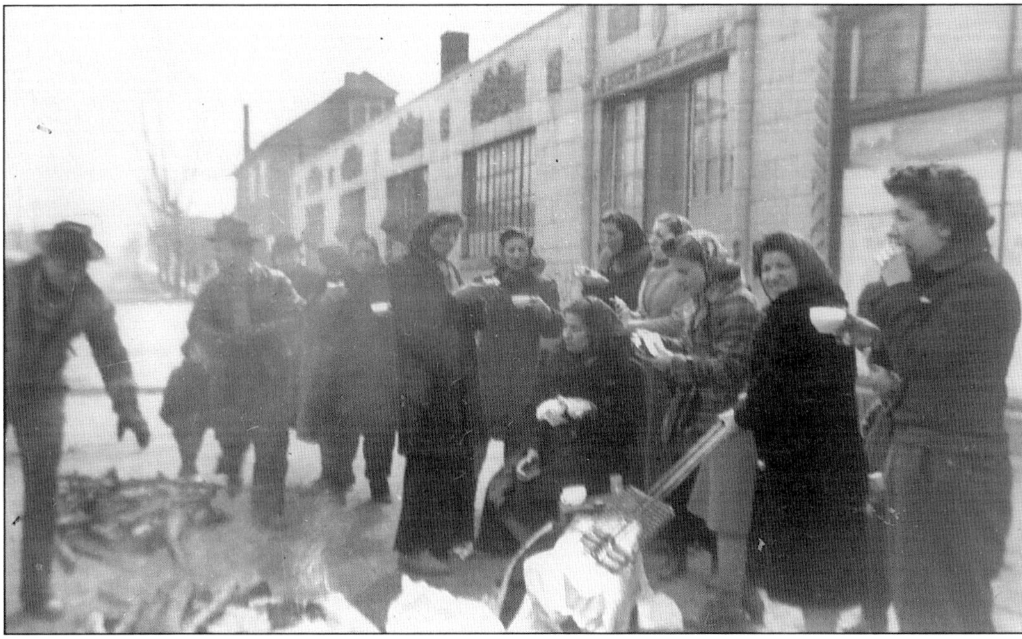

Among those roasting hot dogs in this 1930s picture in front of the Beverly Frocks dress factory at 22nd and Union are Genevieve Mazacco, Lucy Santestafano, Amelia DeLiberty, and Mary Tribo. Beautifully ornamented with terra-cotta eagles, this remarkable building also served as a Volkswagen garage.

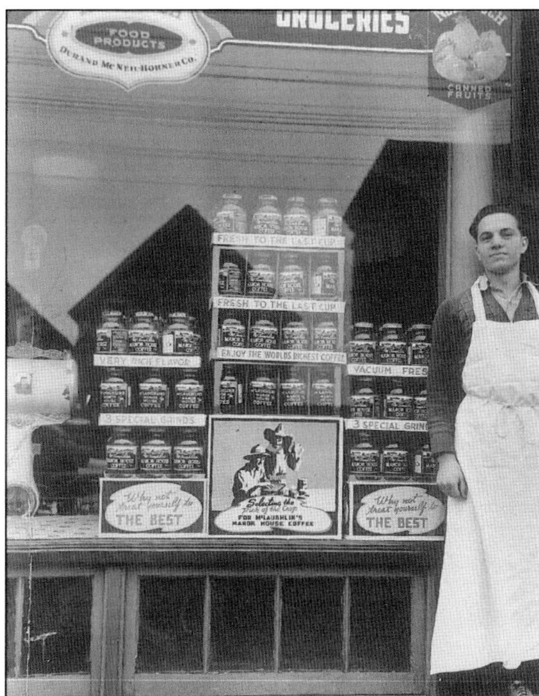

As a teenager in the 1930s, Albert Petrarca worked in his grandfather's (Gaetano D'Amico) grocery store on 22nd Street. Though this particular store survives, as La Granja's, the vast majority of corner stores from the era have been converted to apartments.

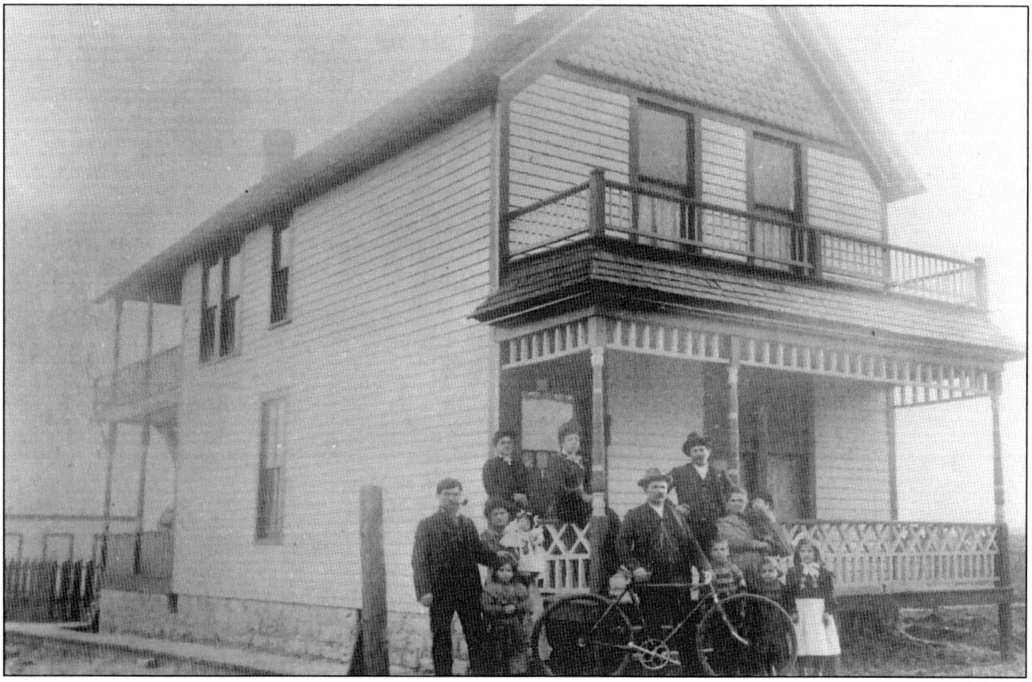

The Frank Piacenti family poses in front of their home on the Hill at 176 East 23rd Street around the turn of the 20th century. Notice the fancy porches and the outbuildings.

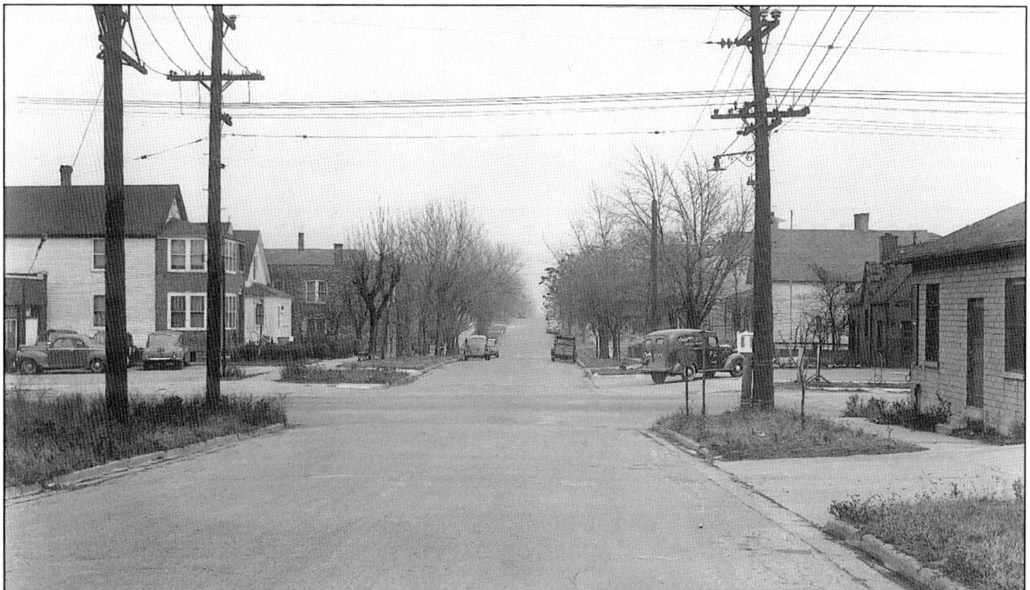

Looking east on 23rd Street at East End Avenue in 1944 reveals the Johnson Oil Storage Company on the right, the Cafarelli Phillips 66 gas station across East End, the cab-stand on the left, a tree-lined parkway, few cars, and the hill leading up to Garfield School. The Guzzino Grocery truck was an efficient way to market fresh groceries in an era when few residents owned automobiles. The small white structure near the hood of the truck is a display honoring neighborhood residents serving in WW II.

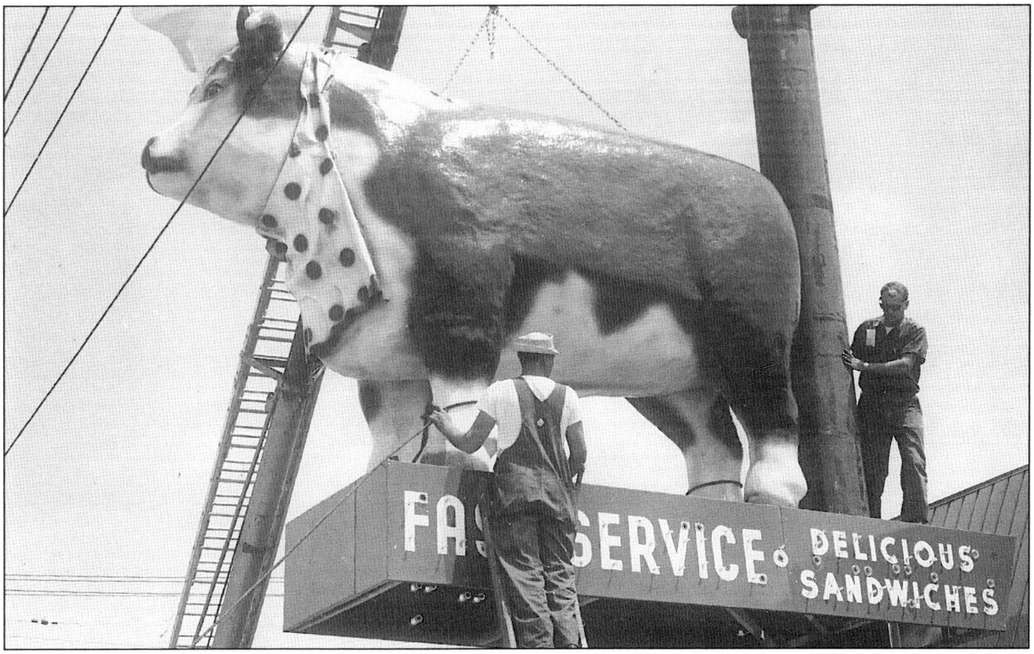

Workers install a giant cow at Leo's Beef, later La Vaquita Mexican restaurant (on Chicago Road near Main Street). Displays such as this and the Tower Restaurant (on Halsted and Broadway) became local pop culture landmarks of our city.

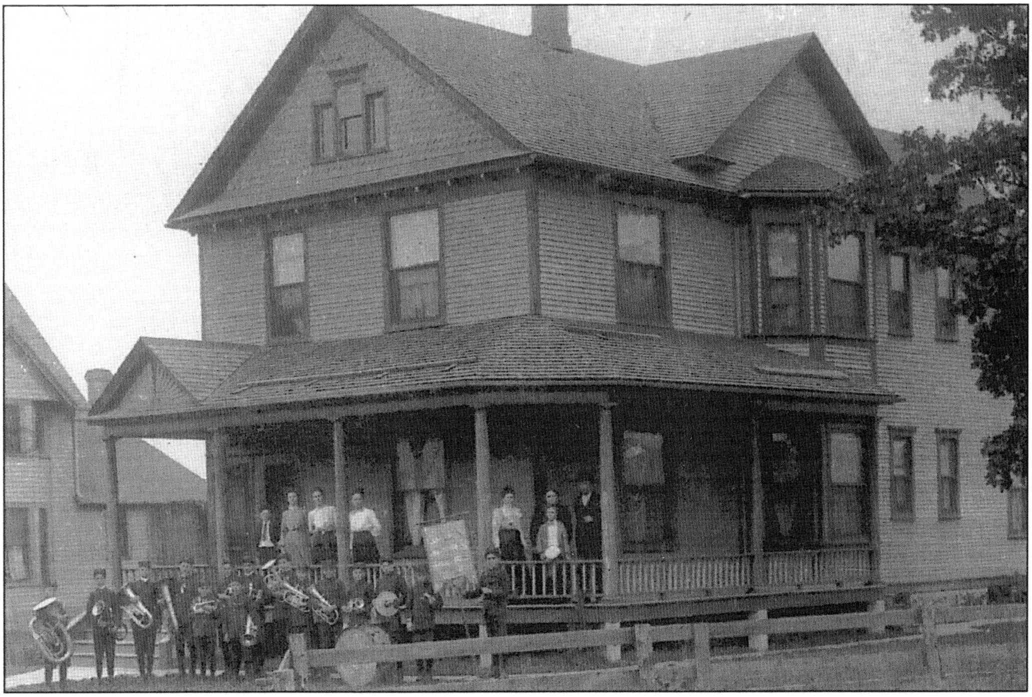
A band of youngsters gathered at the home of E.E. Somes at 1927 Circle Court. The wrap-around porch and the spacious multi-windowed design suggest a gracious lifestyle for the home's residents. The house is said to have been constructed in the 1880s.

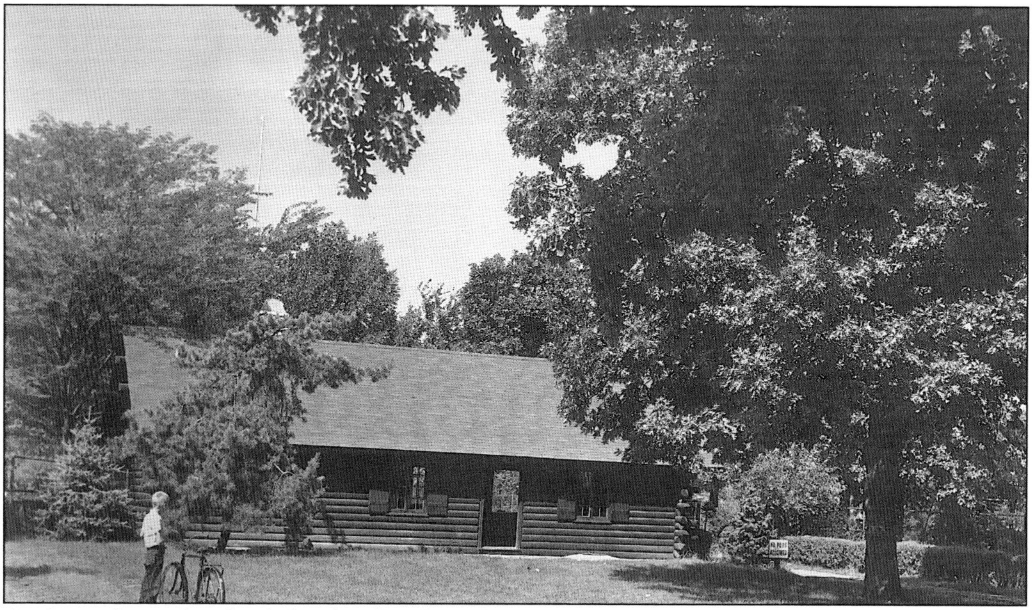

A classic log cabin built by the Civilian Conservation Corps in the late 1930s provides an idyllic summertime photo of the Euclid Park Fieldhouse. The west end of the park borders the forest preserve and the Thorn Creek, which runs diagonally to the northwest through the heart of Chicago Heights.

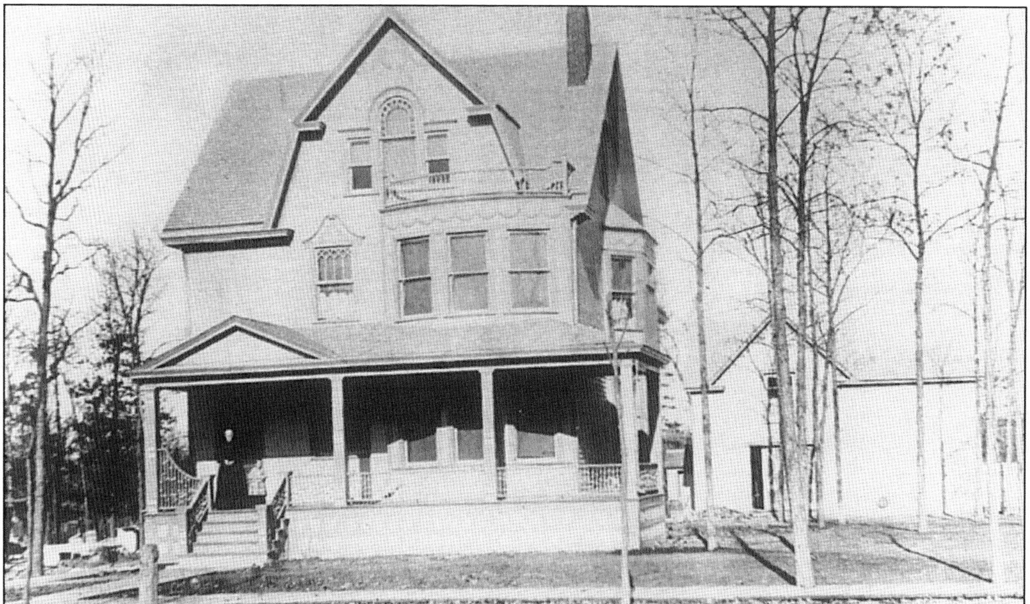

Built in 1892, this Queen Anne was occupied by Robert P. Wallace and his family. He was the son of John Wallace, a pioneer settler who came to Thorn Grove from Ireland in 1835. Wallace was born 1852 in a little home at 19th Street and Chicago Road, when what is now Chicago Heights was nothing more than a concentrated group of farm houses and a few stores. After completing his education, Wallace built this home on Main Street and became a highly successful insurance agent and real estate broker.

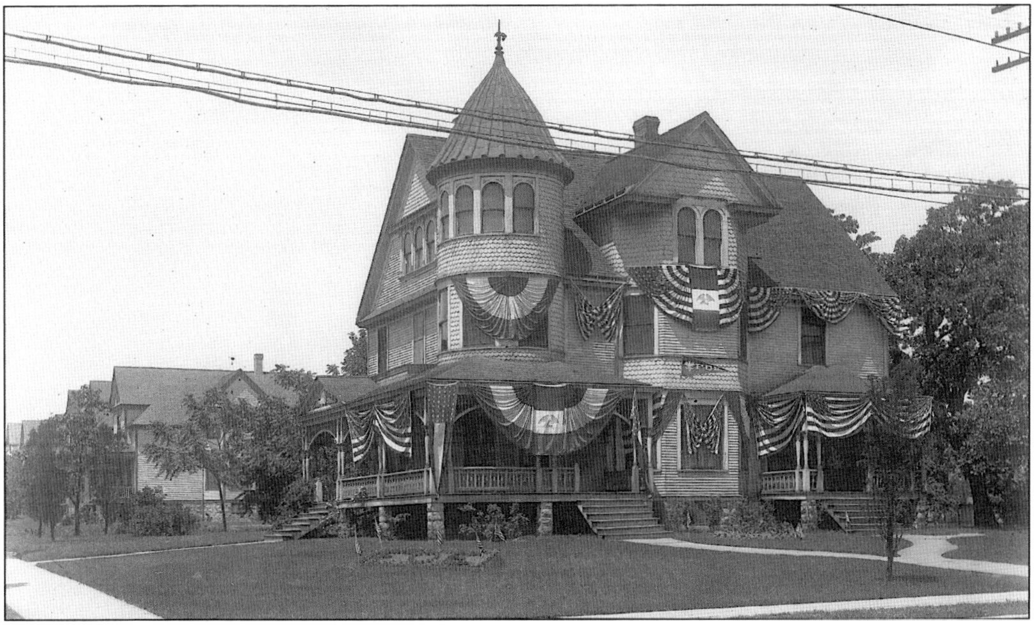

The Fraternal Order of Eagles (FOE) headquarters was located in the former James McEldowney house on the northwest corner of 21st Street and Chicago Road. The FOE was just one of the dozens of fraternal organizations and clubs including the Odd Fellows, Moose, Masons, Kiwanis, Rotary, Lions Club, and others which thrived in Chicago Heights during the 1920s.

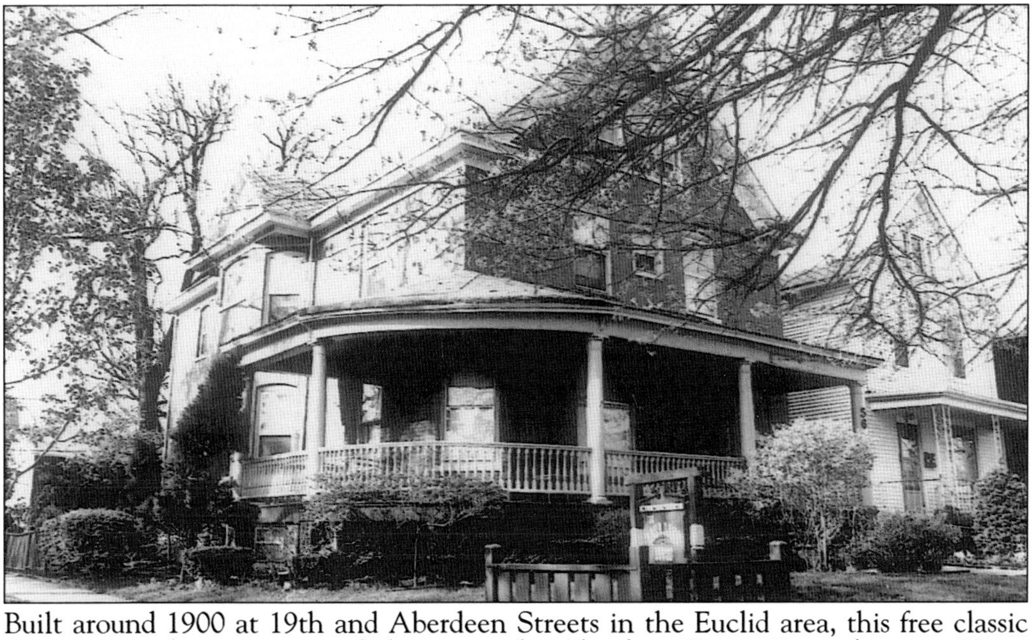

Built around 1900 at 19th and Aberdeen Streets in the Euclid area, this free classic Queen Anne home is currently known as the Aberdeen House. It was home to Harry and Clara Belle Helfrich from at least 1905 until their deaths in the mid-1950s. A carpenter and building contractor, Helfrich brought his family to the growing community of Chicago Heights from Manon, Indiana in 1900.

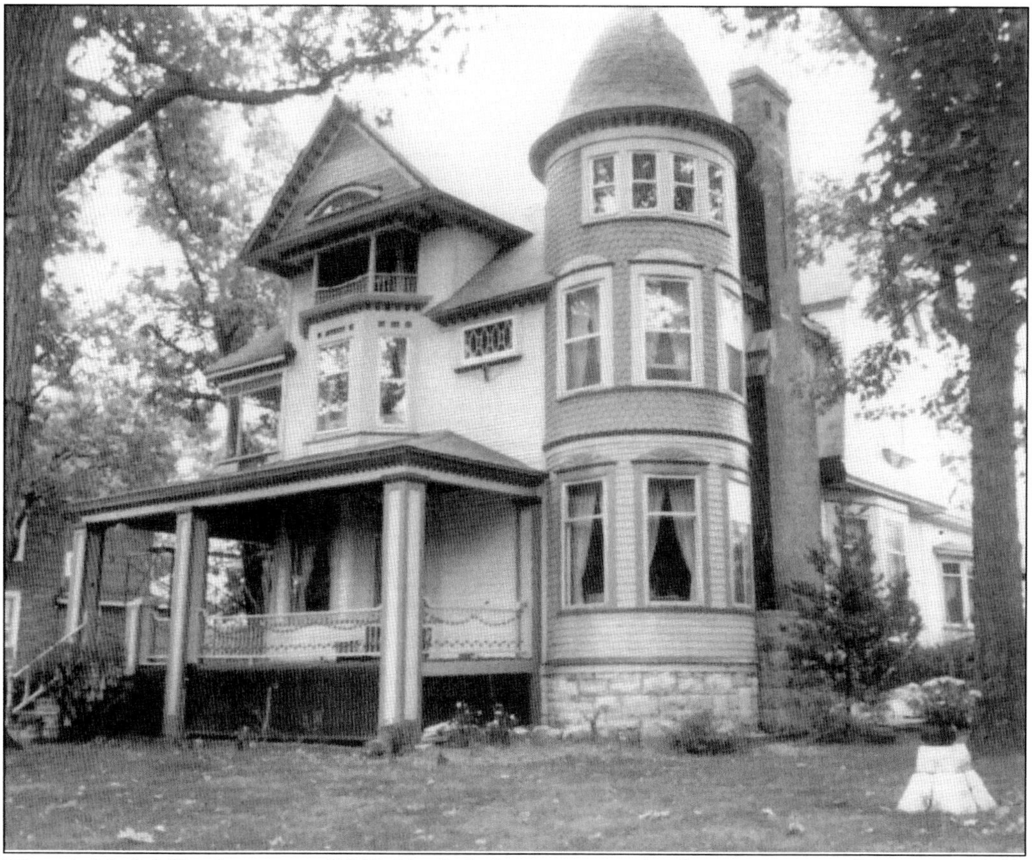

The A.J.J. Miller home at 2002 Euclid Avenue was built in 1893. It features a full-height corner tower and alternating clapboard and shingles on the exterior wall surfaces. Active in Bloom Township and Village affairs, Miller was in the lumber business and served as a trustee of the Chicago Heights Land Association and president of the Village of Bloom from 1898 to 1899.

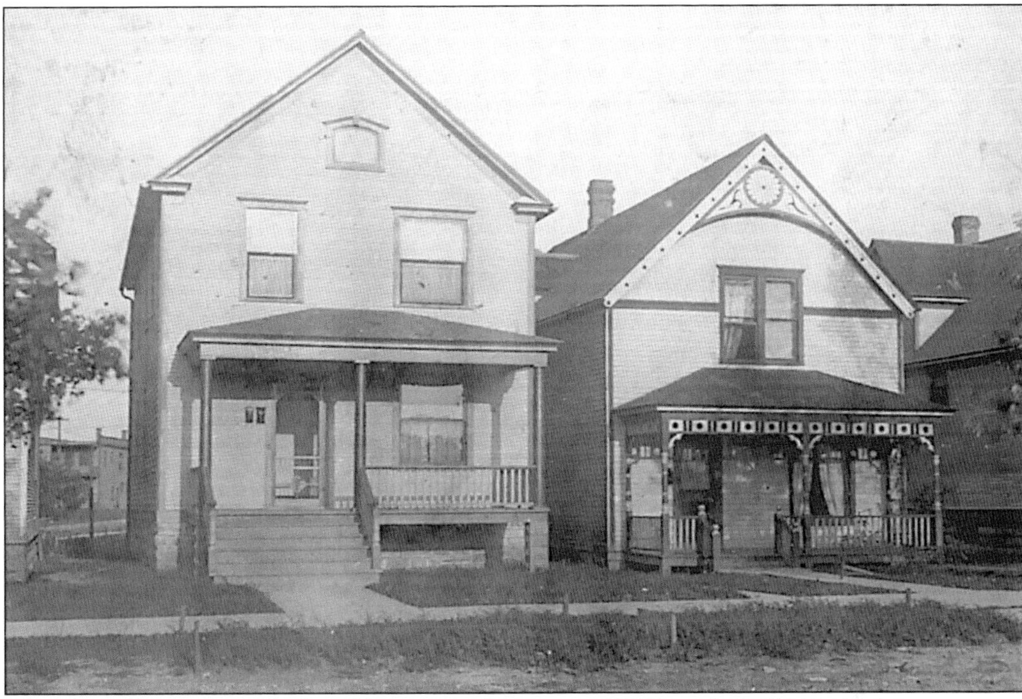

The Agrell home and the Champene home at 1235 and 1237 Park Avenue were photographed c. 1910, before the street was paved. The Champene home illustrates the manner in which homeowners delighted in elaborate exterior architectural decoration. Aluminum-clad, these homes are still standing.

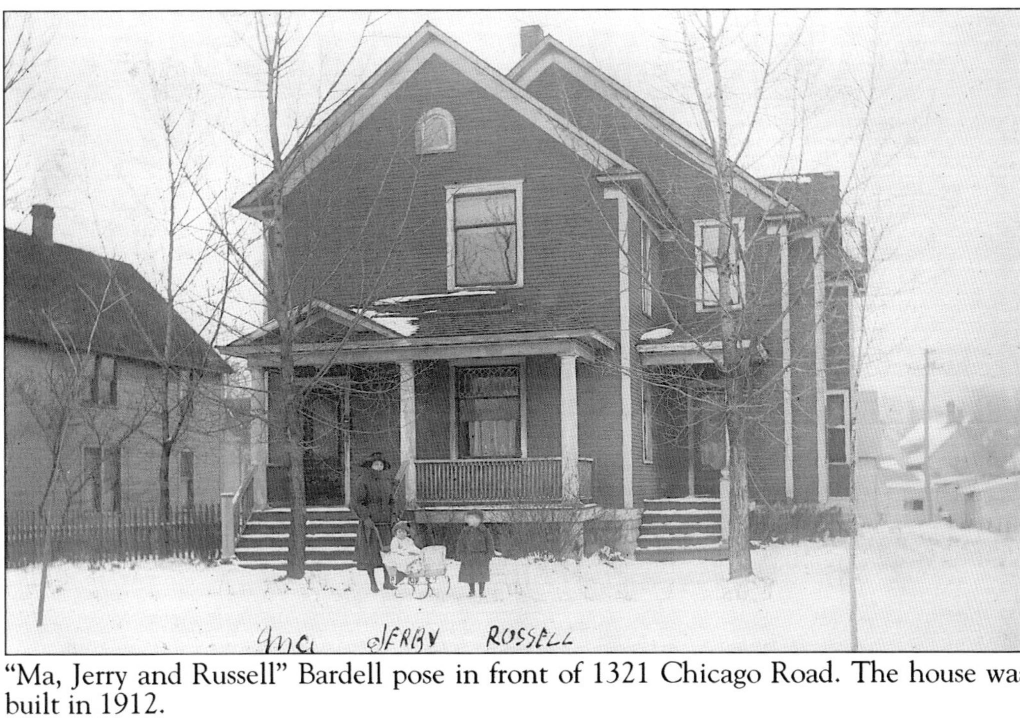

"Ma, Jerry and Russell" Bardell pose in front of 1321 Chicago Road. The house was built in 1912.

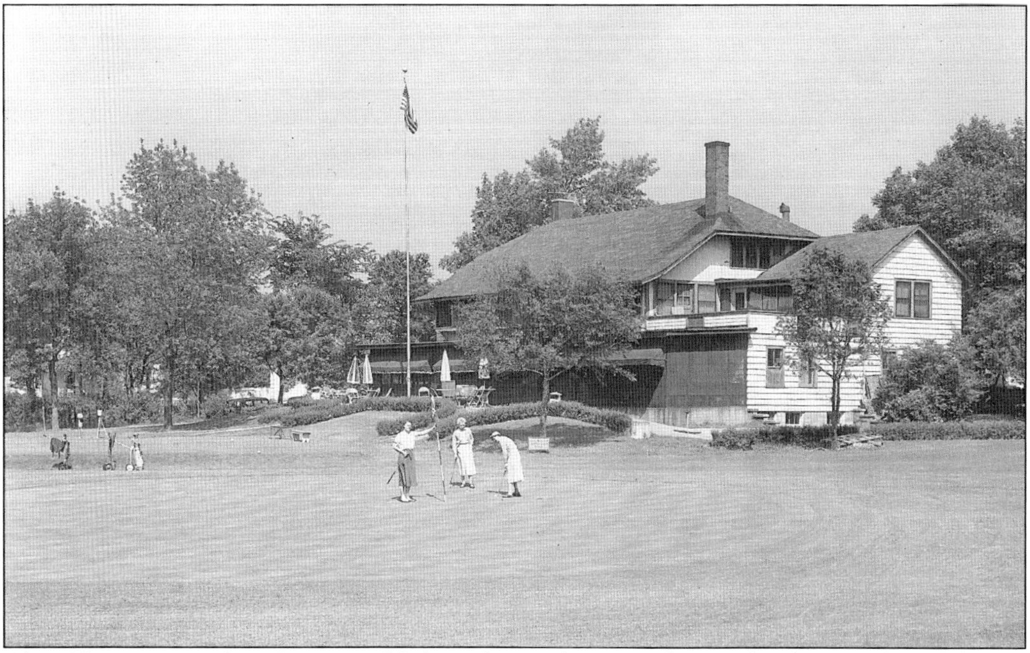

The Chicago Heights Country Club is shown here in this 1951 photo. The club was founded in 1912 by leading citizens who wanted to learn the game of golf and have a center for social activities. It was the pride of the community for many years.

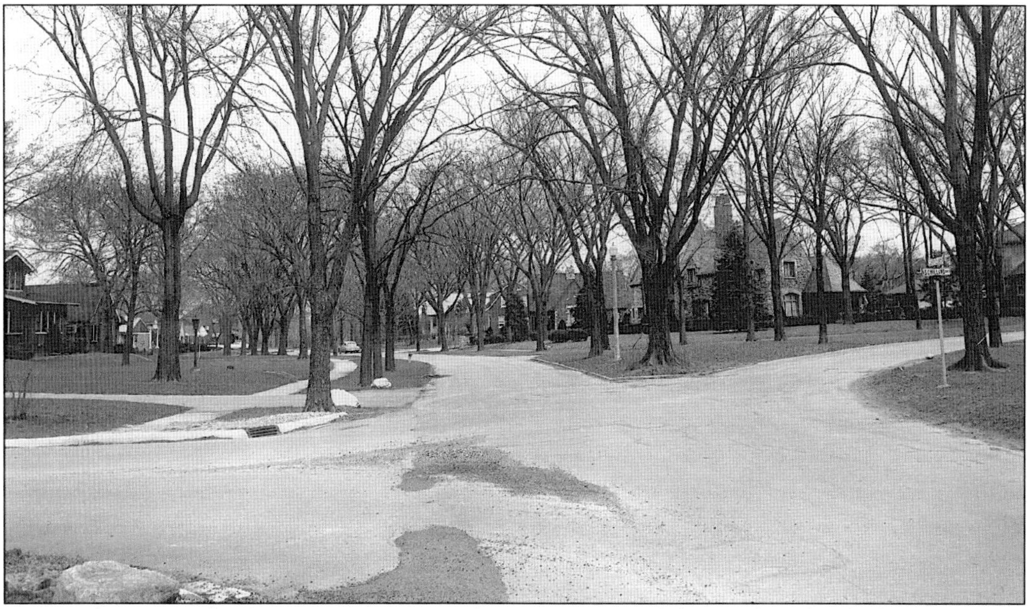

Pictured is a view looking east in winter from Country Club Road and Schilling Avenue in the late 1940s. This scene reveals the profusion of parkway elm trees, the "landscape islands" that grace Country Club Road, and the "castle" built originally by Gene Oliver c. 1930. The movers and shakers of Chicago Heights—leading doctors, lawyers, the postmaster, elected officials, school administrators, bankers, and merchants—chose this neighborhood for their residences.

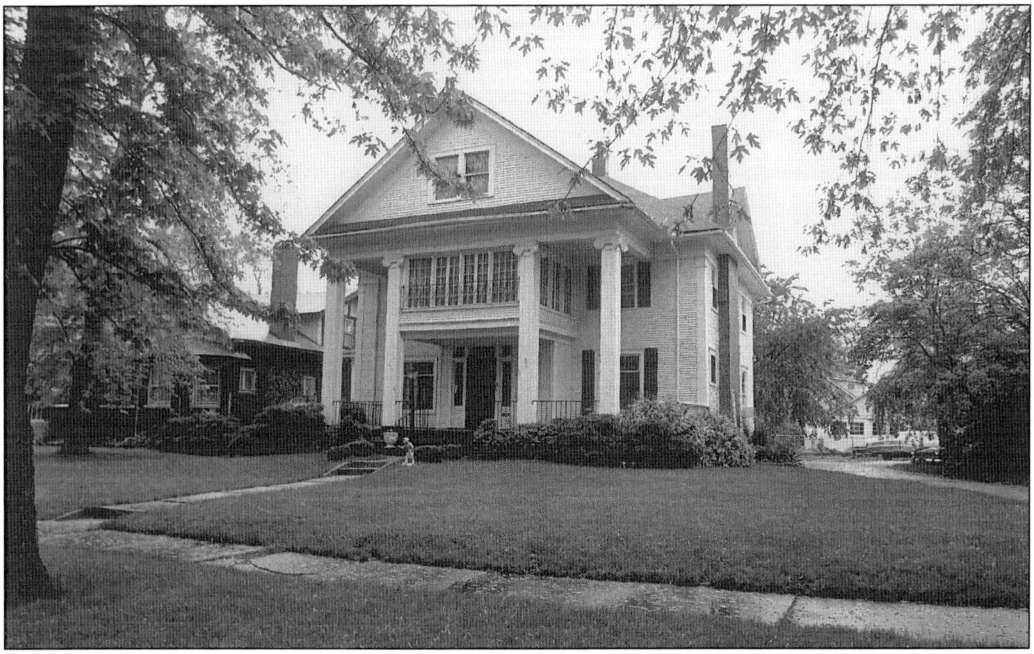

The Hall house at 309 West 16th Street was built by Louis Schilling around 1912 as part of his Schilling Highlands Subdivision. The building was, at one point, used as a hospital. Several other nearby homes bear the mark of Schilling's craftsmanship including 270 West 15th Place, which was designated Chicago Heights' first landmark home in 1997.

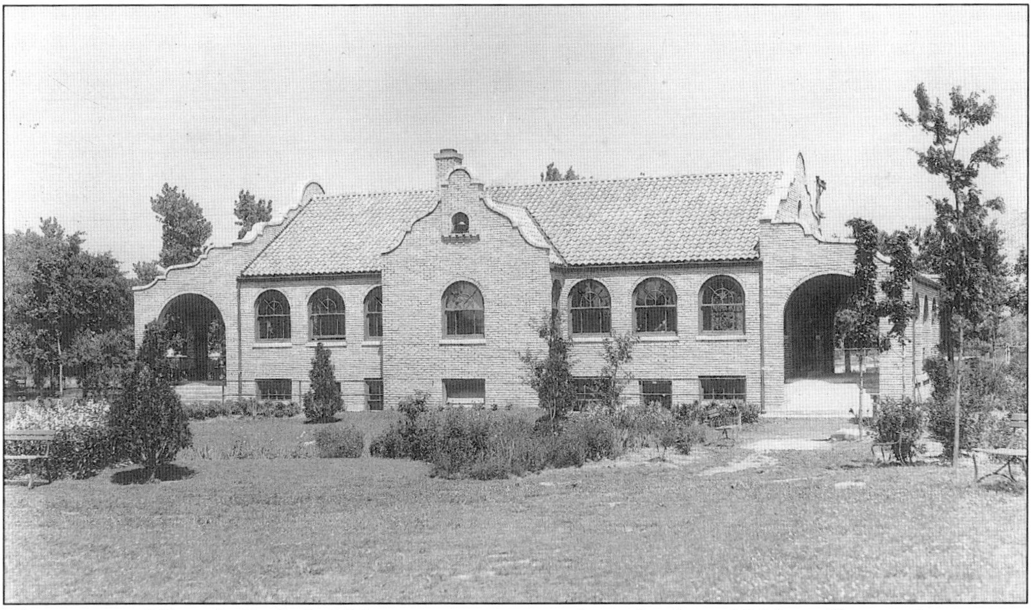

This view of Smith Park field house, constructed in the late 1920s, offers a clear sense of the Spanish motif. Other park district field houses have distinctive architecture—log cabins (Wacker and Euclid parks), an enclosed brick pavilion (Jirtle park), and contemporary (Commissioners park) reflecting the era of their construction.

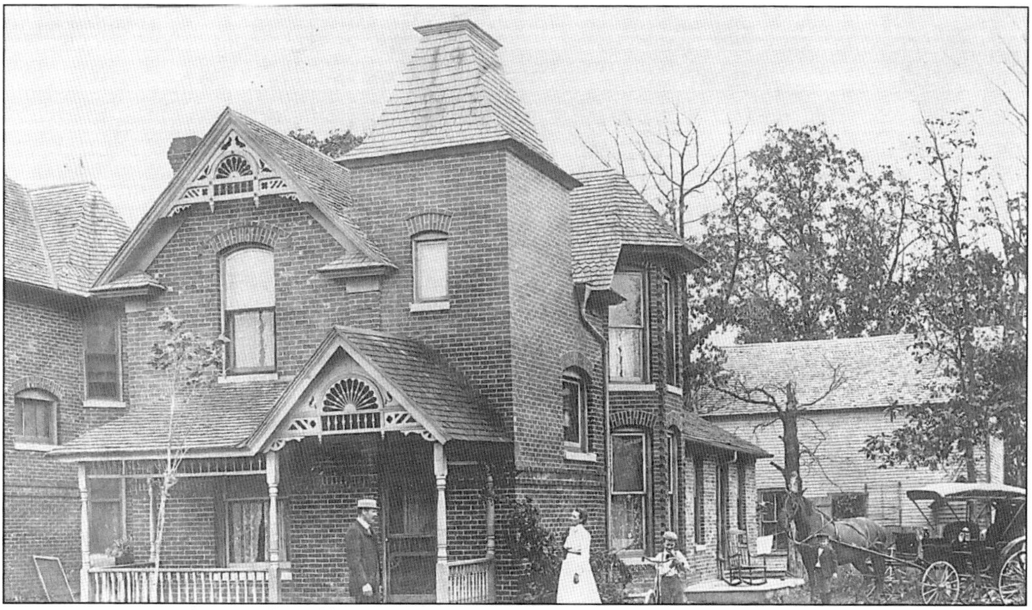

Joe, Maggie, Rufus, and William Orr pose in front of their home at 15th and Vincennes (now the St. James parking garage) at the turn of the century. Joe Orr is the person after whom Joe Orr Road was named. He was the president of the Chicago Heights Coal Company, which later became the Orr Construction Company. The family of Mrs. Orr, the former Maggie McCurdy, maintained a farm near the corner of Dixie Highway and what is now Joe Orr Road.

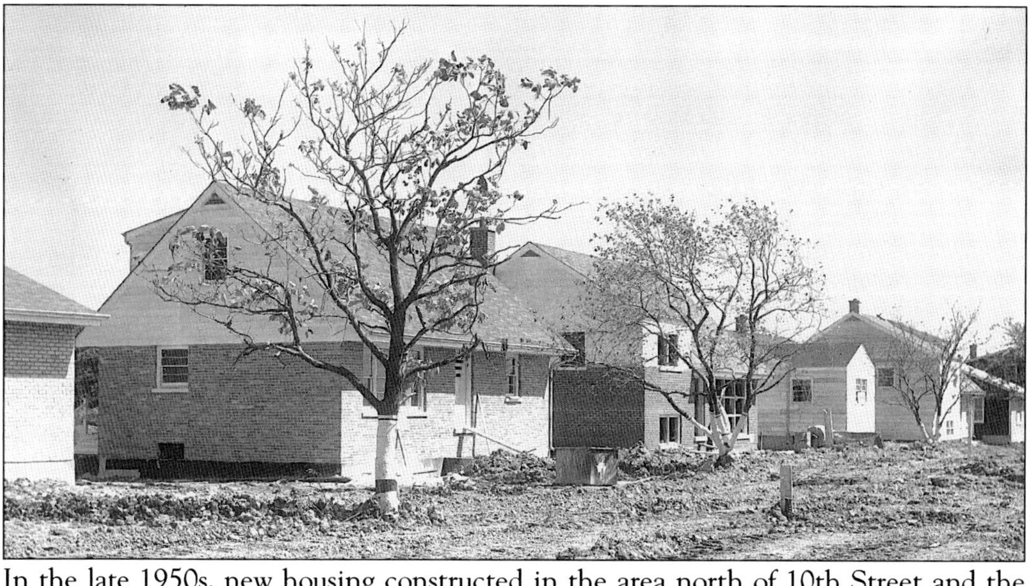

In the late 1950s, new housing constructed in the area north of 10th Street and the Longwood Farms area (shown here) expanded the population of the city while creating a suburban environment architecturally distinct from the older, southern portion of the town built before 1930. This north/south split, extending to the social arena, has replaced the east/west socio-economic division that characterized Chicago Heights earlier in the century.